T0185542

Progressive Web Apps with Angular

Create Responsive, Fast and Reliable PWAs Using Angular

Majid Hajian

Apress®

Progressive Web Apps with Angular

Majid Hajian
Oslo, Norway

ISBN-13 (pbk): 978-1-4842-4447-0   ISBN-13 (electronic): 978-1-4842-4448-7
https://doi.org/10.1007/978-1-4842-4448-7

Managing Director, Apress LLC: Welmoed Spahr
Acquisitions Editor: Louise Corrigan
Development Editor: James Markham
Coordinating Editor: Nancy Chen

Cover designed by eStudioCalamar

Cover image designed by Freepik (www.freepik.com)

Distributed to the book trade worldwide by Springer Science+Business Media New York, 233 Spring Street, 6th Floor, New York, NY 10013. Phone 1-800-SPRINGER, fax (201) 348-4505, e-mail orders-ny@springer-sbm.com, or visit www.springeronline.com. Apress Media, LLC is a California LLC and the sole member (owner) is Springer Science + Business Media Finance Inc (SSBM Finance Inc). SSBM Finance Inc is a **Delaware** corporation.

For information on translations, please e-mail rights@apress.com, or visit http://www.apress.com/rights-permissions.

Apress titles may be purchased in bulk for academic, corporate, or promotional use. eBook versions and licenses are also available for most titles. For more information, reference our Print and eBook Bulk Sales web page at http://www.apress.com/bulk-sales.

Any source code or other supplementary material referenced by the author in this book is available to readers on GitHub via the book's product page, located at www.apress.com/9781484244470. For more detailed information, please visit http://www.apress.com/source-code.

Printed on acid-free paper

*To my lovely wife and daughter, who give me a reason to write,
accept me for me, support my drive and ambitions.*

Table of Contents

About the Author

 **Majid Hajian** is a software developer that has developed and architected complex web applications since 2007 – after he graduated as a software engineer.

Majid is passionate about web platforms, especially hardware connectivity and performance; and, in particular, Progressive Web Apps.

He loves sharing his knowledge with the community by writing on his blog majidhajian.com and tweeting @mhadaily, speaking at conferences, visiting developers to help them, contributing to open source, and organizing meetups and events.

He is a co-organizer of a few meetups in Norway dedicated to front end and mobile in Oslo, including Mobile Meetup, Vue.js Oslo, and Angular Oslo. Majid is also orginizer and an active contributor to Mobile Era and ngVikings, which are the main Nordic conferences for mobile and Angular.

About the Technical Reviewer

Maxim Salnikov (@webmaxru) is an Oslo-based Web Full-Stack Engineer, a Google Developer Expert in Web Technologies and IoT, and a Microsoft MVP in Development Technologies. He's been architecting complex web applications since the end of the last century and has extensive experience with all aspects of web platforms focusing on apps managing real-time data from IoT devices and Progressive Web Apps.

Maxim is a founder and active contributor to two conferences: Mobile Era and ngVikings – Nordic's main conferences for mobile and Angular developers, respectively. He also leads Norway's largest meetups dedicated to web front end and mobile: Angular Oslo, Mobile Meetup, and Oslo PWA.

Maxim is passionate about sharing his web platform experience and knowledge with the community. He travels extensively for developer events and speaking/training at conferences and meetups around the world.

Acknowledgments

Writing this book was a truly enjoyable and great experience and believe or not, it was way more difficult than it looks. There is a lot of work to be done and lots of people that need to help.

First, I want to start by thanking my wonderful wife, Shirin, for all of her support, encouragement, and patience while I was writing this book. I always run to you with my crazy ideas, but you are always patient enough to listen and motivate me!

I'd like to thank my lovely daughter, Hournaz, who was supportive and so patient because I didn't have time for her when I was writing this book.

Many of the technical aspects of this book would not have been possible without the help of Maxim Salnikov. In other words, I believe and always say, this is a book by me and my true friend Maxim. Thanks for all of your efforts and encouragement.

A special thanks to the Apress team: Jade Scard; Nancy Chen for being so calm and insightful; and James Markham for the editing process, which made it a breeze – and I guess it was fun, too!

Thanks to all Angular and PWA community leaders and members, and thank you to Addy Osmani, Jake Archibald, Alex Rickabaugh, and many other PWA devs that I have never met – you don't even know how much I learned from you.

Finally, I am extremely grateful to you, the Reader. Despite the fact that there are tons of videos, tutorials, and blogs available on the internet, you have chosen this book, which might not have been an easy purchase. Thanks for your faith. I hope you enjoy reading it as much as I enjoyed writing it.

Introduction

Progressive Web Apps by Angular are amazing ways to build web applications that utilize PWAs' great features: they are fast, engaging, and resilient. In this book, I will start by exploring the basics of PWAs and soon will dive into Angular Service Worker and its capabilities in different chapters – not only to improve your own PWAs – but also to explore tips and tricks and best practices to build an outstanding web application. My approach in this book is to create an Angular application and slowly improve it and turn it to a PWA; thus, you will see gradually how we will progressively build and deploy a real-world application.

Web development, especially in the front end, was different 12 years ago. The web is evolving very fast. PWAs, Hardware connectivity APIs on the web, and new modern APIs help to create not only much faster and more reliable applications but also ones that are much more native like and pleasant for our customers. So, in this book, I am going to review some of the newest modern APIs that are exciting and will open a new era on the web, in particular, for mobile web development in the feature.

Last but not least, different applications have different needs. Therefore, in this book, I am going to cover building Progressive Web Apps using Angular by implementing Workbox. You will see in this book how different features are being used in Angular Service Worker and Workbox, respectively, and you can make a decision to use either one of them based on your particular application requirements.

CHAPTER 1

Setup Requirements

In this book, I strive to take you on a journey where you can create the most comprehensive Progressive Web Apps (PWAs) with Angular. But before I start, we'll review some PWA fundamentals and set up the environment that will be used throughout the book.

Progressive Web App Fundamentals

PWAs are applied to those web applications that are **fast, engaging, reliable,** and will try to progressively enhance user experience regardless of their browsers, platforms, or devices. In other words, a PWA is not only one framework, tool, or fancy buzzword, but it is a mindset for constant enhancement by leveraging browsers' modern APIs, which leads to satisfaction for every single user.

No matter which framework you choose to work with, no matter which language you choose to write your code with, PWAs must have special characteristics:

1. **Instant loading:** Application should load fast and must be interactive very quickly.

2. **Connectivity independent:** With either no network or a slow and unstable connection, the application must continue working.

3. **Responsive, mobile-first, offline-first design:** Let's focus and optimize for mobile first, which has lower hardware capacity, and the application should be completely usable on mobile.

4. **Re-engaging:** A push notification is one way to send a reminder to a user.

1

© Majid Hajian 2019
M. Hajian, *Progressive Web Apps with Angular*, https://doi.org/10.1007/978-1-4842-4448-7_1

5. **Native-like features:** Having UI architecture like App Shell and using hardware APIs like Web Bluetooth can make our web app more like a native app.

6. **Secure:** Security is the highest priority, and every PWA must serve via HTTPs.

7. **Installable:** Being installable means it'll be added to the device's home screen and launched like a native app.

8. **Progressive:** Regardless of browsers or devices, our app should evolve and embrace new features and give every single one of them the best user experience.

Why Angular?

A couple of years ago, the front-end world was dominated by Angular 1.x even before React came to the market. By establishing and finalizing ES6 and TypeScript appearances as well as new browser features and standards that have been adapted widely, the Angular team, which has been backed by Google, decided to rewrite AngularJS, formerly known as Angular 1.x, leading toward Angular 2, called Angular nowadays. Angular is backed by Observable APIs with Rxjs and TypeScript and has unique features such as robust change detection and routing, animation, lazy loading, a headache-free bundle process, CLI, and tons of other APIs. These make it an exceptional, capable, and full-fledged front-end framework that is trusted by many companies worldwide to build and distribute complex web applications.

Additionally, the Angular Service Worker module has been introduced in version 5, improved in version 6,[1] and is now getting updates regularly in order to add more features and become stable. Although Angular Service Worker along with Angular CLI is not the only option to create a PWA, it is very well maintained, which allows us to effortlessly create or convert an Angular app to a PWA.

All in all, it's not that far off to say you have an all-in-one framework to create a web and mobile application, and this makes Angular unique.

---

[1]At the time I am writing this book, Angular is in version 6, but when you read this book, it may have a higher version.

Installing Node and NPM

You need to make sure that you have Node and NPM installed on your machine. Simply run the following commands to check your Node and NPM version or to see if you have already installed them:

```
$ node -v
$ npm -v
```

Node 8 or higher and NPM 5 or higher are needed. You can visit the Node website at `https://nodejs.org` and download the latest version based on your operating system (Figure 1-1).

Figure 1-1. *Node official website where you can download the latest version of NodeJS*

YARN is an alternative to NPM and has been around for a while. If you prefer to use it, you should visit https://yarnpkg.com/en/docs/install and then install the latest version based on your operating system. To check if you have YARN installed, simply run the following command:

```
$ yarn -v
```

Installing Chrome

Although we create a PWA that will work regardless of browsers of your choice, I will stick to Chrome and its dev tools to develop and debug Service Worker as well as other PWA features. At the time of writing the book, Chrome has a PWA auditing tool called **Lighthouse** that is built in under the *Audit* tab. If you would like to download Chrome, you can visit https://www.google.com/chrome/.

I will evaluable our application with Lighthouse and boost our PWA score later in this book. We continuously use the *applications* tab to debug our Service Worker, IndexedDB, Web App manifest, etc.

Scaffolding Our Project

It is time to scaffold our project using Angular CLI. So, before we proceed, first install Angular CLI globally by running the following:

```
$ npm install -g @angular/cli
```

Or

```
$ yarn global add @angular/cli
```

Now that CLI is installed globally, we can generate a new Angular application.

Generating New Angular App with CLI

As soon as Angular CLI version 6 is installed (you may have a higher version when you read this book), you have the ***ng*** command available globally in your terminal. Let's scaffold our project simply by running the following:

```
$ ng new lovely-offline --routing --style=scss
```

Lovely-offline is our application name, *routing* will generate the route module, and *style=scss* indicates the scss prefix for our styling files.

Adding Angular Material Design

The Angular Material module is, perhaps, one of the best UI libraries for a web app. It will let us develop our application rapidly and flawlessly. You are not limited to this library only, but I recommend it for this project. To install:

```
$ npm install --save @angular/material @angular/cdk @angular/animations
```

Now open the project in your editor or Idea, and then under /src/app, find the app.module.ts, and import BrowserAnimationsModule into your application to enable animations support.

```
import { BrowserModule } from '@angular/platform-browser';
import { NgModule } from '@angular/core';
import { BrowserAnimationsModule } from '@angular/platform-browser/
animations';

import { AppRoutingModule } from './app-routing.module';
import { AppComponent } from './app.component';

@NgModule({
  declarations: [
    AppComponent
  ],
  imports: [
    BrowserModule,
    BrowserAnimationsModule,
    AppRoutingModule
  ],
  providers: [],
  bootstrap: [AppComponent]
})
export class AppModule { }
```

To use each component, we should import their relevant module into ngModule, for instance:

```
import { BrowserModule } from '@angular/platform-browser';
import { NgModule } from '@angular/core';
import { BrowserAnimationsModule } from '@angular/platform-browser/
animations';
import { MatToolbarModule } from '@angular/material/toolbar';
import { MatIconModule } from '@angular/material/icon';

import { AppRoutingModule } from './app-routing.module';
import { AppComponent } from './app.component';

@NgModule({
  declarations: [
    AppComponent
  ],
  imports: [
    BrowserModule,
    BrowserAnimationsModule,
    MatToolbarModule,
    MatIconModule,
    AppRoutingModule
  ],
  providers: [],
  bootstrap: [AppComponent]
})
export class AppModule { }
```

A theme is required; therefore, I will add one of the available themes to style.scs in our project:

```
@import "~@angular/material/prebuilt-themes/indigo-pink.css";
```

It is recommended that you install and include hammer.js as Gestures in Material design are relied on in this library.

```
$ npm install hammerjs
```

After installing, import it in src/main.ts

```
import { enableProdMode } from '@angular/core';
import { platformBrowserDynamic } from '@angular/platform-browser-dynamic';

import { AppModule } from './app/app.module';
import { environment } from './environments/environment';

import 'hammerjs';

if (environment.production) {
  enableProdMode();
}

platformBrowserDynamic().bootstrapModule(AppModule)
  .catch(err => console.log(err));
```

Icons requires the Google Material Icons font; thus, we will add the font CDN link to our index.html file:

```
<!doctype html>
<html lang="en">
<head>
  <meta charset="utf-8">
  <title>LovelyOffline</title>
  <base href="/">

  <meta name="viewport" content="width=device-width, initial-scale=1">
  <link href="https://fonts.googleapis.com/icon?family=Material+Icons"
  rel="stylesheet">
  <link rel="icon" type="image/x-icon" href="favicon.ico">
</head>
<body>
  <app-root></app-root>
</body>
</html>
```

Now our project is ready to use. Simply run *ng serve* or *npm start*. You can access the project in your browser by entering localhost:4200.

Setting Up a Mobile Device

There is nothing better than testing our application in a real device to see how it looks. Android, along with Chrome, is supporting most of the PWA features including Service Worker, Push notification, and background sync as well as even more modern browser APIs.

Please read the article below on the Google developer website, `https://developers.google.com/web/tools/chrome-devtools/remote-debugging`, if you have a real device and want to conveniently connect it to Chrome dev tools. Keep in mind that the real device is not necessary; you can always test your app via Android and iOS emulators.

Setting Up a Mobile Emulator

To run an Android Emulator, I recommend you install **Android Studio** and follow the instructions placed on the Android developer website: `https://developer.android.com/studio/run/emulator`.

Mac Users are also able to install xCode and run an iPhone simulator on their Mac. After installing xCode from `https://developer.apple.com/xcode/`, you should be able to find *Open Developer Tool* under the *xCode* menu, and then you can open *Simulator* to open your selected iPhone / iPad.

Connecting Android Simulator to Chrome Dev Tools

You now should be able to connect your Android simulator to Chrome dev tools. Please refer to the "Set Up Mobile Device" section.

Summary

In this chapter, we have looked at PWA fundamentals, and then we scaffolded our projects using CLI. Angular Material has been added to our project in order to style our app.

Moreover, we have reviewed other tools that we will need throughout this course such as Node, NPM, YARN, and Chrome; and we learned how to set up our real device as well as our simulators in order to properly test our app.

CHAPTER 2

Deploying to Firebase as the Back End

Firebase is considered a Backend as a Service, which is now part of the Google Cloud Platform while it's still serving as an independent entity. It offers different services such as hosting, real-time databases, and cloud functions.

In this chapter, I am going to show you how we can deploy our app to Firebase. It's important to mention that Firebase is not the only option. However, since it's easy to set up and deploy, I encourage you to use Firebase as our host server.

Additionally, we may need to write a bit of back-end logic for our application; therefore, Firebase Function is one of the best choices, in order to leverage serverless architecture and reduce our concerns regarding a back-end system, while the front end will remain our main focus.

Last but not least, to persist our data, we will use Firebase Firestore, which gives us the best passivity to store and retrieve our data as quickly and possible with built-in JSON access to each collection and document where needed.

Setting Up Your Account

Let's get started by opening *firebase.google.com*. Sign in with your Gmail credentials, but if you don't have any, please continue by first registering a Google account.

After you have signed in, continue and hit "GO TO CONSOLE." You will be redirected to your console where you can see your projects.

© Majid Hajian 2019

M. Hajian, *Progressive Web Apps with Angular*, https://doi.org/10.1007/978-1-4842-4448-7_2

Creating a Project

Now it's time to add your project; simply click **Add project**, as shown in Figure 2-1.

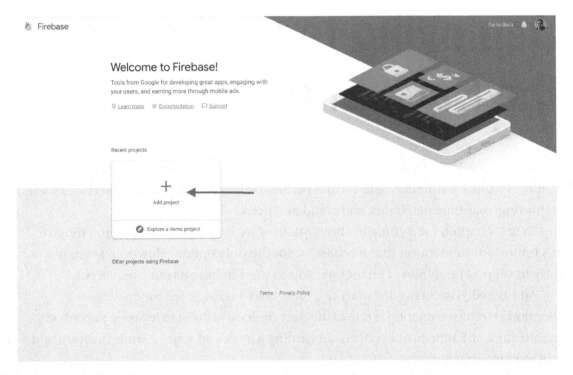

Figure 2-1. *Firebase console, where you should hit **Add Project** to create a new project*

You should see a new view where it is going to ask you about your project details such as your project name. **Awesome-Apress-PWA** is what I have chosen to name my project.

You may need to change your organization or Cloud Firestore location; however, the default setting should be enough to get started. Keep in mind that if you change the Cloud Firestore location, you will not be able to alter it until your project is created.

I will leave **"Use the default settings for sharing Google Analytics for Firebase data"** and **"Terms and Condition"** checked. Now, it's time to hit **Create project** button, as shown in Figure 2-2.

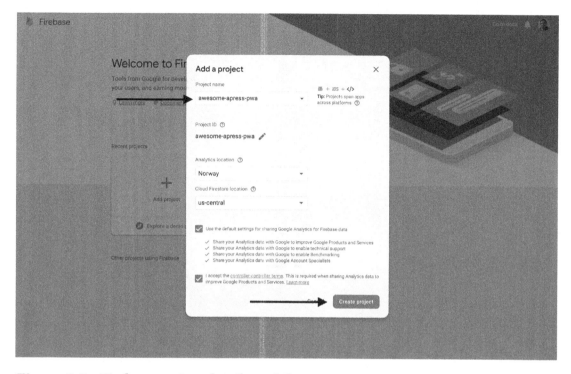

Figure 2-2. *Firebase project detail modal*

It may take several seconds before your project gets ready. As soon as the project is ready, you can continue to your project's dashboard (see Figure 2-3).

Figure 2-3.   *After several seconds, the project is ready, so simply click on the "Continue" button to be redirected to the dashboard*

Deploying to Firebase

We have chosen Firebase as it's easy to work with for our project, and you'll see in a minute how painless deployment is with Firebase CLI (Command-Line Interface).

Generating a New Angular App

Before we start, we need to generate a new Angular app using Angular CLI (Command-Line Interface). If you don't have @angular/cli installed globally on your machine, you should run the following command first:

```
$ npm install -g @angular/cli
```

To generate a new Angular app with **routing** and **scss** set up, we can run:

```
$ ng new lovely-offline      --routing               --style=scss
    Name of project        enable routing       styling with scss
```

After installing all NPM dependencies, you will have your app ready for building and then deploying.

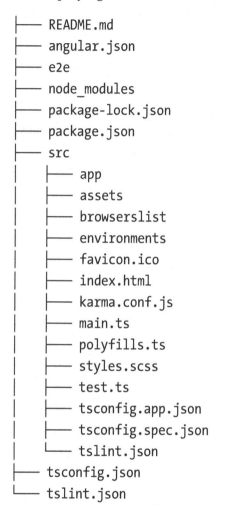

```
├──── README.md
├──── angular.json
├──── e2e
├──── node_modules
├──── package-lock.json
├──── package.json
├──── src
│       ├──── app
│       ├──── assets
│       ├──── browserslist
│       ├──── environments
│       ├──── favicon.ico
│       ├──── index.html
│       ├──── karma.conf.js
│       ├──── main.ts
│       ├──── polyfills.ts
│       ├──── styles.scss
│       ├──── test.ts
│       ├──── tsconfig.app.json
│       ├──── tsconfig.spec.json
│       └──── tslint.json
├──── tsconfig.json
└──── tslint.json
```

Let's now build our app for production.

```
$ ng build --prod
> ng build
Date: 2018-08-26T17:20:35.649Z
Hash: e6da8aa80ad79bc41363
Time: 6332ms
chunk {main} main.js, main.js.map (main) 11.6 kB [initial] [rendered]
chunk {polyfills} polyfills.js, polyfills.js.map (polyfills) 227 kB
[initial] [rendered]
```

```
chunk {runtime} runtime.js, runtime.js.map (runtime) 5.22 kB [entry] [rendered]
chunk {styles} styles.js, styles.js.map (styles) 16 kB [initial] [rendered]
chunk {vendor} vendor.js, vendor.js.map (vendor) 3.18 MB [initial] [rendered]
```

The build is a success, and now it's time to deploy our app to Firebase. Let's install Firebase CLI.

```
$ npm install -g firebase-tools
```

Now the **firebase** command is available globally in our command line. Before we can deploy, we need to make sure we have enough privileges; thus, we should now log in to Firebase to set our credentials, so simply run:

```
$ firebase login
```

A questionnaire appears like that below:

```
Allow Firebase to collect anonymous CLI usage and error
reporting  information? (Y/n) Y

Visit this URL on any device to log in:
https://accounts.google.com/o/oauth2/........

Waiting for authentication...
```

As soon as you see **Authentication URL,** you will be redirected to a browser in order to sign in to your Google account. Then, you should grant enough permission to Firebase CLI by clicking **Allow** access, as shown in Figure 2-4.

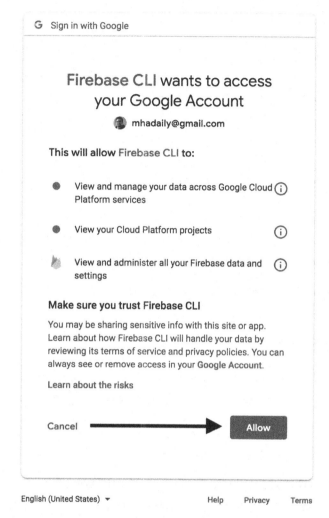

Figure 2-4. *Click **Allow** to give Firebase CLI permission to access your account*

As quickly as permission is given, you should see a **success** message in your browser, as shown in Figure 2-5.

Figure 2-5. Success message in your browser after giving permission to Firebase CLI

You will also see a success message as seen below in your terminal, which means that Firebase CLI now has enough access to your Firebase projects.

✓ Success! Logged in as mhadaily@gmail.com

Initializing the App

The next step is to initialize your Firebase project. This will link your local Angular app to the Firebase application that we just created. To do this, make sure you are in the root of the project and run:

$ firebase init

Once you hit the command above, Firebase CLI asks you a few questions, appearing in your terminal, in order to scaffold your Firebase project and create necessary requirements that are essential to deploy our application to Firebase. Let's review each question step by step.

Features Selection

The first question, as shown below, is about which Firebase features we would like to use:

Which Firebase CLI features do you want to set up for this folder? Press Space to select features, then Enter to confirm your choices.
　　◯ Database: Deploy Firebase Realtime Database Rules
＞ ◉ Firestore: Deploy rules and create indexes for Firestore

16

- ◉ Functions: Configure and deploy Cloud Functions
- ◉ Hosting: Configure and deploy Firebase Hosting sites
- ○ Storage: Deploy Cloud Storage security rules

Firebase Realtime Database[1] and Firestore[2] are two NoSQL databases services to store and sync data for client- and server-side development. Cloud functions for Firebase lets you automatically run back-end code in response to events triggered by Firebase features and HTTPS requests. Your code is stored in Google's cloud and runs in a managed environment. Firebase Hosting provides fast and secure hosting for your web app, static and dynamic content, and microservices. Cloud storage is built for app developers who need to store and serve user-generated content, such as photos or videos.

I will select **Firestore**, **Functions**, and **Hosting features** for this project as I am going to use them throughout this book. Once you have selected what is needed, press **enter** to go to the next step.

Project Selection

The second question, as shown below, shows your projects in Firebase, and since we have created one project, I will select that one and continue by pressing **enter**. **Note that you can also create a project in this step, too.**

```
Select a default Firebase project for this directory: (Use arrow keys)
[don't set up a default project]
> awesome-apress-pwa (awesome-apress-pwa)
  [create a new project]
```

Database Setup

Firebase Firestore is a scalable and flexible NoSQL[3] real-time database to store and sync data for a client- or server-side app development. This database keeps our data in sync across multiple client apps and offers offline capabilities. Data in Firestore saves documents that contain fields mapping to values. Collections are containers of documents that allow us to not only organize our data but also to build queries.

---

[1]https://firebase.google.com/docs/database/
[2]https://firebase.google.com/docs/firestore/
[3]Read more at https://en.wikipedia.org/wiki/NoSQL.

Since we have selected Firestore service already in the step features selection step, the third question, as shown below, is about a database rules file to write all rules regarding our project database. I continue with the default name, which is database. rules.json:

```
What file should be used for Database Rules? (database.rules.json)
```

Functions Setup

Cloud functions in Firebase let us run back-end code over HTTPS requests without having an actual server to maintain and manage and store our code in Google's cloud-managed environment. In order to achieve **serverless**[4] architecture in our app, we are going to use Functions to write and run our essential back-end code.

Since we have selected to use the Firebase Functions feature already in the feature selection step, the fourth question, as shown below, asks to choose our desired language to write **Functions**.

```
What language would you like to use to write Cloud Functions? (Use arrow keys)
> JavaScript
  TypeScript
```

JavaScript is my choice now as we are not going to have a lot of functions in this book; therefore, I kept it simple. Feel free to continue with TypeScript if this is what you like.

Followed by the language of choice, Firebase CLI offers to set up a linting tool to help us find possible bugs and styling issues in the next question, as shown below. If you like to enforce styling and catch possible bugs in your cloud functions, continue with Y.

```
Do you want to use ESLint to catch probable bugs and enforce style? (Y/N) y
```

Final Setup

I will continue for the last three questions in order to complete my project initialization.

If you like to install dependencies now, enter Y in the next question.

```
Do you want to install dependencies with npm now? (Y/n)
```

---

[4]Read more at https://en.wikipedia.org/wiki/Serverless_computing.

In the next step, we need to define where our ready-to-deploy app is located. By default, in Angular it's dist directory; thus, I also enter dist to set my public directory. So, I will continue to answer the question as shown below:

```
What do you want to use as your public directory? (public) dist
```

Finally, our application is going to have a routing system in the front end, which means we are going to create a single-page application. Therefore, when Firebase CLI is questioned about rewriting all URLs to index.html, we should answer Y to make sure our front end is handling routes individually, regardless of our server routing.

Although we are moving forward with a single-page application, it's definitely not required for creating a PWA. Notice that in this book, we will make a single-page PWA by Angular. Let's continue the final question with Y as shown below:

```
Configure as a single-page app (rewrite all urls to /index.html)? (y/N) y
```

Initializing our app with Firebase CLI has been completed! Our app structure will look like the following tree after initialization.

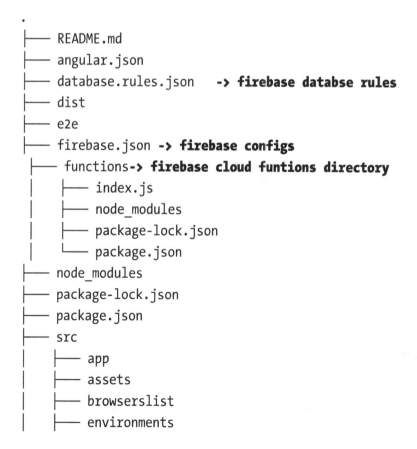

```
|     ├── favicon.ico
|     ├── index.html
|     ├── karma.conf.js
|     ├── main.ts
|     ├── polyfills.ts
|     ├── styles.scss
|     ├── test.ts
|     ├── tsconfig.app.json
|     ├── tsconfig.spec.json
|     └── tslint.json
├── tsconfig.json
└── tslint.json
```

Adjustment in Angular Project Settings

Before we can deploy our app, we need to apply a minor change to our Angular setting located in **Angular.json.** Angular CLI is capable of building multiple apps, and each app could simply be placed in a **dist** folder. However, we want to deal with only one app at the moment, and we need to build it in the **dist** folder where Firebase will find and deploy it. Therefore, we should change from

```
"architect": {
    "build": {
      "builder": "@angular-devkit/build-angular:browser",
      "options": {
        "outputPath": "dist/lovely-offline",  // outputPath showes
          where to build
```

to

```
"architect": {
    "build": {
      "builder": "@angular-devkit/build-angular:browser",
      "options": {
        "outputPath": "dist ",  // build app just in dist
```

By removing our app name from **outputPath**, we enforce Angular CLI to build and place all files in the **dist** folder instead. Now it's time to finally deploy our app to Firebase.

Deploying Our App

While we are in the root of the project directory, we can simply run the following command:

```
$ firebase deploy
```

Deployment starts...

```
> firebase deploy

=== Deploying to 'awesome-apress-pwa'...

i  deploying database, functions, hosting
Running command: npm --prefix "$RESOURCE_DIR" run lint

> functions@ lint ~/awesome-apress-pwa/functions
> eslint .

✓  functions: Finished running predeploy script.
i  database: checking rules syntax...
✓  database: rules syntax for database awesome-apress-pwa is valid
i  functions: ensuring necessary APIs are enabled...
✓  functions: all necessary APIs are enabled
i  functions: preparing functions directory for uploading...
i  hosting[awesome-apress-pwa]: beginning deploy...
i  hosting[awesome-apress-pwa]: found 14 files in dist
✓  hosting[awesome-apress-pwa]: file upload complete
i  database: releasing rules...
✓  database: rules for database awesome-apress-pwa released successfully
i  hosting[awesome-apress-pwa]: finalizing version...
✓  hosting[awesome-apress-pwa]: version finalized
i  hosting[awesome-apress-pwa]: releasing new version...
✓  hosting[awesome-apress-pwa]: release complete

✓  Deploy complete!
```

Project Console: https://console.firebase.google.com/project/awesome-apress-pwa/overview
Hosting URL: https://awesome-apress-pwa.firebaseapp.com

Congratulations – deployment is successfully completed, and now the website is available at https://awesome-apress-pwa.firebaseapp.com.

Setting Up AngularFire[5]

AngularFire2 is an official library for Angular to support Firebase functionalities. It is powered by observable, real-time bindings, authentication, and offline data support. I strongly recommend implementing this library in order to make it way easier for our development process to deal with Firebase.

To install, run the following command:

```
$ npm install firebase @angular/fire --save
```

To add a Firebase configuration, open the **/src/environment/environment.ts** file, and add the following setup:

```
export const environment = {
  production: false,
  firebase: {
    apiKey: '<your-key>',
    authDomain: '<your-project-authdomain>',
    databaseURL: '<your-database-URL>',
    projectId: '<your-project-id>',
    storageBucket: '<your-storage-bucket>',
    messagingSenderId: '<your-messaging-sender-id>'
  }
};
```

To find your app configuration, open the Firebase console and from the project overview page, click **gear** icon and click **project settings**, as shown in Figure 2-6.

---

[5]https://github.com/angular/angularfire2

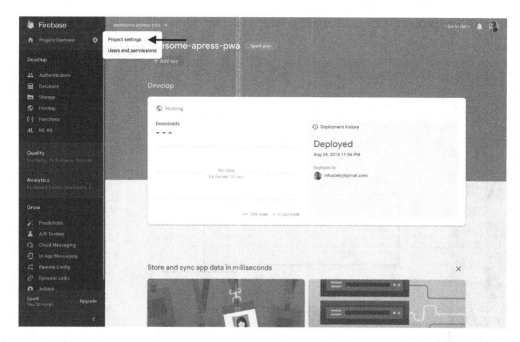

Figure 2-6. *Click the gear icon to see the project setting menu*

From the project setting view, find **Add Firebase to your web app** (see Figure 2-7).

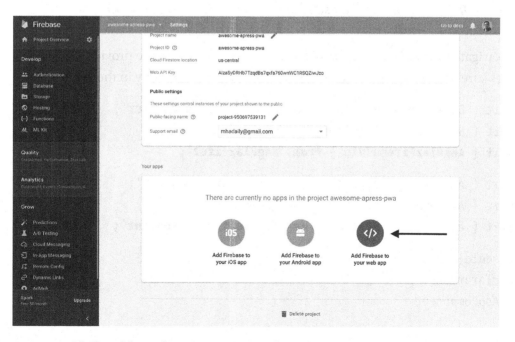

Figure 2-7. *Click Add Firebase to your app button to see project settings*

Replace the project setting in environment.ts. (see Figure 2-8).

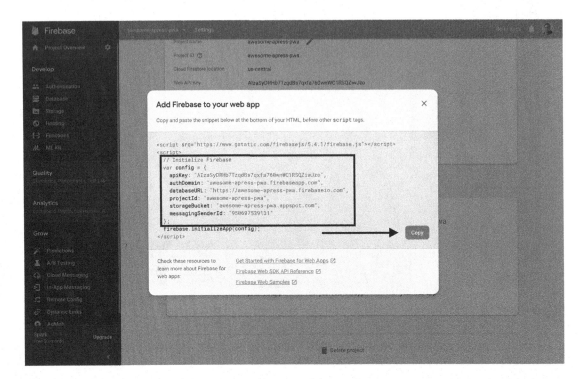

Figure 2-8. *Copy your project setting to replace in environment.ts*

Navigate to **/src/app/app.module.ts** and inject the Firebase provider. Injector makes sure that your Firebase configuration is specified correctly in the app.

```
import { BrowserModule } from '@angular/platform-browser';
import { NgModule } from '@angular/core';
import { AngularFireModule } from 'angularfire2';

import { AppRoutingModule } from './app-routing.module';
import { AppComponent } from './app.component';
import { environment } from '../environments/environment';

@NgModule({
  declarations: [
    AppComponent
  ],
```

```
  imports: [
    BrowserModule,
    AppRoutingModule,
    AngularFireModule.initializeApp(environment.firebase)
  ],
  providers: [],
  bootstrap: [AppComponent]
})
export class AppModule { }
```

AngularFire is a modular package to support different Firebase features. AngularFirestoreModule, AngularFireAuthModule, AngularFireDatabaseModule, and AngularFireStorageModule are available individually to be added to **@NgModules.** For instance, in this app, we would add AngularFireStoreModule and AngularFireAuthModule, respectively, to get support for database and authentication features.

```
import { BrowserModule } from '@angular/platform-browser';
import { NgModule } from '@angular/core';
import { AngularFireModule } from 'angularfire2';
import { AngularFirestoreModule } from 'angularfire2/firestore';
import { AngularFireAuthModule } from 'angularfire2/auth';

import { AppRoutingModule } from './app-routing.module';
import { AppComponent } from './app.component';
import { environment } from '../environments/environment';

@NgModule({
  declarations: [
    AppComponent
  ],
  imports: [
    BrowserModule,
    AppRoutingModule,
    AngularFireModule.initializeApp(environment.firebase),
    AngularFirestoreModule, // needed for database features
    AngularFireAuthModule, // needed for auth features,
  ],
```

```
  providers: [],
  bootstrap: [AppComponent]
})
export class AppModule { }
```

Great, `AngularFirestore` provider is now available in order to get access to Firebase database collections to modify/delete or perform more actions. For example, open **/src/app/app.component.ts** and inject `AngularFirestore`.

```
import { Component } from '@angular/core';
import { AngularFirestore } from 'angularfire2/firestore';

@Component({
  selector: 'app-root',
  templateUrl: './app.component.html',
  styleUrls: ['./app.component.scss']
})
export class AppComponent {
  title = 'lovely-offline';

  constructor(db: AngularFirestore) {

  }
}
```

The nest step is to bind a particular Firestore collection. As an example, in the future, we will create a collection named **notes**. The following code demonstrates how we can get access to all data and show it in our view while it's an observable.

```
import { Component } from '@angular/core';
import { AngularFirestore } from 'angularfire2/firestore';
import { Observable } from 'rxjs';

@Component({
  selector: 'app-root',
```

```
template: `
  <h1>Bind Firestore collection example</h1>
  <ul>
    <li class="text" *ngFor="let note of notes$ | async">
      {{note.title}}
    </li>
  </ul>
  <router-outlet></router-outlet>
  `,
  styleUrls: ['./app.component.scss']
})
export class AppComponent {
  notes$: Observable<any[]>;
  constructor(db: AngularFirestore) {
    this.notes$ = db.collection('notes').valueChanges();
  }
}
```

Summary

This chapter unfolds an easy way to deploy our Angular app to Firebase and introduced services such as Firestore Cloud functions to manage and run our back-end code. Even though we didn't deep dive into each feature, it was enough to start and make the app live.

AngularFire2 is the official Angular library for Firebase, which has been set up in our app, and it was explained how to inject it in our component in order to get access to Firestore and other Firebase features later in the next chapters.

Now that we have prepared deployment requirements, we are ready to move on to the next chapter and create our app skeleton and make it ready to start building a PWA.

Completing an Angular App

Up to this point, we have reviewed fundamentals and requirements and set up prerequisites in order to host, store data, and run functions in the cloud. It may sound a bit boring to you, but as we continue to each chapter, it gets more exciting because we will gradually build a real PWA together by adding more features.

Now, it's time to step into the real world and create an app that works. In this chapter, we are going to implement logics to yield an app that saves personal notes in Firebase. This app will have user authentication functionalities and let a user save, edit, and delete notes in their personal account. We will create UIs and routes, respectively, for each of these functionalities.

Furthermore, there are two goals behind this chapter. First, you will see how we can start an app from scratch and understand how we proceed to convert it to a PWA as we continue to the next chapters. Secondly, you will see how we are going to convert an existing app to a PWA. So, what are we waiting for? Let's get started.

Implementing Our UI

First, we need to create an app that looks good. What we select for our UI must at least contain the following characteristics: **modern**, **fast**, **consistent**, **versatile**, **flexible**, **mobile first**, **responsive**, **and user friendly**. Angular Material[1] is one of the best, which perfectly fits in Angular and helps us to rapidly develop our app while it looks nice and fulfills our needs.

---

[1]https://material.angular.io/

© Majid Hajian 2019
M. Hajian, *Progressive Web Apps with Angular*, https://doi.org/10.1007/978-1-4842-4448-7_3

Installing and Setting Up Angular Material, CDK, and Animations

Angular CLI 6+ provides a new command ng add in order to update an Angular project with correct dependencies, perform configuration changes, and execute initialization code, if any.

Installing @angular/material Automatically with Angular CLI

We can now use this command to install @angular/material:

ng add @angular/material

You should see the following messages:

```
> ng add @angular/material

Installing packages for tooling via npm.
npm WARN @angular/material@6.4.6 requires a peer of @angular/cdk@6.4.6 but
none is installed. You must install peer depen
dencies yourself.
```

+ @angular/material@6.4.6
```
added 2 packages from 1 contributor and audited 24256 packages in 7.228s
found 12 vulnerabilities (9 low, 3 high)
  run `npm audit fix` to fix them, or `npm audit` for details
Installed packages for tooling via npm.
```
UPDATE package.json (1445 bytes)
UPDATE angular.json (3942 bytes)
UPDATE src/app/app.module.ts (907 bytes)
UPDATE src/index.html (477 bytes)
UPDATE src/styles.scss (165 bytes)
```
added 1 package and audited 24258 packages in 7.297s
```

Awesome – Angular cli has taken care of all configurations for us. However, for a better understanding of how it works in detail, I will also continue to add Angular material to my project manually, as described below.

Installing @angular/material Manually

You can use either NPM or YARN to install packages, so use whichever is most appropriate for your project. I will continue with npm.

```
npm install --save @angular/material @angular/cdk @angular/animations
```

To enable animation support once packages are installed, **BrowserAnimationsModule** should be this:

```
imported into our application.
import { BrowserModule } from '@angular/platform-browser';
import { NgModule } from '@angular/core';
import { AngularFireModule } from 'angularfire2';
import { AngularFirestoreModule } from 'angularfire2/firestore';
import { AngularFireAuthModule } from 'angularfire2/auth';

import { AppRoutingModule } from './app-routing.module';
import { AppComponent } from './app.component';
import { environment } from '../environments/environment';
import { BrowserAnimationsModule } from '@angular/platform-browser/
animations';

@NgModule({
  declarations: [
    AppComponent
  ],
  imports: [
    BrowserModule,
    AppRoutingModule,
    AngularFireModule.initializeApp(environment.firebase),
    AngularFirestoreModule, // needed for database features
    AngularFireAuthModule,  // needed for auth features,
    BrowserAnimationsModule,
  ],
  providers: [],
  bootstrap: [AppComponent]
})
export class AppModule { }
```

To enable animation support once packages are installed, **BrowserAnimationsModule** should be imported.

Fonts and icons help our app look nicer and feel better. Therefore, we will add **Roboto and Material Icons fonts** into our application. To include them, modify index. html, and add the following links between <head></head>:

```
<link href="https://fonts.googleapis.com/icon?family=Material+Icons"
rel="stylesheet">
<link href="https://fonts.googleapis.com/css?family=Roboto:300,400,500"
rel="stylesheet">
```

Finally, we need to include a theme. There are prebuilt themes in the @angular/ material library, which at the time I am writing this book, are the following:

- deeppurple-amber.css

- indigo-pink.css

- pink-bluegrey.css

- purple-green.css

Open angular.json, and add one of the theme CSS files to architect ➤ build ➤ styles, so it looks like the following configuration:

```
"architect": {
      "build": {
        "builder": "@angular-devkit/build-angular:browser",
        "options": {
          "outputPath": "dist",
          "index": "src/index.html",
          "main": "src/main.ts",
          "polyfills": "src/polyfills.ts",
          "tsConfig": "src/tsconfig.app.json",
          "assets": [
            "src/favicon.ico",
            "src/assets"
          ],
```

```
"styles": [
  {
    "input": "node_modules/@angular/material/prebuilt-themes/
    indigo-pink.css"
  },
  "src/styles.scss"
],
"scripts": []
},
```

Great – we have added what we need for our UI; now let's create a basic skeleton for our app.

Creating a Core Module / Shared Module

One of the common ways in Angular to benefit from lazy loading and code splitting is to modularize an application while it still keeps its components-based approach. It means that we will encapsulate as many components as make sense into one module and will reuse this module by importing into other modules. To start, we will generate **SharedModule** to import into all other modules and expose all common components and modules that will be reused across our app and **CoreModule**, which will only be imported once in our root module, AppModule, and contains all providers that are singletons and will initialize as soon as the application starts.

Run the following commands to generate a core module.

```
ng generate module modules/core
> ng g m modules/core
CREATE src/app/modules/core/core.module.spec.ts (259 bytes)
CREATE src/app/modules/core/core.module.ts (188 bytes)
```

Angular CLI generates CoreModule located in the **modules** folder. Let's do this command one more time to generate SharedModule located in the **modules** folder:

```
ng generate module modules/shared
> ng g m modules/shared
CREATE src/app/modules/shared/shared.module.spec.ts (275 bytes)
CREATE src/app/modules/shared/shared.module.ts (190 bytes)
```

To make sure that CoreModule will not be imported multiple times, we can create a guard for this module. Simply add the following code to your module:

```
export class CoreModule {
  constructor(@Optional() @SkipSelf() parentModule: CoreModule) {
    if (parentModule) {
      throw new Error(`CoreModule has already been loaded. Import Core
      modules in the AppModule only.`);
    }
  }
}
```

So, our core module looks like the following:

```
import { NgModule, Optional, SkipSelf } from '@angular/core';
import { CommonModule } from '@angular/common';

@NgModule({
  imports: [
    CommonModule,
  ],
  providers: []
})
export class CoreModule {
  constructor(@Optional() @SkipSelf() parentModule: CoreModule) {
    if (parentModule) {
      throw new Error(`CoreModule has already been loaded. Import Core
      modules in the AppModule only.`);
    }
  }
}
```

Let's import CoreModule into AppModule. Now we are ready to start creating our first shared components.

Header, Footer, and Body Components

In this section, we are going to create our first application – a main application layout – based on the simple sketch that is shown in Figure 3-1.

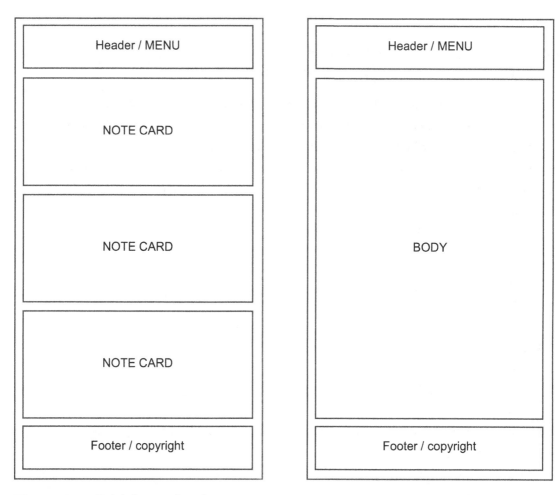

Figure 3-1. *Initial app sketch*

We will continue developing while we have this sketch in mind. To begin, let's create a module named LayoutModule that contains a footer, header, and menu components and then import this module into AppModule to reuse header/footer in the app. component.ts file.

```
ng g m modules/layout
import LayoutModule into AppModule:
```

```
...imports: [
    CoreModule,
    LayoutModule,...
```

By running the following command, footer and header components are generated, respectively.

```
ng generate component modules/layout/header
ng generate component modules/layout/footer
```

We have already created SharedModule; however, we need some changes in this module. First, what we imported as share modules or share components should be exported, too. Angular Material is a modular package; with that said, we should import modules that are needed for our UI. Then, I will add as many modules from Angular Material as we need in this application. It will be possible to add or remove modules and components later.

Lastly, our SharedModule looks like the code below:

```
const SHARED_MODULES = [
    CommonModule,
    MatToolbarModule,
    MatCardModule,
    MatIconModule,
    MatButtonModule,
    MatDividerModule,
    MatBadgeModule,
    MatFormFieldModule,
    MatInputModule,
    MatSnackBarModule,
    MatProgressBarModule,
    MatProgressSpinnerModule,
    MatMenuModule,
    ReactiveFormsModule,
    FormsModule,
    RouterModule
];
```

```
const SHARED_COMPONENTS = [];
@NgModule({
  imports: [ ...SHARED_MODULES² ],
  declarations: [ ...SHARED_COMPONENTS ],
  exports: [ ...SHARED_MODULES,    ...SHARED_COMPONENTS ],
})
export class SharedModule { }
```

After importing SharedModule into LayoutModule, we are able to design our header/footer based on material components that are required.

Following is the Header component:

```
// header.component.html
<mat-toolbar color="primary">
  <span>ApressNote-PWA</span>
  <span class="space-between"></span>
  <button mat-icon-button [mat-menu-trigger-for]="menu">
    <mat-icon>more_vert</mat-icon>
  </button>
</mat-toolbar>
<mat-menu x-position="before" #menu="matMenu">
  <button mat-menu-item>Home</button>
  <button mat-menu-item>Profile</button>
  <button mat-menu-item>Add Note</button>
</mat-menu>
```

```
// header.component.scss
.space-between {
    flex:1;
}
```

```
// header.component.ts
import { Component, OnInit } from '@angular/core';
@Component({
  selector: 'app-header',
```

---

[2]The pread operator (three dots ...) helps to concatenate arrays.

```
  templateUrl: './header.component.html',
  styleUrls: ['./header.component.scss']
})
export class HeaderComponent { }
```

Following is the Footer component:

// footer.component.html

```
<footer>
  <div class="copyright">Copyright Apress - Majid Hajian</div>
</footer>
<div class="addNote">
  <button mat-fab>
    <mat-icon>add circle</mat-icon>
  </button>
</div>
```

// footer.component.scss

```
footer{
    background: #3f51b5;
    color: #fff;
    display: flex;
    box-sizing: border-box;
    padding: 1rem;
    flex-direction: column;
    align-items: center;
    white-space: nowrap;
}
.copyright {
    text-align: center;
}
.addNote {
 position: fixed;
 bottom: 2rem;
 right: 1rem;
 color: #fff;
}
```

// footer.component.ts

```
import { Component, OnInit } from '@angular/core';

@Component({
  selector: 'app-footer',
  templateUrl: './footer.component.html',
  styleUrls: ['./footer.component.scss']
})
export class FooterComponent { }
```

Now add a few custom CSS lines in style.scss file to adjust our layout:

```
html, body { height: 100%; }
body { margin: 0; font-family: 'Roboto', sans-serif; }
.appress-pwa-note {
    display: flex;
    flex-direction: column;
    align-content: space-between;
    height: 100%;
}
.main{
    display: flex;
    flex:1;
}
mat-card {
 max-width: 80%;
 margin: 2em auto;
 text-align: center;
}

mat-toolbar-row {
 justify-content: space-between;
}
```

Lastly, add the footer, header, and necessary changes to `app.component.ts`:

```
import { Component } from '@angular/core';

@Component({
  selector: 'app-root',
  template: `
  <div class="appress-pwa-note">
    <app-header></app-header>
    <div class="main">
      <router-outlet></router-outlet>
    </div>
    <app-footer></app-footer>
  </div>
  `,
})
export class AppComponent { }
```

So far, so good – the initial skeleton based on the sketch is now ready as shown in Figure 3-2.

Let move on and create different pages and routes.

Note   You'll find all the codes in the www.github.com/mhadaily/awesome-apress-pwa/chapter03/01-material-design-and-core-shared-modules-setup.

Figure 3-2. *Initial application shell*

Login / Profile Page

We need to create pages so that my users can register, log in, and see their profiles. To begin, we create `UserModule,` including routing:

```
ng generate module modules/user --routing
```

As we are going to lazy load this module, we need at least one path and one component. To generate a component, continue running the following command:

```
ng generate component modules/user/userContainer --flat
flag --flat ignores creating a new folder for this component.
```

Once the component is generated, we should add it to UserModule declarations and then define our path in UserModuleRouting – path /user could be lazy loaded in AppRoutingModule accordingly.

// UserModuleRouting

```
import { NgModule } from '@angular/core';
import { Routes, RouterModule } from '@angular/router';

import { UserContainerComponent } from './user-container.component';

const routes: Routes = [
  {
    path: '',
    component: UserContainerComponent
  }
];

@NgModule({
  imports: [RouterModule.forChild(routes)],
  exports: [RouterModule]
})
export class UserRoutingModule { }
```

//AppModuleRouting

```
import { NgModule } from '@angular/core';
import { Routes, RouterModule } from '@angular/router';

const routes: Routes = [
  {
    path: 'user',
    loadChildren: './modules/user/user.module#UserModule',
  }
];

@NgModule({
  imports: [RouterModule.forRoot(routes)],
  exports: [RouterModule]
})
export class AppRoutingModule { }
```

Adding Login, Signup, and Profile UI and Functionalities

Before we continue to add login/signup functionalities, we must activate Sign-in providers in Firebase. Hence, go to your project Firebase console, find Authentication under the develop group on the left menu list, and then move the current tab to Sign-in methods. To keep it simple, we will use Email/Password providers; however, you should be able to add more providers as you wish (see Figure 3-3).

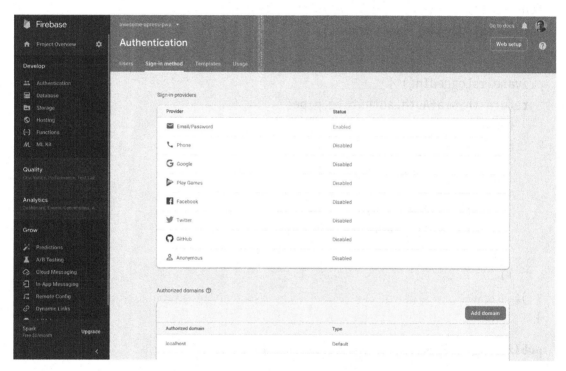

Figure 3-3. *Enable Email/Password authentication*

Let's move on and create an Angular service that handles all Firebase authentication methods. Continue by running the following command:

```
ng generate service modules/core/firebaseAuthService
```

We need to write several methods, checking the user login state and doing log in, sign up, and log out.

Take your time and look at Listing 3-1 where we implement FirebaseAuthService in order to invoke necessary methods from AngularFireAuth service and share the state across the app. The service methods are self-explanatory.

Listing 3-1. App/modules/core/auth.service.ts

```
export class AuthService {
  // expose all data
  public authErrorMessages$ = new Subject<string>();
  public isLoading$ = new BehaviorSubject<boolean>(true);
  public user$ = new Subject<User>();

  constructor(private afAuth: AngularFireAuth) {
    this.isLoggedIn().subscribe();
  }

  private isLoggedIn() {
    return this.afAuth.authState.pipe(
      first(),
      tap(user => {
        this.isLoading$.next(false);
        if (user) {
          const { email, uid } = user;
          this.user$.next({ email, uid });
        }
      })
    );
  }

  public signUpFirebase({ email, password }) {
    this.isLoading$.next(true);
    this.handleErrorOrSuccess(() => {
      return this.afAuth.auth.createUserWithEmailAndPassword(email, password);
    });
  }

  public loginFirebase({ email, password }) {
    this.isLoading$.next(true);
    this.handleErrorOrSuccess(() => {
      return this.afAuth.auth.signInWithEmailAndPassword(email, password);
    });
  }
```

```
public logOutFirebase() {
  this.isLoading$.next(true);
  this.afAuth.auth
    .signOut()
    .then(() => {
      this.isLoading$.next(false);
      this.user$.next(null);
    })
    .catch(e => {
      console.error(e);
      this.isLoading$.next(false);
      this.authErrorMessages$.next("Something is wrong when signing out!");
    });
}

private handleErrorOrSuccess(
  cb: () => Promise<firebase.auth.UserCredential>
) {
  cb()
    .then(data => this.authenticateUser(data))
    .catch(e => this.handleSignUpLoginError(e));
}

private authenticateUser(UserCredential) {
  const {
    user: { email, uid }
  } = UserCredential;

  this.isLoading$.next(false);
  this.user$.next({ email, uid });
}

private handleSignUpLoginError(error: { code: string; message: string })
{
  this.isLoading$.next(false);
  const errorMessage = error.message;
```

```
    this.authErrorMessages$.next(errorMessage);
  }
}
```

Lastly, the application should provide a UI to log in and sign up as well as user information. Going back to our userContainerComponent, we will implement UI and methods respectively. Listings 3-2 through 3-4 show our TypeScript, HTML, and CSS.

Listing 3-2. User-container.component.ts

```
export class UserContainerComponent implements OnInit {
  public errorMessages$ = this.afAuthService.authErrorMessages$;
  public user$ = this.afAuthService.user$;
  public isLoading$ = this.afAuthService.isLoading$;
  public loginForm: FormGroup;
  public hide = true;

  constructor(
    private fb: FormBuilder,
    private afAuthService: FirebaseAuthService
  ) {}

  ngOnInit() {
    this.createLoginForm();
  }

  private createLoginForm() {
    this.loginForm = this.fb.group({
      email: ["", [Validators.required, Validators.email]],
      password: ["", [Validators.required]]
    });
  }

  public signUp() {
    this.checkFormValidity(() => {
      this.afAuthService.signUpFirebase(this.loginForm.value);
    });
  }
```

```
  public login() {
    this.checkFormValidity(() => {
      this.afAuthService.loginFirebase(this.loginForm.value);
    });
  }

  private checkFormValidity(cb) {
    if (this.loginForm.valid) {
      cb();
    } else {
      this.errorMessages$.next("Please enter correct Email and Password value");
    }
  }

  public logOut() {
    this.afAuthService.logOutFirebase();
  }

  public getErrorMessage(controlName: string, errorName: string): string {
    const control = this.loginForm.get(controlName);
    return control.hasError("required")
      ? "You must enter a value"
      : control.hasError(errorName)
        ? `Not a valid ${errorName}`
        : "";
  }
}
```

Listing 3-3. User-container.component.html

```
<mat-card *ngIf="user$ | async as user">
  <mat-card-title>
    Hello {{user.email}}
  </mat-card-title>
  <mat-card-subtitle>
    ID: {{user.uid}}
  </mat-card-subtitle>
```

```
  <mat-card-content>
    <button mat-raised-button color="secondary" (click)="logOut()">Logout
    </button>
  </mat-card-content>
</mat-card>

<mat-card *ngIf="!(user$ | async)">
  <mat-card-title>
    Access to your notes
  </mat-card-title>
  <mat-card-subtitle class="error" *ngIf="errorMessages$ | async as
  errorMessage">
    {{ errorMessage }}
  </mat-card-subtitle>
  <mat-card-content>
    <div class="login-container" [formGroup]="loginForm">
      <mat-form-field>
        <input matInput placeholder="Enter your email" formControl
        Name="email" required>
        <mat-error *ngIf="loginForm.get('email').invalid">{{getErrorMessage
        ('email', 'email')}}</mat-error>
      </mat-form-field>
      <br>
      <mat-form-field>
        <input matInput placeholder="Enter your password" [type]="hide ?
        'password' : 'text'" formControlName="password">
        <mat-icon matSuffix (click)="hide = !hide">{{hide ? 'visibility' :
        'visibility_off'}}</mat-icon>
        <mat-error *ngIf="loginForm.get('password').invalid">{{getErrorMess
        age('password')}}</mat-error>
      </mat-form-field>
    </div>
    <button mat-raised-button color="primary" (click)="login()">Login
    </button>
  </mat-card-content>
```

```
<mat-card-content><br>----- OR -----<br><br></mat-card-content>
<mat-card-content>
  <button mat-raised-button color="accent" (click)="signUp()">Sign Up
  </button>
</mat-card-content>
<mat-card-footer>
  <mat-progress-bar *ngIf="isLoading$ | async" mode="indeterminate">
  </mat-progress-bar>
</mat-card-footer>
</mat-card>
```

Listing 3-4. User-container.component.scss

```
.login-container {
  display: flex;
  flex-direction: column;
  > * {
    width: 100%;
  }
}
```

Figure 3-4 shows the result of what we have done up to this point.

Figure 3-4. *Login, Signup, and Profile UI in the app*

Note   You'll find all the codes in the www.github.com/mhadaily/awesome-apress-pwa/chapter03/02-login-signup-profile.

Although what we need to proceed has been achieved, you are not limited and can continue adding more and more Firebase features such as forgot password link, password-less login, and other providers for log in.

Firebase CRUD[3] Operations for Note Module

In the following section, we are going to work on different views and methods in order to list, add, delete, and update notes in our application; let's do it step by step.

Set Up Firestore Database

First things first: a quick start to show how to set up our Firestore database.

1. Open your browser and go to Firebase project console.

2. In the **Database** section, click **the Get Started** or **Create database** button for Cloud Firestore.

3. Select **Locked mode** for your Cloud Firestore Security Rules.[4]

4. Click Enable as shown in Figure 3-5.

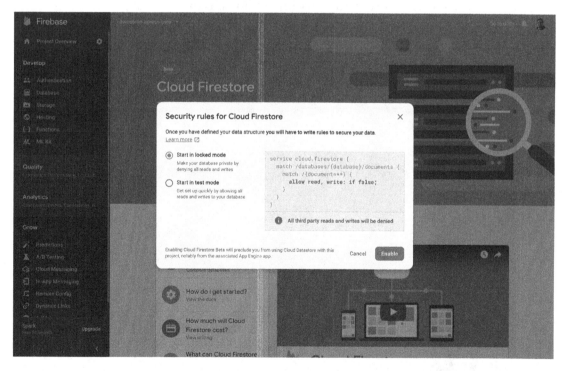

Figure 3-5. *Select locked mode when creating a new database in Firebase*

---

[3]https://en.wikipedia.org/wiki/Create,_read,_update_and_delete
[4]https://firebase.google.com/docs/firestore/quickstart

51

Below is the Database schema[5] that we aim to create in order to store our users and their notes.

```
----- users // this is a collection
        ------- [USER IDs] // this is a document
               ------ notes // this is a collection
                      ----- [NOTE DOCUMENT]
                      ----- [NOTE DOCUMENT]
                      ----- [NOTE DOCUMENT]
        ------- [USER IDs] // this is a document
               ------ notes // this is a collection
                      ----- [NOTE DOCUMENT]
                      ----- [NOTE DOCUMENT]
                      ----- [NOTE DOCUMENT]
```

It is possible to create collections and documents in Firestore manually; but we will do it programmatically later by implementing proper logics in our application (see Figure 3-6).

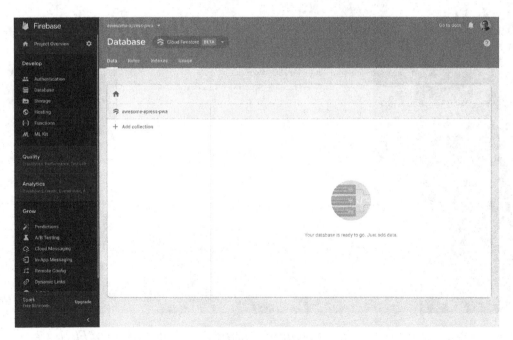

Figure 3-6. *Firestore view once it is enabled*

---

[5]https://en.wikipedia.org/wiki/Database_schema

The last step is to set Firestore rules to require a user unique id (uid) in request in order to give sufficient permission to do create/read/update/delete actions. Click on the *Rules* tab and copy and paste the following rules (see Figure 3-7).

```
service cloud.firestore {
  match /databases/{database}/documents {
    // Make sure the uid of the requesting user matches name of the user
    // document. The wildcard expression {userId} makes the userId variable
    // available in rules.
    match /users/{userId} {
      allow read, update, delete: if request.auth.uid == userId;
      allow create: if request.auth.uid != null;
      // make sure user can do all action for notes collection if userID is
      matched
        match /notes/{document=**} {
          allow create, read, update, delete: if request.auth.uid == userId;
        }
    }
  }
}
```

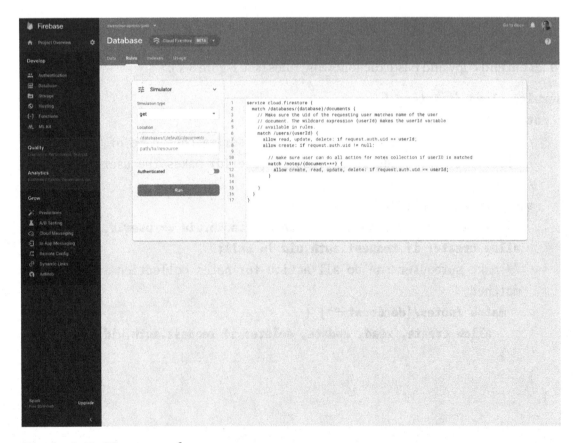

Figure 3-7. *Firestore rules*

List, Add, and Detail Note Views

The next step, once the Firestore setup is done, is to create our components in order to show a list of notes, add a note, and detail the note view along with their relevant functionalities.

To begin, generate a notes module, including routing, by running the following command:

```
ng generate module modules/notes --routing
```

Let's take a look at NotesRoutingModule:

```
const routes: Routes = [
```

```
  {
    path: "",
    component: NotesListComponent
  },
  {
    path: "add",
    component: NotesAddComponent
  },
  {
    path: ":id",
    component: NoteDetailsComponent
  }
];

@NgModule({
  imports: [RouterModule.forChild(routes)],
  exports: [RouterModule]
})
export class NotesRoutingModule {}
```

As you see, three paths have been defined; therefore we should generate related components by running each command separately:

```
ng generate component modules/notes/notesList
ng generate component modules/notes/notesAdd
ng generate component modules/notes/noteDetails
```

Finally, lazy load NotesModule by adding NotesRoutingModule into the AppRoutingModule:

```
const routes: Routes = [
  {
    path: "",
    redirectTo: "/notes",
    pathMatch: "full"
  },
```

```
  {
    path: "user",
    loadChildren: "./modules/user/user.module#UserModule",
  },
  {
    path: "notes",
    loadChildren: "./modules/notes/notes.module#NotesModule"
  }
];

@NgModule({
  imports: [RouterModule.forRoot(routes)],
  exports: [RouterModule]
})
export class AppRoutingModule {}
```

Authentication Service

The authentication service is used to log in, log out, and sign up and check if the user has already been authenticated for the application. The credentials were sent to Firebase by calling proper methods on the AngularFire Auth service to perform each function accordingly.

AuthService is required to be injected[6] in order to handle the authentication layer in our app:

```
ng generate service modules/core/auth
```

The following code shows the logic for AuthService:

// auth.service.ts

```
interface User {
  uid: string;
  email: string;
}
```

---

[6]https://angular.io/guide/dependency-injection

```typescript
@Injectable({
  providedIn: "root"
})
export class AuthService {
  public authErrorMessages$ = new BehaviorSubject<string>(null);
  public isLoading$ = new BehaviorSubject<boolean>(true);
  public user$ = new BehaviorSubject<User>(null);

  private authState = null;

  constructor(private afAuth: AngularFireAuth) {
    this.isLoggedIn().subscribe(user => (this.authState = user));
  }

  get authenticated(): boolean {
    return this.authState !== null;
  }

  get id(): string {
    return this.authenticated ? this.authState.uid : "";
  }

  private isLoggedIn(): Observable<User | null> {
    return this.afAuth.authState.pipe(
      map(user => {
        if (user) {
          const { email, uid } = user;
          this.user$.next({ email, uid });
          return { email, uid };
        }
        return null;
      }),
      tap(() => this.isLoading$.next(false))
    );
  }

  public getCurrentUserUid(): string {
    return this.afAuth.auth.currentUser.uid;
  }
```

```
public signUpFirebase({ email, password }) {
  this.isLoading$.next(true);
  this.handleErrorOrSuccess(() => {
    return this.afAuth.auth.createUserWithEmailAndPassword(email, password);
  });
}

public loginFirebase({ email, password }) {
  this.isLoading$.next(true);
  this.handleErrorOrSuccess(() => {
    return this.afAuth.auth.signInWithEmailAndPassword(email, password);
  });
}

public logOutFirebase() {
  this.isLoading$.next(true);
  return this.afAuth.auth.signOut();
}

private handleErrorOrSuccess(
  cb: () => Promise<firebase.auth.UserCredential>
) {
  cb()
    .then(data => this.authenticateUser(data))
    .catch(e => this.handleSignUpLoginError(e));
}

private authenticateUser(UserCredential) {
  const {
    user: { email, uid }
  } = UserCredential;

  this.isLoading$.next(false);
}
```

```
private handleSignUpLoginError(error: { code: string; message: string })
{
    this.isLoading$.next(false);
    const errorMessage = error.message;
    this.authErrorMessages$.next(errorMessage);
  }
}
```

Data Service

This service contains a standard set of CRUD methods (Create, read, update and delete). Functionalities such as fetching all notes; add, update and delete; and fetch detail note by calling proper methods or requesting from proper APIs. In fact, it acts as an interface between the Angular application and the back-end APIs.

To generate **DataService**, run the command below:

```
ng generate service modules/core/data
```

The following code shows the logic for DataService:

// data.service.ts

```
interface Note {
  id: string;
  title: string;
  content: string;
}

@Injectable({
  providedIn: "root"
})
export class DataService {
  protected readonly USERS_COLLECTION = "users";
  protected readonly NOTES_COLLECTION = "notes";
  public isLoading$ = new BehaviorSubject<boolean>(true);

  get timestamp() {
    return new Date().getTime();
  }
```

```
  constructor(private afDb: AngularFirestore, private auth: AuthService) {}

  getUserNotesCollection() {
    return this.afDb.collection(
      this.USERS_COLLECTION + "/" + this.auth.id + "/" + this.NOTES_COLLECTION,
      ref => ref.orderBy("updated_at", "desc")
    );
  }

  addNote(data): Promise<DocumentReference> {
    return this.getUserNotesCollection().add({
      ...data,
      created_at: this.timestamp,
      updated_at: this.timestamp
    });
  }

  editNote(id, data): Promise<void> {
    return this.getUserNotesCollection()
      .doc(id)
      .update({
        ...data,
        updated_at: this.timestamp
      });
  }

  deleteNote(id): Promise<void> {
    return this.getUserNotesCollection()
      .doc(id)
      .delete();
  }

  getNote(id): Observable<any> {
    return this.getUserNotesCollection()
      .doc(id)
      .snapshotChanges()
      .pipe(
        map(snapshot => {
```

```
            const data = snapshot.payload.data() as Note;
            const id = snapshot.payload.id;
            return { id, ...data };
          }),
          catchError(e => throwError(e))
      );
  }

  getNotes(): Observable<any> {
    return this.getUserNotesCollection()
      .snapshotChanges()
      .pipe(
        map(snapshot =>
          snapshot.map(a => {
            //Get document data
            const data = a.payload.doc.data() as Note;
            //Get document id
            const id = a.payload.doc.id;
            //Use spread operator to add the id to the document data
            return { id, ...data };
          })
        ),
        tap(notes => {
          this.isLoading$.next(false);
        }),
        catchError(e => throwError(e))
      );
  }
}
```

Authentication Guard

Since this application requires a user to be authenticated before performing any action, we should make sure that all routes are protected by a guard.

AuthGuard helps to protect access to authentication routes. Since we need to put this guard on a lazy load module, CanLoad should be implemented.

Ng generate guard modules/notes/auth

The following code shows the logic for AuthGuard:

// auth.guard.ts

```
@Injectable()
export class AuthGuard implements CanLoad {
  constructor(private auth: AuthService, private router: Router) {}

  canLoad(): Observable<boolean> {
    if (!this.auth.authenticated) {
      this.router.navigate(["/user"]);
      return of(false);
    }
    return of(true);
  }
}
```

We should provide AuthGuard in our AppRoutingModule. It's important to remember to add this guard into providers.

```
  {
    path: "notes",
    loadChildren: "./modules/notes/notes.module#NotesModule",
    canLoad: [AuthGuard]
  }

@NgModule({
  imports: [RouterModule.forRoot(routes)],
  providers: [AuthGuard],
  exports: [RouterModule]
})
```

NoteList, NoteAdd, and NoteDetail Components

We have prepared all the service layers and routing that are needed in the application. The rest of the application is to just implement proper UI and components logics for NotesList, NoteAdd, and NoteDetail components (Listings 3-5 through 3-13). Since it's easy, I would like you to just take a look at the components, and at the end, Figure 3-8 will demonstrate the result.

Listing 3-5. // Notes-list.component.ts

```
export class NotesListComponent implements OnInit {
  notes$: Observable<Note[]>;
  isDbLoading$;

  constructor(private db: DataService) {}

  ngOnInit() {
    this.notes$ = this.db.getNotes();
    this.isDbLoading$ = this.db.isLoading$;
  }
}
```

Listing 3-6. // Notes-list.component.html

```
<div *ngIf="notes$ | async as notes; else notFound">
  <app-note-card *ngFor="let note of notes" [note]="note" [loading]="isDb
  Loading$ | async" [routerLink]="['/notes', note.id]">
  </app-note-card>
</div>
<ng-template #notFound>
  <mat-card>
    <mat-card-title>
      Either you have no notes
    </mat-card-title>
  </mat-card>
</ng-template>
```

Listing 3-7. // Notes-card.component.ts

```
@Component({
  selector: "app-note-card",
  templateUrl: "./note-card.component.html",
  styleUrls: ["./note-card.component.scss"]
})
export class NoteCardComponent {
  @Input()
  note;

  @Input()
  loading;

  @Input()
  edit = true;
}
```

Listing 3-8. // Notes-card.component.html

```
<mat-card>
  <mat-card-title>{{ note.title }}</mat-card-title>
  <mat-card-subtitle>{{ note.created_at | date:"short" }}</mat-card-
  subtitle>
  <mat-card-content>{{ note.content }}</mat-card-content>
  <mat-card-footer class="text-right">
    <button color="primary" *ngIf="edit"><mat-icon>edit</mat-icon></button>
    <mat-progress-bar *ngIf="loading" mode="indeterminate"></mat-progress-
    bar>
  </mat-card-footer>
</mat-card>
```

Listing 3-9. // Notes-add.component.ts

```
export class NotesAddComponent {
  public userID;
  public errorMessages$ = new Subject();
```

```
constructor(
  private router: Router,
  private data: DataService,
  private snackBar: SnackBarService
) {}

onSaveNote(values) {
  this.data
    .addNote(values)
    .then(doc => {
      this.router.navigate(["/notes"]);
      this.snackBar.open(`Note ${doc.id} has been succeffully saved`);
    })
    .catch(e => {
      this.errorMessages$.next("something is wrong when adding to DB");
    });
}

onSendError(message) {
  this.errorMessages$.next(message);
}
}
```

Listing 3-10. // Notes-add.component.html

```
<mat-card>
  <mat-card-title>New Note</mat-card-title>
  <mat-card-subtitle class="error" *ngIf="errorMessages$ | async as
  errorMessage">
    {{ errorMessage }}
  </mat-card-subtitle>
  <mat-card-content>
    <app-note-form (saveNote)="onSaveNote($event)" (sendError)="onSendError
    ($event)"></app-note-form>
  </mat-card-content>
</mat-card>
```

Listing 3-11. // Notes-form.component.ts

```
export class NoteFormComponent implements OnInit {
  noteForm: FormGroup;

  @Input()
  note;

  @Output()
  saveNote = new EventEmitter();

  @Output()
  sendError = new EventEmitter();

  constructor(private fb: FormBuilder) {}

  ngOnInit() {
    this.createForm();

    if (this.note) {
      this.noteForm.patchValue(this.note);
    }
  }

  createForm() {
    this.noteForm = this.fb.group({
      title: ["", Validators.required],
      content: ["", Validators.required]
    });
  }

  addNote() {
    if (this.noteForm.valid) {
      this.saveNote.emit(this.noteForm.value);
    } else {
      this.sendError.emit("please fill all fields");
    }
  }
}
```

Listing 3-12. // Notes-form.component.html

```html
<div class="note-container" [formGroup]="noteForm">
  <mat-form-field>
    <input matInput placeholder="Enter your title" formControlName="title"
    required>
  </mat-form-field>
  <br>
  <mat-form-field>
    <textarea matInput placeholder="Leave a comment"
    formControlName="content" required cdkTextareaAutosize></textarea>
  </mat-form-field>
</div>
<br>
<br>
<div class="text-right">
  <button mat-raised-button color="primary" (click)="addNote()">Save</
button>
</div>
```

Listing 3-13. // Notes-details.component.ts

```typescript
export class NoteDetailsComponent implements OnInit {
  public errorMessages$ = new Subject();
  public note$;
  public isEdit;

  private id;

  constructor(
    private data: DataService,
    private route: ActivatedRoute,
    private snackBar: SnackBarService,
    private router: Router
  ) {}
```

```
ngOnInit() {
  const id = this.route.snapshot.paramMap.get("id");
  this.id = id;
  this.note$ = this.data.getNote(id);
}

delete() {
  if (confirm("Are you sure?")) {
    this.data
      .deleteNote(this.id)
      .then(() => {
        this.router.navigate(["/notes"]);
        this.snackBar.open(`${this.id} successfully was deleted`);
      })
      .catch(e => {
        this.snackBar.open("Unable to delete this note");
      });
  }
}

edit() {
  this.isEdit = !this.isEdit;
}

saveNote(values) {
  this.data
    .editNote(this.id, values)
    .then(() => {
      this.snackBar.open("Successfully done");
      this.edit();
    })
    .catch(e => {
      this.snackBar.open("Unable to edit this note");
      this.edit();
    });
}
```

```
  sendError(message) {
    this.errorMessages$.next(message);
  }
}
```

Listing 3-14. // Notes-details.component.html

```html
<div *ngIf="note$ | async as note; else spinner">

    <mat-card *ngIf="isEdit">
        <mat-card-subtitle class="error" *ngIf="errorMessages$ | async as
        errorMessage">
            {{ errorMessage }}
        </mat-card-subtitle>
        <mat-card-content>
            <app-note-form [note]="note" (saveNote)="saveNote($event)"
            (sendError)="sendError($event)"></app-note-form>
        </mat-card-content>
    </mat-card>

    <app-note-card *ngIf="!isEdit" [note]="note" [loading]="isDbLoading$ |
    async"></app-note-card>

    <button mat-raised-button color="accent" (click)="delete()"><mat-
    icon>delete</mat-icon></button>
    <button mat-raised-button color="primary" (click)="edit()"><mat-
    icon>edit</mat-icon></button>
</div>

<ng-template #spinner>
    <mat-spinner></mat-spinner>
</ng-template>
```

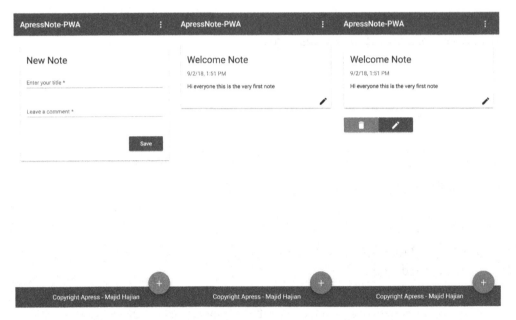

Figure 3-8. *Add note, details, and notes list view*

Note   If you are comfortable, check out the final code. You will find it in github. com/mhadaily/chapter03/03-note-list-add-edit-update-delete/. Clone the project and navigate to the folder. Then run the following commands:

```
npm install // to install dependencies

npm start // to run development server

npm run deploy // to deploy to firebase
```

Summary

The first three chapters' goal was to reveal PWA fundamentals; tools; and creating an app, step by step, together. It may sound unrelated to PWA; however, as we continue in this book, chapter by chapter, section by section, we will try to make our app progressively better to finally have a great PWA with Angular.

Beginning with the next chapter, we will dive into implementing offline capabilities, caches, push notifications, new modern browsers' APIs, and more just to create a native-like app for better user experiences on the mobile and web. While this was not possible just a few years ago, these days it's widely supported in major browsers.

CHAPTER 4

Angular Service Worker

Up to this point, the application that we built has no PWA characteristics. From this chapter on, we are going to gradually add PWA features and dive into them in depth. Angular provides a module called `service-worker` to handle caching strategies and push notifications out of the box. Angular Service Worker is highly configurable and can satisfy Angular app requirements. However, before we start implementing this module, we should have a basic understanding of Service Worker.

This chapter begins with Service Worker fundamentals and cache APIs as it's crucial to know what's going on behind the scenes when we code with Angular Service Worker. Then, Angular CLI will help us to scaffold and turn our project to PWA by using `@angular/pwa` schematics.

Although, the focus is on CLI v6, each modification will be broken down in order to give us a better picture of what needs to be done if it is implemented manually, for instance, in Angular version 5 or even lower.

Service Workers: The Brain of PWAs

Your brain is the center of decision making and has full control of your body. Server workers resemble our brain. At their core, they are worker scripts written in JavaScript, enabled with a few lines of code in modern browsers and runs in the background. Once activated, developers are able to intercept network requests, handle push notifications, manage caches, and perform many different tasks.

You may ask, what if it's not supported?[1]

---

[1]All major browsers, support Service Worker. Check `https://caniuse.com/#feat=serviceworkers`

© Majid Hajian 2019
M. Hajian, *Progressive Web Apps with Angular*, https://doi.org/10.1007/978-1-4842-4448-7_4

If it is not implemented in a user's browser, it simply falls back, and the website will function normally. The beautify of PWA is, by its definition, that anyone – regardless of browser and operating system of choice – should be able to surf the website and get the best user experience. This description refers to a phrase known as "perfect progressive enhancement."

Understanding Service Worker

In order to understand Service Worker, think of yourself sitting in the center of your brain. You are provided with different tools to gain control of your body. You see everything, and you can make any decision. It's up to you either let your body do what it does normally or redirect the decision to a different direction. You may even stop the brain from functioning completely. This is what you can do with network requests in Service Worker; it acts similar to a proxy between a website and server. The ability to totally take over a network request makes Service Worker extremely powerful and allows you to react and respond!

It's crucial to mention that although Service Worker is written in JavaScript, it has slightly different behavior such as the following:

- Runs in different threads from the main JavaScript that empowers your app. Figure 4-1 illustrates how Service Worker sits on a different thread and intercepts a network request.

- Runs in its own global context.

- Designed to be fully asynchronous; therefore, it doesn't have access to things such as synchronous XHR and LocalStorage.

- Runs in worker context – thus, it doesn't have access to DOM.

- Runs HTTPS-Only in production, in addition to Localhost for development.

- Runs in 1:1 scope, meaning there can be only one Service Worker per scope.

- Can be terminated any time.

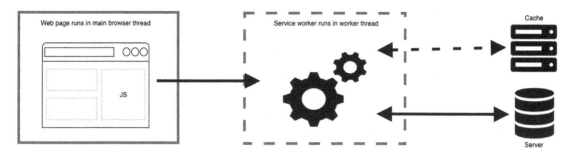

Figure 4-1. *Service Worker can run in different threads and intercept requests*

Service Workers are event driven. As a consequence, it is easier than you think to get started with them once the basics of the events are understood. Simply pick and choose which event you want to tap into, and you are good to go. Let's take a look at primary events in Service Workers.

The Service Worker Life Cycle

Service Worker in its life cycle has different stages. Take your time and look at Figure 4-2, which demonstrates how the Service Worker life cycle takes place in four steps. Imagine that your website is going to be served by a Service Worker:

Step 1, when the user navigates to the website, by calling the `register()` function, the browser detects the Service Worker JavaScript file; therefore, it downloads, parses, and the execution phase begins. The Register function retunes a Promise[2] in which in case of error, the registration gets rejected and the Service Worker registration process stops.

Step 2, however, if registration goes well and gets resolved, the Service Worker state turns into **installed**. Therefore, an **install** event fires where it is the best place to precache all of the static assets. Keep in mind that an **install** event happens only the first time after registration.

Step 3, as soon as install has completed successfully, Service Worker is then **activated**, and has total control under its own scope. Similar to the **install** event, activate only happens for the first time after registration and once **install** has completed.

---

[2]https://developer.mozilla.org/en/docs/Web/JavaScript/Reference/Global_Objects/
 Promise

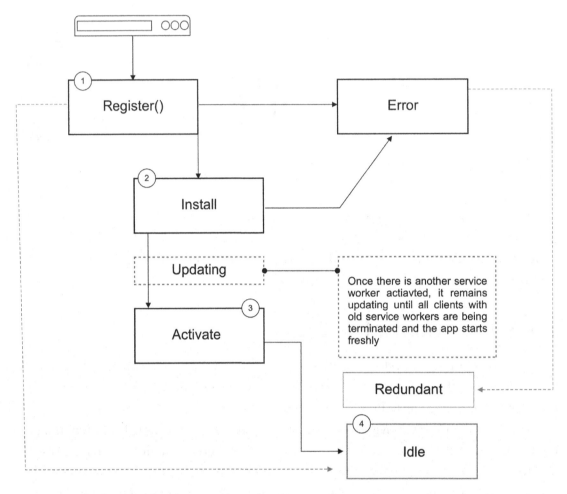

Figure 4-2. *Server worker life cycle*

Note   Scope is used to specify the subset of your content that you want the server worker to control and can be defined either by the optional parameter `scope` in second argument in `register()` function or by default where the server worker JavaScript file is located. For instance, if the server worker file is in the root of the application, it has control over all pages. However, `/sw-test/` specifies only access to all pages under this origin. Figure 4-3 demonstrates how the scope works.

Step 4, once install and activate events are completed with no errors, Service Worker will be effective. However, if it fails during installation, activation, or is replaced by a new one, it remains redundant and does not affect the app.

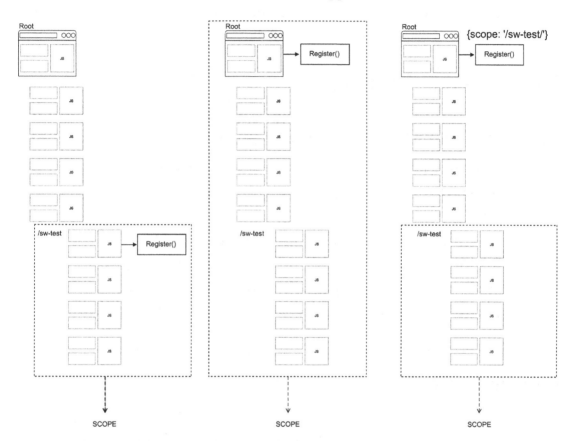

Figure 4-3. *Service worker scope demonstration*

As mentioned, a website without Service Worker won't handle any requests; however, as soon as it's installed and activated, it can control every single request under its own scope. Hence, to kick the logic off in Service Worker after the first installation and activation, the website needs to be refreshed, or we should navigate to another page.

Last but not least, it may happen that we want to alter a registered and activated Service Worker. If there is byte-size change in the registered file, the browser considers it, and all the steps, as mentioned above, will happen again. However, since we already had a Service Worker activated, the process is slightly different. This time, Service Worker will not get activated immediately; therefore, the logic in Service Worker does not execute.

It remains **waiting** until all tabs and clients that have old Service Worker running are terminated. In other words, all the tabs that have the website open must be closed and reopened again. As we are developers and know ninja tricks, we can simply skip waiting from DevTools, or if we want, we can do it programmatically in Service Worker logic, too. We will review this in detail, shortly, in this chapter.

Service Worker Functional Events

Along with **Install** and **Activate** events, **Fetch**, **Push**, and **Sync** events are also available in Service Worker and are known as **functional events**. In short:

- **Fetch**: happens every time the browser requests static assets or dynamic content; for instance, request for an image, video, CSS, JS, HTML, and even an ajax request.

- **Push**: happens when web app receives a push notification.

- **Sync**: Lets you defer actions until the user has stable connectivity. This is useful to ensure that whatever the user wants to send is actually sent. This API also allows servers to push periodic updates to the app so the app can update when it's next online.

Chrome DevTools

No developer feels comfortable without an appropriate debugging tool. Among all browsers, at the time of writing this book, Chrome DevTools is the best choice to debug Service Workers. Let's catch a glimpse Chrome DevTools and see what options it provides to assist us in making debugging easier and enhancing PWAs even better.

Console, Application, and Audits are main panels for debugging Service Worker in Chrome DevTools. Audits panel leverages **Lighthouse**,[3] which is an open source, automated tool for improving the quality of websites and can be used to run accessibility, performance, SEO, best practices, and a PWA audit test. We use the **Audits** panels to qualify web pages, especially **Progressive Web App**, which is in our target (see Figure 4-4).

---

[3]https://developers.google.com/web/tools/lighthouse/

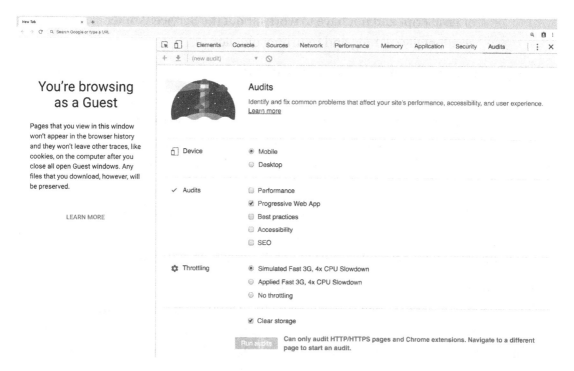

Figure 4-4. *Audits panel in Chrome where we run auditing tests on web pages*

Having looked at **Application** panel, we see the following:

- **Manifest**: where we can debug *Web App Manifest.*[4]

- **Service Workers**: where we debug Service Worker and have many options such as update Service Worker, remove, skip waiting, and different options to work with the network (Figure 4-5).

  - **Offline**: simulate a no-internet-access in browser.

  - **Update on reload**: where it downloads Service Worker every time a page is reloaded, and therefore all life-cycle events, including install and activate, happen on reload. This is incredibly useful for debugging.

  - **Bypass for network**: Will force the browser to ignore any active Service Worker and fetch resources from the network. This is extremely useful for situations where you want to work on CSS

[4]Chapter 6 is dedicated to Web App Manifest.

or JavaScript and not have to worry about the Service Worker
accidentally caching and returning old files.

- **Clear storage**: where we can delete all caches.

- LocalStorage, Session Storage, **Indexed DB**, Web SQL, and cookies
  are all different type of storages you may be familiar with. Indexed
  DB will be in our main focus in this book since it's asynchronous and
  Service Worker has access to it.

- **Cache Storage**: it's a new cache API in browsers, key-value base, and
  capable of storing requests and responding. We open this cache to
  store most of our assets and dynamic content. This cache is extremely
  powerful and is available in both application and Service Worker.

If you are interested in learning more about Chrome DevTools, you can check the
detailed documents at the Google developer website found in `https://developers.`
`google.com/web/tools/chrome-devtools/`. I strongly recommend that you take your
time and explore, in depth, the information about DevTools, which I believe makes you
much more productive.

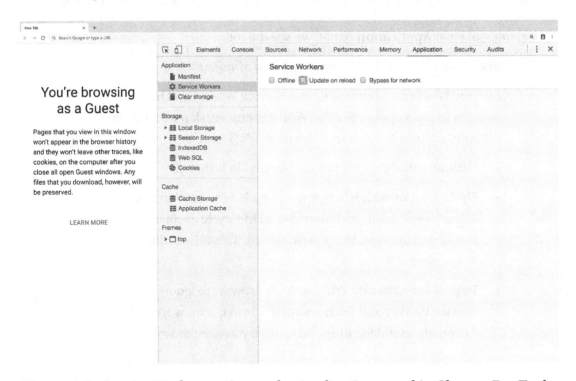

Figure 4-5. *Service Workers option under Application panel in Chrome DevTools*

I know that you are impatient to start coding and see sample codes, so let's get started.

Service Worker Example Code

It is time to write a few lines of code to see how we can register a Service Worker and explore its own life cycle. To begin, I'll create a simple html file, and right before `</body>` I'll open a `<script>` tag and will register `service-worker.js` file where it is located in the root next to `index.html`.

```html
<!DOCTYPE html>
<html lang="en">
<head>
    <meta charset="UTF-8">
    <meta name="viewport" content="width=device-width, initial-scale=1.0">
    <meta http-equiv="X-UA-Compatible" content="ie=edge">
    <title>Apress Simple Service Worker Registartion</title>
</head>
<body>
    <div style="text-align: center; padding: 3rem">
        <h1>Apress Simple Service Worker Registartion</h1>
    </div>
    <script>
        if ('serviceWorker' in navigator) {
            navigator.serviceWorker
                .register('/service-worker.js')
                .then(registration => {  // registeration object
                    console.log('Service worker is registered', registration);
                })
                .catch(e => {
                    console.error('Something went wrong while registaring
                    service worker.')
                });
        }
    </script>
</body>
</html>
```

Progressive enhancement is meant to allow all users to load our web pages whether they are using the oldest or latest versions of browsers. Consequently, we should always check for features that may not be available in different browsers. Code above has started by a feature-checking statement if ('serviceWorker' in navigator) {}. Once availability is ensured, the register method has been called register('/service-worker.js') by passing the Service Worker path. This method has a second argument that is optional to pass extra options to the method: for instance, defining scope. Since, there is no second argument in the register method, scope is supposed to be the default; and in this case it is the root where the Service Worker file is located. then and catch return the registration or error object when the register promised is resolved or rejected respectively.

Logic in server-worker.js is listeners for **activate** and **install** events where we log two messages in the console in the callback function. Self in this context refers to ServiceWorkerGlobalScope.

```
//service-worker.js

self.addEventListener("install", (event) => {
  console.log("[SW.JS] Step 2, Service worker has been installed");
});

self.addEventListener("activate", (event) => {
  console.log("[SW.JS] Step 2, Service worker has been activated");
});
```

You will be able to see logs when you open devTools in console panel (see Figure 4-6).

Note   You can pull down www.github.com/mhadaily/awesome-apress-pwa/chapter04/01-simple-service-worker. Run npm install and then run npm start. It runs a web server on port 8080. You can navigate to localhost:8080. If you copy and paste code from the book to your project, you need a web server to run your code.

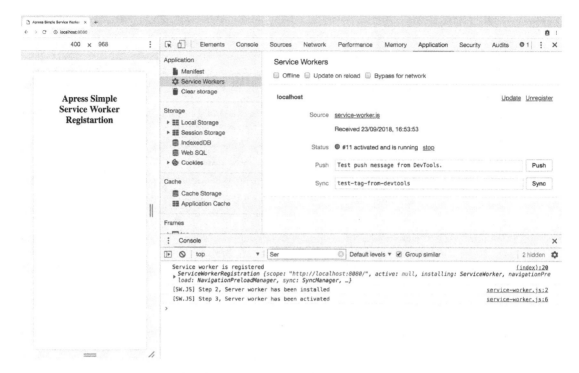

Figure 4-6. *Service worker life cycle when it's registered for the first time. As you see, install and activate events happen.*

Reload the web page; from now on until the new change in `service-wokrer.js`, you'll only see the registration object logged in the console, and install and activate does not get fired anymore (see Figure 4-7).

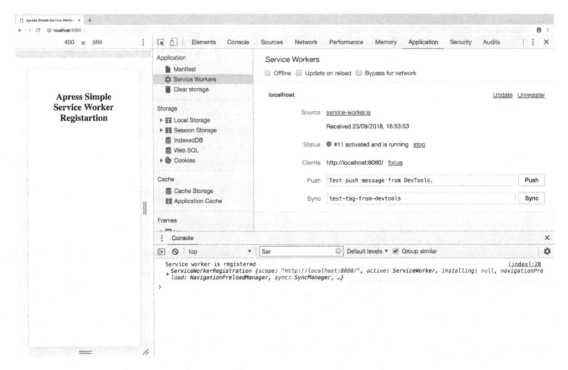

Figure 4-7. *Once Service Worker is activated, second reload doesn't fire install and activate event anymore*

Add just a few lines to the Service Worker file and then reload the application while watching Service Workers in the application panel.

```
// modified service-worker.js
// this is equivalent to following addEventistener
// self.oninstall = (event) => { };
self.addEventListener("install", event => {
  console.log("[SW.JS] Step 2, Service worker has been installed");
  console.log("Just added something;");
});

// this is equivalent to following addEventistener
// self.onactivate = (event) => { };
self.addEventListener("activate", event => {
  console.log("[SW.JS] Step 3, Service worker has been activated");
});
```

After reloading, you'll see that a new Service Worker is waiting until all clients are terminated. Once the browser detects a new change in Service Worker, then, this file gets installed; however, it does not activate until all clients get claimed– in other words, all tabs need to be closed and reopened again, programmatically performing skipWaiting in Service Worker, or you can manually click on SkipWaiting in Chrome DevTools as shown in Figure 4-8.

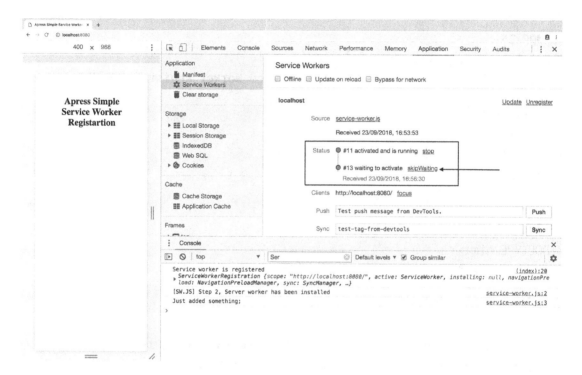

Figure 4-8. *In DevTools, you can click SkipWaiting to activate new Service Worker*

So far, we have discovered how Service Worker and its life cycle work. Now it's time to unfold Cache API capability and see it in action in the next section.

Cache API

Connectivity independence is a top-notch PWAs trait that makes them phenomenal. Cache API is a new caching storage in browsers where we can store a request as key and a response as value. In this section, we are going to have a quick glimpse of Cache API in order to understand how offline features work under the hood.

I change the app structure to include app.js file where it manipulates DOM to display title and style.css where it contains a title to make the headline center.

```
.
├── app.js
├── index.html
├── service-worker.js
└── style.css
```

// app.js
```
const title = document.querySelector(".title");
title.innerHTML = "<h1>Apress Simple Service Worker Registartion</h1>";
```

// style.css
```
.title {
  text-align: center;
  padding: 3rem;
}
```

// index.html
```
<!DOCTYPE html>
<html lang="en">

<head>
    <meta charset="UTF-8">
    <meta name="viewport" content="width=device-width, initial-scale=1.0">
    <meta http-equiv="X-UA-Compatible" content="ie=edge">
    <title>Apress Simple Service Worker Registartion</title>
    <link href="/style.css" rel="stylesheet">
</head>

<body>
    <div class="title"></div>
```

```
<script src="/app.js"></script>
<script>
    if ('serviceWorker' in navigator) {
        navigator.serviceWorker.register('/service-worker.js')
    }
</script>
</body>

</html>
```

Precache Static Assets

Every web application contains many static assets including styles, JavaScript, and images. As mentioned earlier in this chapter, once an install event fires, it's possible to tap into the event and write desired logics. It fires once per installation right before Service Worker takes control over all content; thus, here is one of the best places to open cache and add data to cache storage in which it is essential to load application fundamentals.

server-worker.js
```
// always add version to your cache
const CACHE_VERSION = "v1";
const PRECACHE_ASSETS = ["/", "/style.css", "/index.html", "/app.js"];

self.oninstall = event => {
  console.log("Install event, start precaching...");
  event.waitUntil(
    caches.open(CACHE_VERSION).then(cache => {
      return cache.addAll(PRECACHE_ASSETS);
    })
  );
};
```

Let's break down the code. First, we have defined a cache storage name, which is specified as a version name. Secondly, this app requires that some of its static assets, in order to run without having an internet connection, must be listed in an array.

As soon as the install event in Service Worker fires, regardless of what the result of logic in callback is, it is closed. So, we need a mechanism to tell Service Worker to stand still until actions are resolved. Hence, `waitUntil()` is a method that tells browsers to remain in the same event until the promise or promises that are going to be passed into the method are resolved.

Lastly, `caches.open()` accepts a name and open cache to store data into it. Other Caches methods are:

- **delete(cacheName)**: delete whole cache name and returns Boolean.

- **has(cacheName)**: find cache name and returns Boolean.

- **keys()**: retrieve all caches name and returns array of strings.

- **match(request)**: matches a request, if any.

- **open(cacheName)**: it opens a cache storage to add request/response.

All cache APIs are Promised Based.

Once a cache opens, we can add all of our assets either one by one or as an array. Other available methods on cache are the following:

- **add(request)**: add a request, and you can add a name as string.

- **addAll(requests)**: add array of requests or arrays of strings.

- **delete(request)**: deletes request or name string and returns a Boolean.

- **keys()**: retrieve all caches names and returns array of strings.

- **match(request)**: matches a request, if any.

- **matchAll(requests)**: matches array of requests, if any.

- **put(request, response)**: modifies an existing request with new response.

You may ask, where should I dump my cache? Great question – it's right before Service Worker controls all pages under its scope, which means to activate an event. Imagine we already bumped up our cache version to **v2** and we want to delete all outdated caches, which helps to clean up outdated caches and free up space (see Figure 4-9).

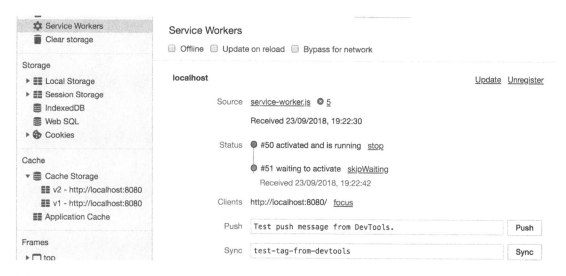

Figure 4-9. *Two versions of caches are available in install event since new Service Worker is not activated yet*

We need to filter out all other caches expect the current one and delete all of them.

// service-worker.js

```
self.onactivate = event => {
  console.log("activate event, clean up all of our caches...");
  event.waitUntil(
    caches.keys().then(cacheNames => {
      return Promise.all(
        cacheNames
        .filter(cacheName => cacheName !== CACHE_VERSION)
        map(cacheName => caches.delete(cacheName));
      })
    );
};
```

We call `waitUntil()` method to tell browser to stay in the activate event until all Promises passed into this method have been resolved. As you see in the code above, all keys are retrieved and then are being filtered where it's not equal to current version, and then deletes all previous caches (see Figure 4-10).

Figure 4-10. *Once new Service Worker is activated, all previous oudated caches are deleted*

Having reviewed the Service Worker and cache API, I am impatiently looking forward to starting off the Angular Service Worker module.

Angular Service Worker Module

Conceptually, Angular Service Worker is similar to a forward cache or a CDN edge installed in the end user's web browsers, which satisfies requests made by an Angular app for resources or data from a local cache without needing to wait for the network. Like any cache, it has rules for how content is expired and updated.

Before adding anything to the project, let's analyze our application using Lighthouse in the Audit panel.

Navigate to awesome-apress-pwa.firebaseapp.com[5] or your Firebase URL where you have already deployed the application.

---

[5]Alternatively, you can run run `ng serve --prod` to run `production ready app served a locally runned server, then nagivate to localhost:4200.`

Note   You can pull down `www.github.com/mhadaily/awesome-apress-pwa/chapter04/03-analyze-using-lighthouse`. Run `npm install` and then run `npm run serve:prod`. It runs a production app on a web server. You can navigate to `localhost:4200`. You may need to also deploy this code to Firebase in order to evaluate your app before adding a Service Worker.

Next, open developer tools[6] in Chrome and click on the Audit panel. Our main target group is mobile users. So, preferably select emulation on *Mobile* and uncheck all check boxes expect *Progress Web App*[7] and select *Simulated Fast 3G, 4x CPU slowdown* in throttling[8] option to make sure our test environment is similar to average real mobile user devices. Ensure *clear storage* is also selected as focused visitors are those who load the web for the first time.

Press *run audits* and wait until Lighthouse generates a report. Result indicates a 54/100[9] score; that's because we have some audits passed. Six failures are mainly related to Service Workers, Progressive Enhancement, and Web App Manifest as shown in Figure 4-11.

Note   If you run auditing on localhost, keep in mind that since you are not running your app with HTTPS, you may see a lower score.

---

[6]Press Ctrl + Shift + I in Windows or Cmd + Shift + I in Mac.

[7]We do run all other options in this book as we go and optimize to hit a 100/100 score.

[8]Read more about network throttling in Lighthouse: `https://github.com/GoogleChrome/lighthouse/blob/master/docs/throttling.md`.

[9]Lighthouse validates many aspects of PWA which is specifically based on `https://developers.google.com/web/progressive-web-apps/checklist`.

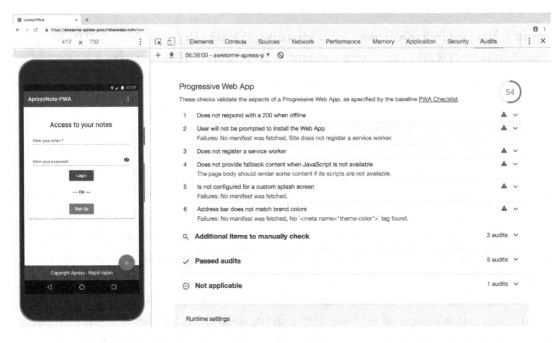

Figure 4-11. *Initial result before adding any new optimization to the project*

Support for Service Worker in Angular

Angular schematics[10] has been introduced to Angular CLI 6 and has had a notable impact on how quickly we can scaffold our Angular app. Due to this, Adding PWA features, including Service Worker, is a straightforward process and incredibly easy. Since @angular/cli has been installed globally, simply run the following command in your terminal.

ng add @angular/pwa

This command[11] will automatically modify some of the existing files by extending boilerplate codes and adding new files into the Angular app structure. Let's take a close look at the modifications.

---

[10]Learn more about schematics at https://blog.angular.io/schematics-an-introduction-dc1dfbc2a2b2.

[11]Version 6.1.3 of Angular cli and PWA schematics is buggy. So please upgrade or downgrade to a lower version, possibly 6.1.0 or 6.2+.

```
CREATE ngsw-config.json (441 bytes)
CREATE src/manifest.json (1085 bytes)
CREATE src/assets/icons/icon-128x128.png (1253 bytes)
CREATE src/assets/icons/icon-144x144.png (1394 bytes)
CREATE src/assets/icons/icon-152x152.png (1427 bytes)
CREATE src/assets/icons/icon-192x192.png (1790 bytes)
CREATE src/assets/icons/icon-384x384.png (3557 bytes)
CREATE src/assets/icons/icon-512x512.png (5008 bytes)
CREATE src/assets/icons/icon-72x72.png (792 bytes)
CREATE src/assets/icons/icon-96x96.png (958 bytes)
UPDATE angular.json (4049 bytes)
UPDATE package.json (1646 bytes)
UPDATE src/app/app.module.ts (1238 bytes)
UPDATE src/index.html (652 bytes)
```

As you have seen, different icons sizes, `ngsw-config.json`, `manifest.json`, and `ngsw-worker.js`[12] have been added to the project while `angular.json`, `app.module.ts`, `index.html`, and `package.json` have been modified.

Let's break down the changes and see what and where it has changed:

1. **package.json**: Angular Service Worker `"@angular/service-worker"` has been added to list of dependencies, and by the time of writing this book, version 6.1.0 has been installed. It may upgrade or add a new version by the time you read this book.

2. **ngsw-config.json**: added to *root* of project, and it contains a Service Worker configuration. In this chapter we will take a look at it and walk through the basics, and in the next chapter we will dive into it and add more advanced configurations along with tips and tricks.

   ```
   {
     "index": "/index.html",
     "assetGroups": [
   ```

---

[12]You need to build for production to find this file under /dist folder.

```
    {
      "name": "app",
      "installMode": "prefetch",
      "resources": {
        "files": [
          "/favicon.ico",
          "/index.html",
          "/*.css",
          "/*.js"
        ]
      }
    }, {
      "name": "assets",
      "installMode": "lazy",
      "updateMode": "prefetch",
      "resources": {
        "files": [
          "/assets/**"
        ]
      }
    }
  ]
}
```

3. **manifest.json**: added to */src/* folder in the project. it contains a configuration to make the app installable. In Chapter 6, `manifest. json` will be reviewed in depth.

```
{
  "name": "lovely-offline",
  "short_name": "lovely-offline",
  "theme_color": "#1976d2",
  "background_color": "#fafafa",
  "display": "standalone",
  "scope": "/",
  "start_url": "/",
```

```
"icons": [
  {
    "src": "assets/icons/icon-72x72.png",
    "sizes": "72x72",
    "type": "image/png"
  },
  {
    "src": "assets/icons/icon-96x96.png",
    "sizes": "96x96",
    "type": "image/png"
  },
  {
    "src": "assets/icons/icon-128x128.png",
    "sizes": "128x128",
    "type": "image/png"
  },
  {
    "src": "assets/icons/icon-144x144.png",
    "sizes": "144x144",
    "type": "image/png"
  },
  {
    "src": "assets/icons/icon-152x152.png",
    "sizes": "152x152",
    "type": "image/png"
  },
  {
    "src": "assets/icons/icon-192x192.png",
    "sizes": "192x192",
    "type": "image/png"
  },
  {
    "src": "assets/icons/icon-384x384.png",
    "sizes": "384x384",
    "type": "image/png"
  },
```

```
    {
      "src": "assets/icons/icon-512x512.png",
      "sizes": "512x512",
      "type": "image/png"
    }
  ]
}
```

4. **Different icons**: added in *src/assets/icons/* and have been reused
    in manifest.json. We will come back to these icons in Chapter 6.

5. **Angular.json**: as you know, this file contains all Angular CLI
    configurations. Since manifest.json needs to be exposed in a
    public/build folder, it must be added to an assets array in in the
    architect configurations where it's applicable. See the following
    snippet, for example:

```
"architect": {
      "build": {
        "builder": "@angular-devkit/build-angular:browser",
        "options": {
          ...
          "assets": [
            "src/favicon.ico",
            "src/assets",
            "src/manifest.json"
          ],
          "styles": [
            ...
            "src/styles.scss"
          ],
          "scripts": []
        },
        ...
```

There will be one more change here. `serviceWorker` has been added to the production configuration to inform Angular CLI that this feature is enabled. Let take a look at the configuration's snippet:

```
"configurations": {
        "production": {
          "fileReplacements": [
            {
              "replace": "src/environments/environment.ts",
              "with": "src/environments/environment.prod.ts"
            }
          ],
          "optimization": true,
          "outputHashing": "all",
          "sourceMap": false,
          "extractCss": true,
          "namedChunks": false,
          "aot": true,
          "extractLicenses": true,
          "vendorChunk": false,
          "buildOptimizer": true,
          "serviceWorker": true
        }
      }
```

6. **Index.html**: after adding `manifest.json` to the project, it needs to be exposed by `rel=manifest` in the head of index.html to let the browser know that this file is the project's manifest configuration file. Theme color meta tells the browser what color to tint UI elements such as the address bar.

```
<link rel="manifest" href="manifest.json">
<meta name="theme-color" content="#1976d2">
```

7. **app.module.ts**: is our main app module that has been modified to import `ServiceWorkerModule` in order to add Service Worker capabilities and features to the project. This module registers

ngsw-worker.js Service Worker JavaScript file, which has been written and maintained by the Angular team and will be added after a prod build to the root of project. It has a second argument to ensure that this registration is enabled only when the app is ready to be built for production and doesn't interrupt the development environment.

```
ServiceWorkerModule.register("ngsw-worker.js", {
    enabled: environment.production
})
```

Service Worker in Angular can also be registered in two other options:

- Adding registration script in index.html, please refer to the previous section where we register a simple Service Worker. Remember to register ngsw-worker.js. I don't recommend this option; rather, use the next option if necessary.

- Using the same registration code in main.ts after bootstrapModule() is resolved,

```
// main.ts
platformBrowserDynamic().bootstrapModule(AppModule)
  .then(() => {
    if ('serviceWorker' in navigator && environment.production) {
      window.addEventListener('load', () => {
        navigator.serviceWorker.register('/ngsw-worker.js') ;
      });
    }
  })
  .catch(err => console.log(err));
```

Note   ServiceWorkerModule.register() has scope option in addition to enable.

Although @angular/pwa schematic helps to set up an Angular PWA project quickly, there may be use cases that we need to do all of the above steps manually. For instance:

1. If you are running Angular 5 in production, there is still a chance to add Angular Service Worker module to your application. Simply go back to each step and try to add or modify all the changes one by one. Run npm install to make sure @angular/service-worker is successfully installed and that you are good to go!

2. You may need only *ServiceWorker* module alone and not the rest of features: for instance, *manifest.json*.

It seems every piece is in place and ready to build for production. In the next section, we are going to check out the *dist* folder and explore new additions.

ngsw-config.json Anatomy

Angular Server Worker has been designed and programmed for large applications in mind; thus, it's highly configurable.

Rules are written in ngsw-config json file. A Top-Level Angular Service Worker configuration object interface indicates that there are five main properties that can be used.

```
interface Config {
    appData?: {};
    index: string;
    assetGroups?: AssetGroup[];
    dataGroups?: DataGroup[];
    navigationUrls?: string[];
}
```

By default, index.html has been added as the main entry point. Having looked at *assetGroups* interface, it's an array that set rules for static assets such as JavaScript, images, icons, CSS, and HTML files.

```
type Glob = string;
```

```
interface AssetGroup {
    name: string;
    installMode?: 'prefetch' | 'lazy';
    updateMode?: 'prefetch' | 'lazy';
    resources: {
        files?: Glob[];
        versionedFiles?: Glob[];
        urls?: Glob[];
    };
}
```

Note   VersionedFiles is depreciated and as of v6, `versionedFiles` and `files` options have the same behaviors. Use `files` instead.

We have seen that Angular CLI has added default rules to the ngsw-config.json:

```
"assetGroups": [
    {
      "name": "app",
      "installMode": "prefetch",
      "resources": {
        "files": ["/favicon.ico", "/index.html", "/*.css", "/*.js"]
      }
    },
    {
      "name": "assets",
      "installMode": "lazy",
      "updateMode": "prefetch",
      "resources": {
        "files": ["/assets/**"]
      }
    }
  ]
```

As it's shown, there are two objects in this array. Let's explore the first object.

```
{
    "name": "app",
    "installMode": "prefetch",
    "resources": {
      "files": ["/favicon.ico", "/index.html", "/*.css", "/*.js"]
    }
},
```

1. **name**: defines group name and will be part of Cache API storage name.

2. **installMode**: determines how cache strategies should behave for group's resources when they are cached or fetched. It has two options:

   a. **prefetch**: means all the resources are downloaded and should immediately be cached on install event; this is similar to precache assets that we have seen earlier in this chapter. This mode is being used for caching assets that applications require for bootstrapping like app-shell to make the application be fully capable offline.

   b. **lazy**: means each resource is cached individually in runtime when it's requested.

3. **resouces**: the explicit list of resources to cache. There are two ways to set up them: files or urls. VersionedFiles as mentioned are depreciated and have the same behavior as files.

   a. **files**: contains a list of globs matched against files in the root (in this case). * stands for file names which have been defined with appropriate file name extensions. For example, *.js means all JavaScript files and / means they are located in the root. In short, /*.js indicates all JavaScript files located in the root of the project.

   b. **urls**: contains a list of external URLs (either relative, absolute paths, or on different origins) that should be cached: for example, Google Fonts. URLs cannot be hashed, so by changes in configuration, they will be updated. In default configurations, there are no URLs, but we will need it to add our external resources in the next chapter.

Note   Files will have content hashed included in `ngsw.json` file's **hashTable**[13] node. It helps to have an accurate version. Keep in mind that file paths are mapped into the URL space of the application, starting with the base href.

Clearly, it tries to precache essential files that are required to run the Angular application even when there is no network.

Moving forward to the second object, it has similar configurations except that it targets all files regardless of their file extension under /assets folder, which will get cached as soon as they are fetched in runtime. If there is a new change in each of those assets, it'll be fetched and updated immediately.

```
{
    "name": "assets",
    "installMode": "lazy",
    "updateMode": "prefetch",
    "resources": {
      "files": ["/assets/**"]
    }
}
```

1. **installMode**: please refer to object one description.

2. **updateMode**: determines how each cached asset should behave when application has a new version and is downloaded; similar to *installMode*, it has two options:

   a. **prefetch**: means each asset should be refreshed on every new app version (if needed). Angular creates hashTable to compare hashes, and if there is a new change, the asset will be downloaded. URLS in caches, in this manner, will always be refreshed (with an If-Modified-Since[14] request).

   b. **lazy**: performs similar to above flow however, when resource is requested. This mode works only if `installMode` is also lazy.

---

[13]https://en.wikipedia.org/wiki/Hash_table
[14]https://developer.mozilla.org/en-US/docs/Web/HTTP/Headers/If-Modified-Since

3. **resources**: please refer to object one description.

   a. **files**: ** stands for everything. In this case, /assets/** means all files under assets files including images, icons, etc.

Note   Default value for installMode and updateMode is prefetch in ngsw.js

---

I believe in the saying that says *"understand, don't imitate."* Evaluating each object should help us to be more capable of writing our own rule based on what we need in our application. The fundamentals are the same; however, you may need more advanced setups such as writing rules for external resources and navigation URLs, which will, be discussed in the next chapter.

Build Project with Angular Service Worker

ServiceWorker module is only enabled when we run a production build. Run the following command to start building an app in *prod-environment*:

```
npm run build:prod // or ng build --prod
```

ngsw-worker.js is our servicer worker file and ngsw.json our configurations which will be fetched by service worker and will be implemented accordingly.

```
.
├── 0.c570a2562d2874d34dc4.js
├── 1.71eb2445db7dfda9e415.js
├── 2.df6bb6a6fde654fe8392.js
├── 3rdpartylicenses.txt
├── assets
├── favicon.ico
├── index.html
├── main.873527a6348e9dfb2cc1.js
```

```
├── manifest.json
├── ngsw-worker.js
├── ngsw.json
├── polyfills.8883ab5d81bf34ae13b1.js
├── runtime.e14ed3e6d31ff77728e9.js
├── safety-worker.js
├── styles.7a3dc1d11e8502df3926.css
└── worker-basic.min.js
```

ngsw-worker is registered as the Service Worker logic file, and ngsw.json is being created based on ngsw-config.json. All the configurations and resources are generated in ngsw.json manifest, which is automatically fetched by written logic in ngsw-worker and an add, update, or delete cache based on URLs, files, and strategies that have been defined in this file. It contains a hashTable according to build-hash and Angular Service Worker. Check this hash to update resources that are in *dist* folder if there are any changes.

If you open ngsw manifest file, static assets and JavaScript files after the build have been added magically. Eventually, Angular CLI will match all of our files and add them to ngsw, as we need a full path of each file. ngsw.json also informs Angular to fetch these resources into the cache and keep them updated accordingly. It's worth mentioning that even though this file has been designed for Angular Service Worker, it's a pretty readable file for us as developers.

Let's run following the command to fire up the local server:

npm run prod

Navigate to localhost:4200 and open your Chrome DevTools. Open the application panel and check for Service Workers. Figure 4-12 clearly shows that ngsw-worker.js has been successfully installed and how different caches in Cache Storage were created.

In the next chapter, ngsw manifest and ngsw-worker will be reviewed in depth.

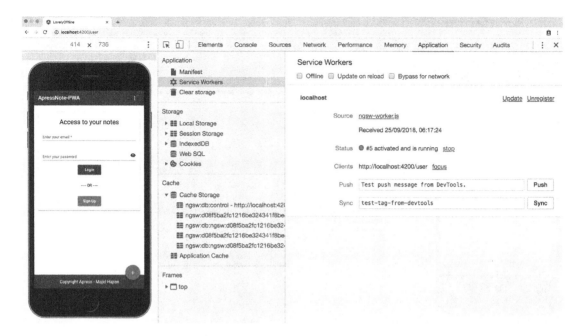

Figure 4-12. `ngsw-worker.js` *has been installed and resouces have been added to Cache storage*

We need to run the following command as always to deploy a new build to Firebase and see how all of our efforts in the setup work in action:

```
npm run deploy
```

Once deployment is done, open audit panel in Chrome DevTools and press *run audits* (see Figure 4-13). Remember, we should keep all the same settings as we did earlier in this chapter.

Yes, this is true: score 100/100 as shown in Figure 4-13 has been achieved for PWA auditing by just adding a few steps in Angular, which was mainly done by the CLI. This is great, but we still have a lot to do.

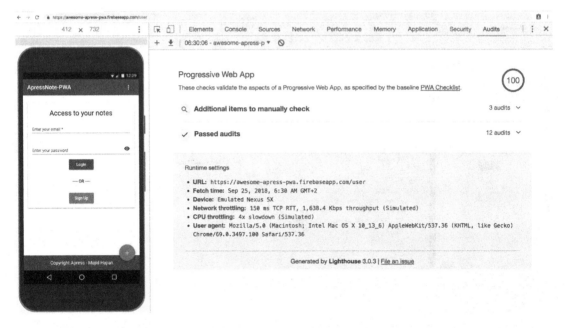

Figure 4-13. *Score 100 after setting up Angular for PWA schematics by ng CLI*

> **Note**   Chapters 13 and 14 are dedicated to building a PWA with Workbox, which is a tool to create our service worker and cache strategies. The goal is to have 100% PWA coverage for all Angular apps regardless of their version. So, do not worry if your Angular version does not have an Angular Service Worker module or the Angular Service Worker does not meet your essential requirements. You'll be covered soon.

Summary

The Angular team aims to make PWA features as easy as possible. As you have seen, it was a trivial process to set up those features in the Angular project. In this chapter, we have seen how we turned our Angular application into a PWA using Angular CLI not only with *pwa schematic* but also with defined steps to reproduce manually while default configurations have been explained.

Although the app got a score of 100, it does not mean we have accomplished all of what we need to run our application for any circumstances. So, bear with me while we dive deeply into more configurations, settings, and advanced techniques in order to meet all production-ready app requirements.

With that said, I encourage you to proceed to the next chapter.

CHAPTER 5

Advanced Angular Service Worker and Runtime Caching

In the previous chapter, we implemented Angular Service Worker and saw that Angular CLI helped us to run PWA out of the box with minimal effort. Basic configuration is the beginning of our journey to create a PWA with Angular. It is obvious that an application will require advanced techniques and strategies as it grows. Hence, Angular Service Worker is providing more features to handle variant situations.

In this chapter, I will expand configurations to an advanced level in order to make a fully offline application. However, we start off by learning complex cache strategies in Service Worker that enable us to understand what underlies Angular Service Worker implementation.

Cache Strategies

There are a few patterns for handling requests and responds in Service Worker. It differs from application to application. Depending on requirements, you may use one or more of the strategies discussed in the following sections.

Cache Only

In this strategy, requests always look for a match in the cache and respond accordingly. This is ideal for "versioned" files when they are supposed to be there for your application and considered static and unchanged until the next deployment. Usually all statics assets that application needs to run, we cache them on install event. Figure 5-1 is a simple illustration to show how it works.

© Majid Hajian 2019
M. Hajian, *Progressive Web Apps with Angular*, https://doi.org/10.1007/978-1-4842-4448-7_5

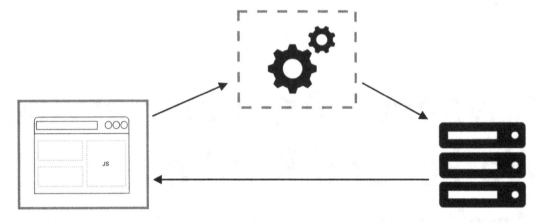

Figure 5-1. *Cache only strategy illustration*

Following snippet shows how we can use this strategy.

```
self.addEventListener("fetch", event => {
  event.respondWith(caches.match(event.request));
});
```

Notice where a request match is not found in the cache, respond will look like a connection error.

Network Only

There are use cases that don't have an offline equivalent. Imagine that you have a stock exchange website and always need to show the latest and most up-to-date rates to your user. Figure 5-2 shows a simple illustration of how this works.

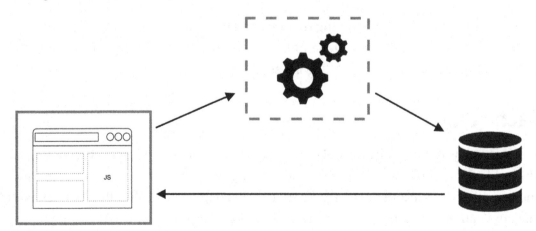

Figure 5-2. *Network Only*

```
self.addEventListener("fetch", event => {
  event.respondWith(fetch(event.request));
});
```

It is possible that you don't call event.respondWith, which ends up in default browser behavior.

Cache Falling Back to Network or Cache-First

This gives you a combination of cache only and network only where it tries to match the request from a cache, and if it doesn't exist, then it falls back to fetch a request from the network. See Figure 5-3 to see how it works.

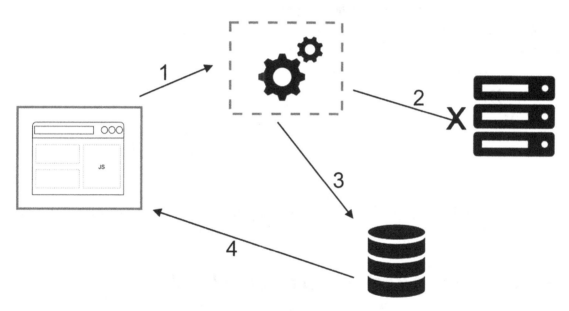

Figure 5-3. *Cache falling back to network or Cache-First*

```
self.addEventListener('fetch', function(event) {
const request = event.request;
  event.respondWith(
    caches.match(event.request).then(function(response) {
      return response || fetch(event.request);
    })
  );
});
```

We can leverage this strategy to cache content dynamically.

```
self.addEventListener("fetch", event => {
const request = event.request;
  event.respondWith(
    caches.match(request).then(res => {
      // Fallback
      return (
        res ||  fetch(request).then(newRes => {
          // Cache fetched response
          caches
            .open(DYNAMIC_CACHE_VERSION)
            .then(cache => cache.put(request, newRes));
// Response can be used once, we need to clone to use it more in the
context
          return newRes.clone();
        })
      );
    })
  );
});
```

Keep in mind that updated-cached content will be available in the next visit of the same request.

Network Falling Back to Cache or Network-First

This strategy is suitable for those resources that should update regardless of what is the app version or what the versioned files are: for instance, showing the latest articles or timeline in social media (see Figure 5-4). Eventually, the most up-to-date content is shown to our online users whereas in offline mode, a user will receive an older cached version of the content. Similar to the previous strategy, it's most likely that we want to update a cache entry when a network request succeeds.

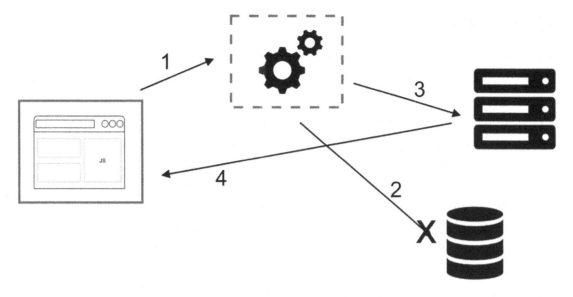

Figure 5-4. *Network falling back to cache or Network-First*

```
self.addEventListener("fetch", event => {
const request = event.request;
  event.respondWith(
    fetch(request)
      .then(res => {
        // Cache latest version
        caches
          .open(DYNAMIC_CACHE_VERSION)
          .then(cache => cache.put(request, res));
        return res.clone();
      }) // Fallback to cache
      .catch(err => caches.match(request))
  );
});
```

However, in case of a slow or intermittent connection, a user faces an unacceptable and unpleasant experience since fetch takes an extremely long time; so it's going to be frustrating from the user's perspective. See the next pattern if you are looking for a better alternative.

Cache and Network

The idea is to first show your user old cached content if it exists and then update the UI when the network request succeeds. In other words, you have to make two fetch requests in the page, and in Service Worker you should always update the cache with the latest fetch response. Figure 5-5 demonstrates how it works.

You have seen this pattern in many social media platforms such as Twitter where they usually show old cached content and then add newer content on top of the timeline and adjust the scroll position so that a user is uninterrupted. All in all, this is ideal for content that needs to be updated frequently such as articles or activity timelines.

Although this strategy gives our user a better experience, it can be disruptive, too: for instance, when a user is reading content on the website. All of sudden, a large piece of that content disappears in order to update the UI and show them fresh data. So, it is important that we ensure users' interactions with the app and never interrupt so it is as smooth as possible. Remember, one of the most important goals of PWA is to give our user a much better experience.

Code in the app looks like this:

```
const hasFetchData = false;
// fetch fresh data
const freshDataFromNetwork = fetch(YOUR_API)
.then((response) => response.json())
.then((data) => {
  hasFetchData = true;
  showDataInPage();
});

// fetch cached data
caches.match(YOUR_API)
.then((response) => response.json())
.then(function(data) {
  if (!hasFetchData) {
    showDataInPage(data);
  }
})
.catch((e)=>{
```

```
// in case if cache is not availble, we hope data is received by network
fetch
return freshDataFromNetwork;
})
```

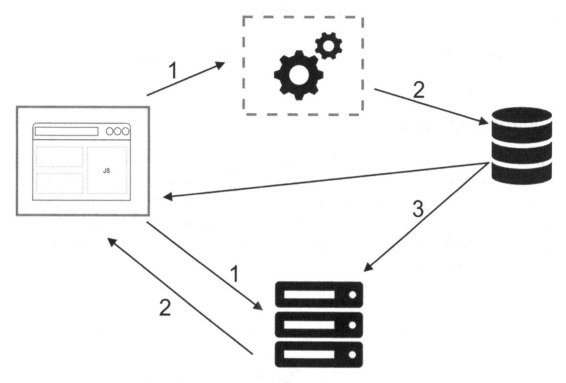

Figure 5-5. *Cache and network*

Note   Cache API is available in Window Object and other Workers in addition to Service Worker.

Code in Service Worker is similar to a network falling back to cache while updating the cache.

```
self.addEventListener("fetch", event => {
  const request = event.request;
  event.respondWith(
    caches.open(DYNAMIC_CACHE_VERSION).then(cache => {
      return fetch(request).then(res => {
```

```
        cache.put(request, res.clone());
        return res;
      });
    })
  );
});
```

You may ask, what if both network and cache fail? See the next pattern to find out more.

Generic Fallback

This pattern is ideal to show a replacement for those requests that are not available in both cache and network: for example, when a user has an avatar and fetch from both the network and cache fails. So, we can simply replace this request with a photo placeholder. Another example is to show our user an offline page when a request fails. You can simply precache offline.html page and match from the cache when necessary. Figure 5-6 illustrates how it works.

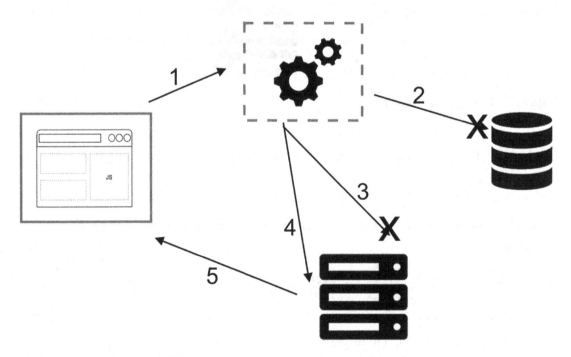

Figure 5-6. *Generic fallback*

```
self.addEventListener("fetch", event => {
  const request = event.request;
  event.respondWith(
    // check with cache first
    caches
      .match(request)
      .then(res => {
        // Fall back to network and if both failes catch error
        return res || fetch(request);
      })
      .catch(() => {
        // If both fail, show a generic fallback:
        return caches.match("/offline.html");
      })
  );
});
```

In a real application, even though you can show an offline replacement to a user, you may want to store data to the indexedDB and let your user know that the request is successfully retained and will be synced. We will review offline storage together in Chapter 9.

Note   It is likely that using all or many of the cache strategies in an application depends on what we need to implement. Evaluate your particular use case and then choose one pattern that suits it.

It is important to understand most of the common cache patterns in Service Worker before we review Angular runtime caching. I am confident that you will get a better understanding of Angular cache strategies since you know how they work. Let's procced to Angular Service Worker advanced configurations.

Runtime Cache in Angular Service Worker

Angular Service Worker is configured using `ngsw-config.json`. Having been helped by Angular CLI, the default setting has been in place to run for a barebones Angular app. But as the application develops, we see the need to cache external files, CDN resources, as well as populate data from a remote API call. It gets more complex and we would like the caching all data or at least partially caching to have an enhanced performance, faster app, and smooth experience. I aim to cover what an application needs regarding data and external file caches in this section. Let's carry on.

Note   Runtime cache may be called dynamic content cache, too. The idea is to cache data when fetched or requested while the application is running, and data has not been stored to cache already on the install event, which is referred to as precache.

External Resources

Font, JavaScript, style, Images, and other type of files that are hosted on a different origin or CDN are considered external resources. Whether we want to precache or lazily add them to cache on runtime, we need to define them in an `ngsw-config.json`. They must be added to `assetGroup` using `urls` key where the value will be an `array of Glob`, meaning we can also use glob pattern to specify urls. URLs are not hashed; thus, whenever a configuration changes, they will update. As mentioned in previous chapters, we had added two fonts in our application.

```
<head>
<link href="https://fonts.googleapis.com/icon?family=Material+Icons"
rel="stylesheet">
<link href="https://fonts.googleapis.com/css?family=Roboto:300,400,500"
rel="stylesheet">
  <base href="/">
  <meta name="viewport" content="width=device-width, initial-scale=1">
  <link rel="manifest" href="manifest.json">
  <meta name="theme-color" content="#1976d2">
</head>
```

Now we want to cache these fonts. Code is similar to the following:

```
// this is our application ngsw-config.json file
{
    "name": "app",
    "installMode": "prefetch",
    "resources": {
      "files": ["/favicon.ico", "/index.html", "/*.css", "/*.js"],
      "urls": [
    https://fonts.googleapis.com/icon?family=Material+Icons,
    https://fonts.googleapis.com/css?family=Roboto:300,400,500,
    https://fonts.gstatic.com/s/roboto/v18/
    KFOlCnqEu92Fr1MmSU5fCRc4AMP6lbBP.woff2,
    https://fonts.gstatic.com/s/materialicons/v41/flUhRq6tzZclQEJ-Vdg-
    IuiaDsNcIhQ8tQ.woff2
            ]
      }
    },
    {
      "name": "assets",
      "installMode": "lazy",
      "updateMode": "prefetch",
      "resources": {
        "files": ["/assets/**"],
      }
    }
```

Here is an example where we could add precise URLs since we already knew those URLs. However, it is not always clear what will be the exact URLs. Thus, we can add a *glob pattern* to cache all *URLs* that are hosted in googleapis.com and gstatic.com in order to host *woff* fonts dynamically.

```
{
    "name": "app",
    "installMode": "prefetch",
```

```
  "resources": {
    "files": ["/favicon.ico", "/index.html", "/*.css", "/*.js"],
  }
 },
 {
   "name": "assets",
   "installMode": "lazy",
   "updateMode": "prefetch",
   "resources": {
     "files": ["/assets/**"],
      "urls": [
    https://fonts.googleapis.com/**,
     https://fonts.gstatic.com/**
         ]
   }
 }
```

Patterns use a limited glob format in configuration unless otherwise it is explicitly noted.

1. ****** matches 0 or more path segments

    a. **/**/*.html** specifies all HTML files

    b. **/**/*.js** specifies all JS files

    c. example.com/** specifies all request which hostname is matched

2. ***** matches 0 or more characters excluding /

    a. **/*.html** specifies only HTML files in the root

    b. **/a/folder/*.png** specified only png files in the /a/folder/

3. **?** matches exactly one character excluding /

    a. **/what?ver.js** specifies all JS files in the root where its 5th character could be anything

4. **The ! prefix** acts negative, meaning that only files that don't match the pattern will be included.

   a. **!/**/*.map** excludes all source-maps

   b. **!/*.pdf** excludes all pdf files in the root

Note   `urls` doesn't have support for negative glob patterns and **?** will be matched literally; that means ? will not match any character other than ? itself.

Run the build command. Once it's done, navigate to /dist folder and open ngsw. json generated based on an ngsw-config.json by Angular CLI.

```
"assetGroups": [
  {
    "name": "app",
    "installMode": "prefetch",
    "updateMode": "prefetch",
    "urls": [
      "/0.c570a2562d2874d34dc4.js",
      "/1.71eb2445db7dfda9e415.js",
      "/2.df6bb6a6fde654fe8392.js",
      "/favicon.ico",
      "/index.html",
      "/main.f224c8a2c47bceb8bef0.js",
      "/polyfills.8883ab5d81bf34ae13b1.js",
      "/runtime.e14ed3e6d31ff77728e9.js",
      "/styles.7a3dc1d11e8502df3926.css"
    ],
    "patterns": []
  },
  {
    "name": "assets",
    "installMode": "lazy",
    "updateMode": "prefetch",
```

```
    "urls": [
      "/assets/icons/icon-128x128.png",
      "/assets/icons/icon-144x144.png",
      "/assets/icons/icon-152x152.png",
      "/assets/icons/icon-192x192.png",
      "/assets/icons/icon-384x384.png",
      "/assets/icons/icon-512x512.png",
      "/assets/icons/icon-72x72.png",
      "/assets/icons/icon-96x96.png"
    ],
    "patterns": [
      "https:\\/\\/fonts\\.googleapis\\.com\\/.*",
      "https:\\/\\/fonts\\.gstatic\\.com\\/.*"
    ]
  }
],
```

By looking into the generated ngsw-worker.js and ngsw.json, we notice that the glob turned into a pattern to be consumed as regex. Here is the piece of code that maps pattern to regex, in class AssetGroup extracted from ngsw-worker.js:

```
// Patterns in the config are regular expressions disguised as
    strings. Breathe life into them.
this.patterns = this.config.patterns.map(pattern => new
RegExp(pattern));
```

And in the future, down in code, it is being used as:

```
// Either the request matches one of the known resource URLs, one of the
patterns for
// dynamically matched URLs, or neither. Determine which is the case for
this request // in order to decide how to handle it.
if (this.config.urls.indexOf(url) !== -1 || this.patterns.some(pattern =>
pattern.test(url))) {
```

These have been added in order to match requests while intercepting and storing them in cache storage.

Revalidate Strategy for Resources with No Hash

Some resources may not have hash while it existed in the cache. Angular Service Worker will check how old is this request and ensure it still can be usable. There are three different strategies applied in Angular Service Worker regarding resource revalidation:

1. The request has a `Cache-Control` header, and thus expiration needs to be based on its age.

   - This specifies directives for caching mechanisms in both requests and responses. Standard Cache-Control directives can be used by the client in an HTTP request.

     ```
     Cache-Control: max-age=<seconds>
     Cache-Control: max-stale[=<seconds>]
     Cache-Control: min-fresh=<seconds>
     Cache-Control: no-cache
     Cache-Control: no-store
     Cache-Control: no-transform
     Cache-Control: only-if-cached
     ```

   - Depends on the condition Angular looks for: **max-age** or **Date** header.

2. The request has an `Expires` header, and expiration is based on the current timestamp.

   - The `Expires` header contains the date/time while Invalid dates, like the value 0, is an indication that a resource is already expired. If there is a `Cache-Control` header with the "max-age" or "s-maxage" directive in the response, the Expires header is ignored.

   - e.g.: `Expires: Wed, 21 Oct 2019 07:28:00 GMT`.

3. The request has no applicable caching headers and must be revalidated.

   - If there is no way to evaluate staleness, assume the response is already stale.

So, it's good practice to add the cache control to your resources; it not only helps browsers to revalidate a response, but also Angular Service Worker helps to stay up to date efficiently.

Data Groups Settings

Beside assetGroups, there are also `dataGroups`. Unlike asset resources, data requests defined in this section are independent of the app version while the assetGroups cache update strategy is different: if the single resource was updated, we recycle the whole version cache. They follow their own manually configured policies, which are most useful for situations such as handling API requests and other data dependencies. We can use them to cache the responses from the external services in case that application goes offline.

Having looked at `DataGroup` Typescript interface, the following properties reveal:

```
export interface DataGroup {
  name: string;
  urls: string[];
  version?: number;
  cacheConfig: {
    maxSize: number;
    maxAge: string;
    timeout?: string;
    strategy?: 'freshness' | 'performance';
  };
}
```

1) **name**:

   (required) name of group that will be included in Cache API storage name. It should be `string`, descriptive to our knowledge, and uniquely identified.

2) **urls**:

   (required) a list of glob patterns that are used to match these URLs for caching accordingly to this data policy. Similar to assetGroups, negative glob patterns are not supported and ? will be matched literally, which means ? will remain the ? character and doesn't match anything.

3) **version**:

(optional) versioning in APIs is quite common. In a way that sometimes a new version format will not be backward compatible with the old API; thus, the existing cache contains an older format and is likely to break the app since it does not match the newer API structure. Although `version` is optional and an integer field defaults to 0, it provides a mechanism to indicate whether an API response that is being cached has been changed in a backward-incompatible way. Hence all old cache entries stored responses for this API must be discarded, eradicated, and replaced with new responses.

4) **cacheConfig**:

(required) settings that define the policies and strategies by which matching requests will be cached:

- **maxSize**:
  (required) when cache is open to accept unlimited number of responses, depends on your app size, it can grow rapidly and eventually exceed the storage quota,[1] calling for eviction. Thus, we can define a maximum number of entries or responses here.

- **maxAge**:
  (required) indicates how long responses are allowed to remain in cache until they flag as invalid and are evicted. It is a string that specifies time duration, which can be set by **d:** days, **h:** hours, **m:** minutes, **s:** seconds and **u:** milliseconds. *10d12h4m*, for instance, will cache content for up to 10 and a half days and 4 minutes.

---

[1]All browsers impose a limit for storage that your web app's origin is allowed to use and that differs from device to device, browser to browser. If the origin eviction couldn't free enough space, the browser will throw a `QuotaExceededError.`

- **timeout**:

  (optional) Although this is optional parameter, it tells Angular Service Worker how long it should wait for the network response before it falls back to content that is cached. This is valid when strategy is *freshness*, which means network first (see next property). Duration specifies time duration similar to maxAge unit. **1d** considers 1 day.

- **strategy**

  (optional) it can have two options for all data resources:

  - **performance**:

    it refers to Cache-First strategy. Content that doesn't change often can fall into this strategy since it has been optimized for faster response.

    It checks cache first and if the resource exists there and it not expired depending on maxAge, the cached version will instantly be served depending on the maxAge, in exchange for better performance. If content expires, it tries to update the cache.

    As an example, we have an endpoint to retrieve a user's wish list. Based on our app, we really do not need to call this API; thus we can set a maxAge of 1 hour and performance strategy to show a faster response to our user.

  - **freshness**:

    This strategy considers as Network-First for which it always tries to fetch data from the network only. Depending on timeout, if the network doesn't respond accordingly, the request fall backs to the cache. It fits all data that needs to be updated frequently.

    For example: a user dashboard that shows user points balance.

Note   By default. Angular Service Worker does not cache any data or files that fetch at runtime. They have to be explicitly defined and configured.

Now it's time to configure our Note application. I will use a Network-First strategy for retrieving notes from a Firebase endpoint using ** glob. I'd like to set size to 100, maximum cache age to 10 days and 5 seconds for timeout after which the request falls backs to cache if it exists.

To have a better understanding, I will create two new methods in data.service.ts to make a GET request to Firestore API directly as well as another method to get a random dad joke. New methods look like the following code:

```
// data.service.ts
// DataService

protected readonly FIRESTORE_ENDPOINT =
    'https://firestore.googleapis.com/v1beta1/projects/awesome-apress-pwa/
    databases/(default)/documents/';
  protected readonly DAD_JOKE = 'https://icanhazdadjoke.com';

// Get a random joke

getRandomDadJoke(): Observable<string> {
    return this.http
      .get<Joke>(this.DAD_JOKE, {
        headers: {
          Accept: 'application/json'
        }
      })
      .pipe(map(data => data.joke));
  }

// Get note Details

getNoteFromDirectApi(id): Observable<any> {
    return this.auth.getToken().pipe(
      switchMap(idToken => {
```

```
      return this.http.get(
        `${this.FIRESTORE_ENDPOINT}users/${this.auth.id}/notes/${id}`,
        {
          headers: {
            Authorization: `Bearer ${idToken}`
          }
        }
      );
    }),
    map(notes => this.transfromNote(notes))
  );
}
```

// List all notes for current user

```
initializeNotes(): Observable<any> {
    return this.auth.getToken().pipe(
      switchMap(idToken => {
        return this.http.get(
          `${this.FIRESTORE_ENDPOINT}users/${this.auth.id}/notes`,
          {
            headers: {
              Authorization: `Bearer ${idToken}`
            }
          }
        );
      }),
      map((data: { documents: { fields: {} }[] }) => data.documents),
      map(notes => this.transfromNotes(notes)),
      tap(notes => {
        this.isLoading$.next(false);
      })
    );
  }
```

```
  private transfromNotes(notes) {
    return notes.map(note => this.transfromNote(note));
  }
```

// since I am calling google API directly, a simple transfromationm make it
easy to use data in our application

```
  private transfromNote(note) {
    const _note = {};
    _note['id'] = note.name.split('/').reverse()[0];
    for (const prop in note.fields) {
      if (note.fields[prop]) {
        _note[prop] =
          note.fields[prop]['stringValue'] || note.fields[prop]['integerValue'];
      }
    }
    return _note;
  }
```

Then I'll replace getNotes() with initializeNotes() and getNote() with getNoteFromDirectApi() in notes-list.component.ts and note-details.component.ts, respectively. Last but not least, I will add a joke to my app.component.ts.

```
@Component({
  selector: 'app-root',
  template: `
  <div class="appress-pwa-note">
    <app-header></app-header>
    <div class="main">
      <div *ngIf="joke$ | async as joke" class="joke">
      {{ joke }}
      </div>
      <router-outlet></router-outlet>
    </div>
    <app-footer></app-footer>
  </div>
  `,
```

```
  styles: [
    `
      .joke {
        margin-top: 0.5rem;
        padding: 1rem;
        border: 1px solid #ccc;
      }
    `
  ]
})
export class AppComponent implements OnInit {
  joke$: Observable<string>;

  constructor(private db: DataService) {}

  ngOnInit() {
    this.joke$ = this.db.getRandomDadJoke();
  }
}
```

Based on my strategy in the app, I decided to use freshness for Firestore Google API endpoints and performance for the random joke endpoint since this is unnecessary to be called many times; once after every 15 minutes should be enough. The corresponding configuration will look like this:

```
"dataGroups": [
    {
      "name": "api-network-first",
      "version": 1,
      "urls": ["https://firestore.googleapis.com/v1beta1/**"],
      "cacheConfig": {
        "strategy": "freshness",
        "maxSize": 100,
        "maxAge": "10d",
        "timeout": "5s"
      }
    },
```

```
{
    "name": "api-cache-first",
    "version": 1,
    "urls": ["https://icanhazdadjoke.com"],
    "cacheConfig": {
      "strategy": "performance",
      "maxSize": 20,
      "maxAge": "15m"
    }
  }
]
```

Now I will build my production-ready app and will serve it locally.

`npm run prod`

Navigate to `localhost:4200` and check out cache storage and the Service Worker tab. You'll notice that now we have cache names to store our both strategies as shown in Figure 5-7.

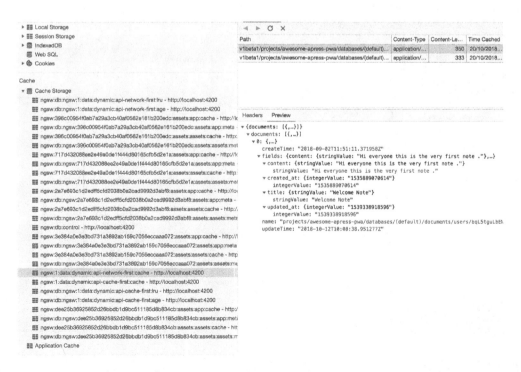

Figure 5-7. *Runtime cache*

Now spend a bit of time with the app and after a few minutes, turn the network off as shown in Figure 5-8 and reload the application.

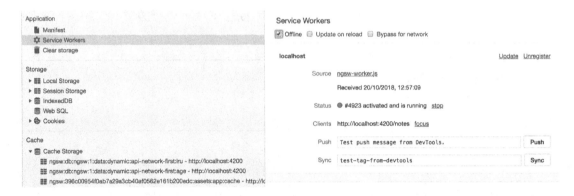

Figure 5-8. *Check offline to disconnect network*

Surprise! All the data that you have seen including notes, static assets, and jokes are now available even though you don't have a network connection whatsoever. Let's take a look at all requests in the network tab. You may notice in Figure 5-9 that there is no request for a joke endpoint.

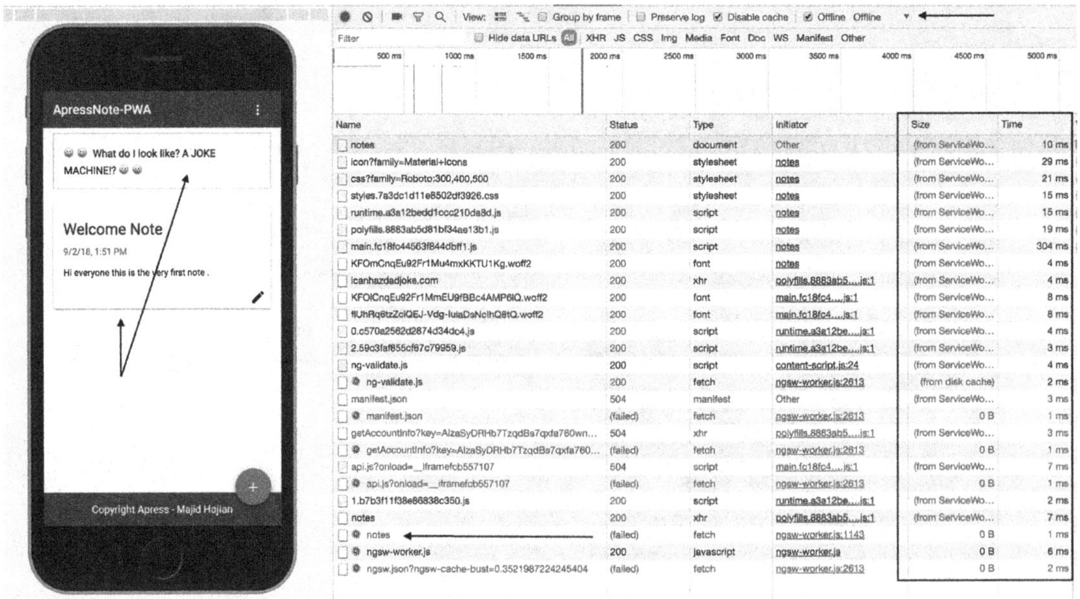

Figure 5-9. *Offline mode network request*

Yes, this is correct, since we have set `performance` (Cache-First) strategy for this endpoint, and it has not been expired due to `maxAge,` which is 15 minutes, Angular Service Worker will drop this request until it expires and then will revalidate this request and update the cache with an appropriate response.

Navigation Cache

In a single page application, routing is being handled in the front end. All routes in the front end are eventually pointed to `index.html` where the framework, in particular Angular Router Module, will match a navigation request to a specific view.

What makes a request considered to be a navigation request falls into three main bullets:

1. Its mode is navigation.

    The *mode* read-only property of the Request interface, is used to determine if cross-origin requests lead to valid responses, and which properties of the response are readable –values of which are cors, no-cors, same-origin, or navigate. **navigate** is a mode for supporting navigation and is intended to be used only by HTML navigation. A navigate request is created only while navigating between documents.[2]

2. It accepts a text/html response (as determined by the value of the Accept header).

3. Its URL matches certain criteria, defaults to:

    a. The URL must not contain a file extension (i.e., *a* .) in the last path segment.

    b. The URL must not contain __.

Having looked at `Config` interface, you will notice that there is a specific property for Angular or custom navigations `navigationUrls`. As you can see, this is optional and enables us to customize a list of URLs.

```
export interface Config {
  appData?: {};
```

---

[2]`https://developer.mozilla.org/en-US/docs/Web/API/Request/mode`

```
  index: string;
  assetGroups?: AssetGroup[];
  dataGroups?: DataGroup[];
  navigationUrls?: string[];
}
```

The URLs can be either an array of URLs and glob-like URL pattern that can be matched at runtime. Negative and nonnegative patterns are both supported.

While the default value is sufficient in most cases, it is sometimes necessary to configure different rules. Let's imagine we have some particular URLs in our application that need to be served in the back end, and we need to pass them through to the server to be handled since they are not Angular routes.

If nagivationUrls is omitted, default values are replaced:

```
"navigationUrls": [
  "/**",           // Include all URLs.
  "!/**/*.*",          // Exclude URLs to files.
  "!/**/*__*",         // Exclude URLs containing `__` in the last
                           segment.
  "!/**/*__*/**"       // Exclude URLs containing `__` in any other
                           segment.
]
```

And the result will look like this:

```
"navigationUrls": [
    {
      "positive": true,
      "regex": "^\\/.*$"
    },
    {
      "positive": false,
      "regex": "^\\/(?:.+\\/)?[^/]*\\.[^/]*$"
    },
    {
      "positive": false,
      "regex": "^\\/(?:.+\\/)?[^/]*__[^/]*$"
```

```
    },
    {
      "positive": false,
      "regex": "^\\/(?:.+\\/)?[^/]*__[^/]*\\/.*$"
    }
  ]
```

As an example, I will implement a route that doesn't need to be cached.
I will generate a component called NoCacheRouteComponent.

```
@Component({
  selector: 'app-no-cache-route',
  template: `
    <div class="appress-pwa-note">No-cache</div>
  `
})
export class NoCacheRouteComponent {}
```

Then I will add a route to app-routing.module.ts.

```
{
  path: 'no-cache-route',
  component: NoCacheRouteComponent
}
```

And finally, I will exclude this URL in ngsw-config.json.

```
"navigationUrls": [
  "/**",
  "!/**/*.*",
  "!/**/*__*",
  "!/**/*__*/**",
  "!/**/no-cache-route"
]
```

> **Note**   You can pull down www.github.com/mhadaily/awesome-apress-pwa/chapter05/03-no-cache-route. Run npm install and then run npm run serve:prod. It runs production app on a web server. You can navigate to localhost:4200.

AppData Config

This property is also optional and may contain application metadata for this specific version. The appData is not used by Service Worker but may be determined in Server Worker update where it can be used to show additional information in UI notifications to inform the user or make an intelligent decision on the app.

For example, information such as release date, build hash, a flag to indicate a sever security bugs which can be applied on the next reload without interrupting users.

I will use this object in the next section and will look at this config in other chapters later.

Dealing with Updates

By implementing Service Worker in our application, sooner or later dealing with a stale version of an app compared to what has been cached and used will become a problem because new versions of Service Worker will only be activated on page reload. Angular Service Worker resolves this issue by providing an SwUpdate class that makes it easy to check for available updates. Let's take a look at the class:

```
class SwUpdate {
  available: Observable<UpdateAvailableEvent>
  activated: Observable<UpdateActivatedEvent>
  isEnabled: boolean
  checkForUpdate(): Promise<void>
  activateUpdate(): Promise<void>
}
```

Let's break this class down:

1. **available**: an observable that emits UpdateAvailableEvent whenever a new app version is available.

```
interface Version {
    hash: string;
    appData?: Object;
}

interface UpdateAvailableEvent {
  type: 'UPDATE_AVAILABLE';
  current: Version
  available: Version;
}
```

UpdateAvailableEvent interface is pretty self-explanatory. As you see, in both current and available properties, appData is an option that will be available if we define it in ngsw-config.json.

For example:

```
{
  "index": "/index.html",
  "appData": {
    "version": "1.0.1"
  },
  "assetGroups": []
}
```

2. **activated**: an observable that emits UpdateActivateEvent whenever the app has been updated to a new version.

```
interface UpdateActivatedEvent {
    type: 'UPDATE_ACTIVATED';
    previous?: Version;
    current: Version;
}
```

3. **isEnabled**: is a Boolean in order to check if Service Worker is supported by the browser and enabled via ServiceWorkerModule.

4. **checkFoUpdate**(): a Promise that will be resolved when an update is available, and it allows us to check for updates periodically.

5. **activateUpdate**(): a Promise that will be resolved by forcing a Service Worker update. We may need to take other actions after getting resolved on this function. For instance, we need to reload the application because the currently loaded resources become invalid.

Now it's time to implement in our application and see the result in action.

```
export class AppComponent implements OnInit {
  joke$: Observable<string>;

  constructor(private db: DataService, private swUpdates: SwUpdate, private
  snackbar: SnackBarService) {}

  ngOnInit() {
    this.joke$ = this.db.getRandomDadJoke();
    this.swUpdateFlow();
  }

  swUpdateFlow() {
    // check if service worker is enabled and only check if it's production
    if (this.swUpdates.isEnabled && environment.production) {
      // subscribe to recieve update when it's available
      this.swUpdates.available.subscribe((event: UpdateAvailableEvent) => {
        // console log version on appData Object defined in ngsw-config.js
        console.log(`Version: ${event.current.appData['version']}`);

        // an update is available, inform user and take an action
        this.snackbar
          .action(
            `${event.type}: current is ${event.current.hash} but available
            is ${event.available.hash}`,
            'Activate'
          )
          .subscribe(() => {
```

```
      // force to activate update
      this.swUpdates
        .activateUpdate()
        .then(() => {
          this.snackbar.open('Update has been applied', 1000);
          // force to reload to ensure new update is in place
          // (<any>window).location.reload();
        })
        .catch(e => {
          this.snackbar.open('Something is wrong, please reload
          manually');
        });
    });
  });

  // subscribe to receive an notification when new version is activated
  this.swUpdates.activated.subscribe((event: UpdateActivatedEvent) => {
    // console log version on appData Object defined in ngsw-config.js
    console.log(`Version: ${event.current.appData['version']}`);

    this.snackbar
      .action(`${event.type}, current is ${event.current.hash} but
      previously was ${event.previous.hash}`, 'Reload')
      .subscribe(() => {
        // force to reload to ensure new update is in place
        (<any>window).location.reload();
      });
  });
  }
 }
}
```

In the app.component.ts, I will inject SwUpdate first. Then, I will ensure that we run the code on production and Service Worker is enabled. I will subscribe to available observables and once an update is available, I will show snackbar notification and inform the user that there is a newer version of app available and ask them to reload the page in order to see the latest and most up-to-date version of the app.

> **Note**   You can pull down www.github.com/mhadaily/awesome-apress-pwa/chapter05/04-notification-updates. Run `npm install` and then run `npm run serve:prod`. It runs a production app on a web server. You can navigate to `localhost:4200`.

Deploy to Firebase

Now we are ready to build our application and deploy to Firebase. As always, simply run:

```
npm run deploy
```

```
✓  hosting[awesome-apress-pwa]: file upload complete
i  database: releasing rules...
✓  database: rules for database awesome-apress-pwa released successfully
i  hosting[awesome-apress-pwa]: finalizing version...
✓  hosting[awesome-apress-pwa]: version finalized
i  hosting[awesome-apress-pwa]: releasing new version...
✓  hosting[awesome-apress-pwa]: release complete
```

✓ **Deploy complete!**

```
Project Console: https://console.firebase.google.com/project/awesome-apress-pwa/overview
Hosting URL: https://awesome-apress-pwa.firebaseapp.com
```

Let's navigate to the website and check Service Worker. As seen in Figure 5-10, new Service Worker has been installed and activated and new caches have been created.

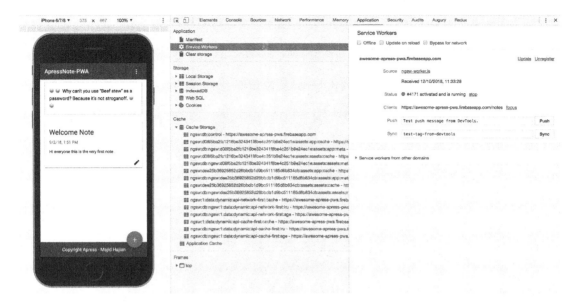

Figure 5-10. *Success deployment to Firebase*

Note   You can pull down www.github.com/mhadaily/awesome-apress-pwa/chapter05/02-runtime-cache. Run npm install and then run npm run serve:prod. It runs a production app on a web server. You can navigate to localhost:4200. You may need to also deploy this code to Firebase in order to evaluate your app before adding Service Worker.

Summary

in the last two chapters, I deep dived into Angular Service Worker configurations and settings, implemented the best strategies for our applications, and deployed an offline-ready app. Although our application works connection independently, there many possibilities to enhance the user experience.

In the next chapter, we will take a detailed look at app manifest, which makes our app installable where our user can run our application from the home screen.

CHAPTER 6

An App Manifest and Installable Angular App

Up until this point in the book, we have focused on the core feature of Progressive Web App (PWA), Service Worker. It enables us to cache our static assets as well as dynamic content. The app will continue to work offline, which is especially important on mobile devices. However, an app's "look and feel" is another important factor that enhances the user experience to truly delight users.

In this chapter, we focus on visual appeal and a few different ways that can help boost engagement on the app. We explore features such as Add to Home Screen and customization, which prompts a user to add the web to their device home screen.

The Web App Manifest

The Web App Manifest is a JSON text file following Web App Manifest specification that provides information about an application such as its name, author, icons, and description. But more importantly, this file enables an application to be installed by a user on their device and allows us to modify the theme, URL that should be opened, splash screen, icons on home page, and more.

Let's take a look at `manifest.json` located in `/src/`, which Angular CLI has created by default.

```
{
  "name": "lovely-offline",
  "short_name": "ApressPWA",
  "theme_color": "#1976d2",
  "background_color": "#fafafa",
  "display": "standalone",
```

© Majid Hajian 2019
M. Hajian, *Progressive Web Apps with Angular*, https://doi.org/10.1007/978-1-4842-4448-7_6

```
"scope": "/",
"start_url": "/",
"icons": [
  {
    "src": "assets/icons/icon-72x72.png",
    "sizes": "72x72",
    "type": "image/png"
  },
  {
    "src": "assets/icons/icon-96x96.png",
    "sizes": "96x96",
    "type": "image/png"
  },
  {
    "src": "assets/icons/icon-128x128.png",
    "sizes": "128x128",
    "type": "image/png"
  },
  {
    "src": "assets/icons/icon-144x144.png",
    "sizes": "144x144",
    "type": "image/png"
  },
  {
    "src": "assets/icons/icon-152x152.png",
    "sizes": "152x152",
    "type": "image/png"
  },
  {
    "src": "assets/icons/icon-192x192.png",
    "sizes": "192x192",
    "type": "image/png"
  },
  {
    "src": "assets/icons/icon-384x384.png",
```

```
    "sizes": "384x384",
    "type": "image/png"
  },
  {
    "src": "assets/icons/icon-512x512.png",
    "sizes": "512x512",
    "type": "image/png"
  }
  ]
}
```

Most of the properties are self-explanatory, but I will try to provide descriptive definitions. Each property in a manifest file has a role and tells the browser information regarding our app's look and feel. Although default manifest.json added by Angular CLI should be fine for most use cases, there are more properties that we can add to better enhance the user experience depending our needs and requirements.

Let's break them down:

- **name**:

    a readable name for the app displayed to user or as a label for an icon.

- **short_name**:

    short name that replaces name if that doesn't fit due to insufficient space.

- **theme_color**:

    defines the default theme color for the application to tint OS or browser-related UIs: for example, browser's toolbar or Android's task switcher. HEX code or color's name can be used.

- **background_color**:

    defines the expected background color for the app even before user agent loads website style sheets. Usually, there is a short gap between launching the web application and loading the site's content. This creates a smooth transition to fill the delay.

You can use color HEX code or standard color's name. Note that this background will not be used by the user agent after the style sheet is available.

- **display**:

  preferred display mode for the website. Four options are available as per spec, but it may not be available in all browsers:

  fullscreen: All of the available display is used. if not supported, falls back to standalone mode.

  standalone: most browser elements are hidden. Feels like a standalone application. In this mode, the user agent will exclude UI elements for controlling navigation but can include other UI elements such as a status bar. If not supported, falls backs to minimal-ui mode.

  minimal-ui: this application looks like a standalone app; however, essential UIs of the browser are still visible such as navigation buttons. It not supported, fall backs to browser mode.

  browser: just conventional browser tab or new window.

  It's interesting to know what there is a feature in CSS where you can detect display-mode. See code below:

  ```
  @media all and (display-mode: minimal-ui) {
    /* ... */
  }
  @media all and (display-mode: standalone) {
    /* ... */
  }
  ```

- **scope**:

  more or less similar to service worker scope that defines the navigation scope of this website's context. If a page is outside of this scope, it retunes to a normal web page inside a browser tab/window. In case of relative URL, the base URL will be the URL of the manifest. If omitted, default is everything under the manifest directory and all subdirectories.

- **start_url**:

    the URL that loads when a user launches the application. It can be different from the main page, for example, if you want your PWA users to go directly to login page or signup page instead of home page. For analytical purposes, start_url can be crafted to indicate that the application was launched from the outside of the browser, which can be translated to PWA. That is: "start_url": "/?launcher=homescreen"

- **icons**:

    an array of image files that specifics the app icons depending on the context. Each image has three properties:

    src: path to the image file; in case of relative URL, the base URL will be the URL of the manifest.

    sizes: specifies an icon size (even multiple sizes that are containing space-separate image dimensions). There are a variety of different screen sizes that we should support; the more dimensions we include, the better result we will get regarding the quality of icons.

    type: the media type[1] of image; if the user agent doesn't support this type, they can quickly ignore it.

- **prefer_related_applications**:

    this asks the browser to indicate to the user a specified native application in which are recommended in the next property, over the PWA. Although it may sound silly, sometimes it happens that we have a very specific native feature that doesn't exist on the web, so we want our user to use a native app instead. If omitted, the default value is false.

---

[1]https://www.iana.org/assignments/media-types/media-types.xhtml#image

- **related_applications**:

  recommended native applications that are installable or
  accessible from underlying platform store. For example, link to
  an Android app from Google Play Store. The objects may contain
  platform, url, and id.

  ```
  {
      "platform": "play",
      "url": "https://play.google.com/store/apps/details?id=com.
      example.app1",
      "id": "com.example.app1"
  }, {
      "platform": "itunes",
      "url": "https://itunes.apple.com/app/example-app1/id123456789"
  }
  ```

- **orientation**:

  sets the app work on default orientation. Orientation may be one
  of the following values:

  ```
  any, natural, landscape, landscape-primary, landscape-secondary
  portrait, portrait-primary, portrait-secondary
  ```

- **dir**:

  specifies the primary text direction for the name, short_name, and
  description. There are two values: ltr, auto, and rtl. When
  the value is omitted, default is auto.

- **lang**:

  together with dir, it specifies correct display language. Default is
  en-US.[2]

- **description**:

  a general description of what the website does.

---

[2]https://developer.mozilla.org/en-US/docs/Web/HTML/Global_attributes/lang

- **serviceWorker**:

  this member represents an intended service worker registration in form of a registration object.

  ```
  "serviceworker": {
    "src": "sw.js",
    "scope": "/foo",
    "update_via_cache": "none"
  }
  ```

  This feature may not work in any browsers.

- **categories**:

  specifies an array of strings of the expected application categories to which the web application belongs, written in lowercase.

- **screenshots**:

  array of image resources that represent the web application in common usage scenarios. This might not work yet in any browser or platform.

- **iarc_rating_id**:

  represents the International Age Rating Coalition (IARC)[3] certification code of the web application.

To reference a manifest file, we need to add a link tag between head to all the pages in our web app. However, we have a single page application with Angular, and ng-cli has added the link to index.html and angular.json to copy this file to the root folder after build.

---

[3]https://www.globalratings.com/

```
// index.html where we added manifest.json link.
<head>
  .

  .

  <base href="/">
  <link rel="manifest" href="manifest.json">

  .

  .

  </head>
```

Debugging Web App Manifest

Now that I have covered the Web App Manifest and referenced the index HTML page, we should be able to run an application and then navigate to the app in the Chrome. In DevTools, go to Application tab and click on manifest option on the left side, right above Service Workers (see Figure 6-1).

The details appear there, including errors if any. There is an option to test the prompt to add the app to the home screen also.

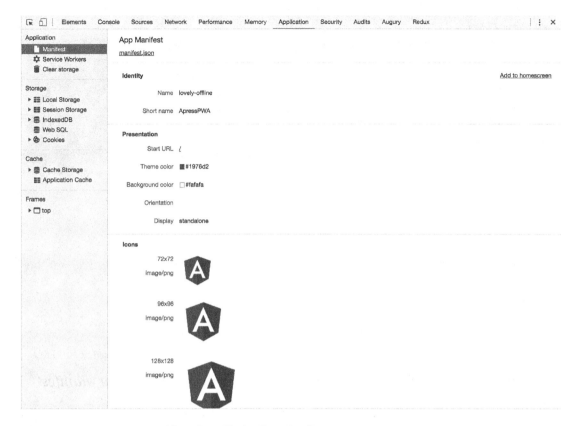

Figure 6-1. *App manifest details in DevTools*

Although Chrome DevTools is fine to debug your manifest file, there are tools that you can check to validate your manifest file against W3C spec. One example is manifest-validator.appspot.com where you can simply audit your manifest file. Figure 6-2 shows a screenshot of Web Manifest Validator.

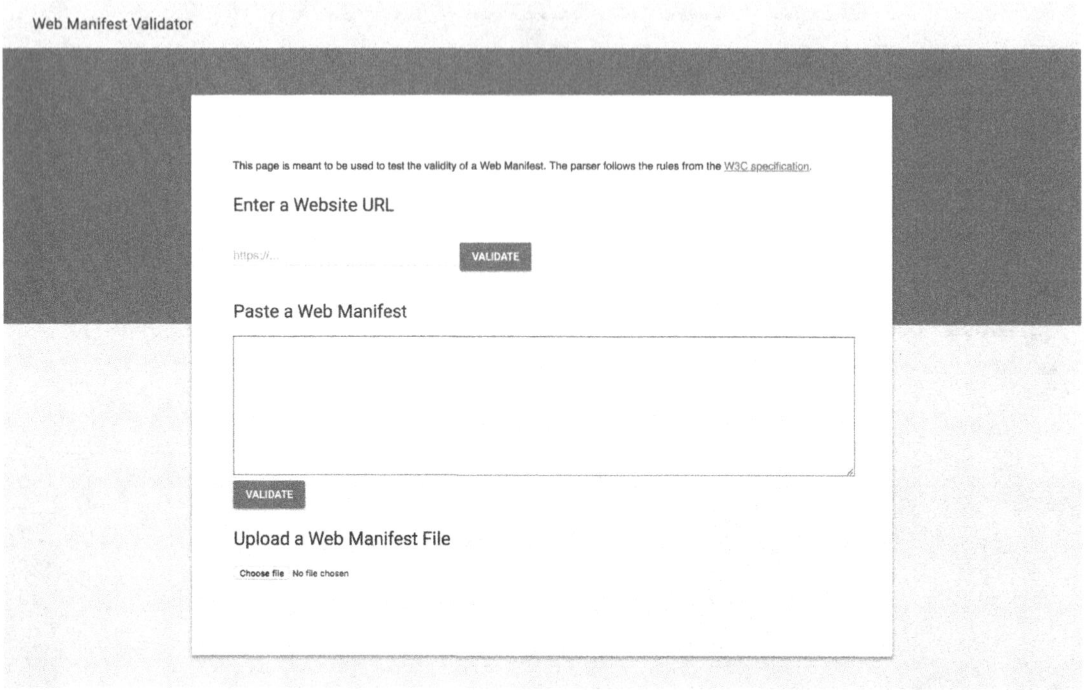

Web Manifest Validator

This page is meant to be used to test the validity of a Web Manifest. The parser follows the rules from the W3C specification.

Enter a Website URL

https://...   VALIDATE

Paste a Web Manifest

VALIDATE

Upload a Web Manifest File

Choose file   No file chosen

Figure 6-2. *Web Manifest Validator is a tool where you can debug your manifest file*

Adding to Home Screen

By default, a native app installs on your home screen. You will see an icon and short name, and when you need to run this application, it's easy to come back to the home screen and tap on the icon to open up the app. As web developers, it is important to engage our users and keep them coming back to our app. So, functionality as a native app is one piece of the puzzle to tackle engagement. A great way to seamlessly allow our users to add our web's app to their home screen is Add to Home Screen (you may see A2HS) capability, also known as a web app install banner.

This feature makes it easy to install a PWA on the mobile or desktop device. It displays a prompt and after the user accepts it, your PWA will added to their launcher or home screen. It will run like any other installed app and looks similar to native apps.

However, the web app install banner prompt will not be shown unless otherwise it meets the following criteria:

1. Serve over HTTPS (this was one of the PWA core concepts and required for Service Worker).

2. Web App Manifest has to include:

    a. `short_name` or `name`

    b. `icons` must include a 192px and a 512px sizes icons

    c. `start_url` must have a proper value

    d. `display` must be one of the: `fullscreen`, `standalone`, or `minimal-ui`

3. The web app is not already installed.

4. An appropriate user engagement heuristic.

    This item may change over time, so you should always keep yourself updated with the latest news and check different browsers' criteria lists time to time. At the time of writing this book, a user must interact with the domain for at least 30 seconds.

5. App has a registered Service Worker with a `fetch` event handler.

While this list is in a bit of flux and is updated frequently, if these criteria are met, Google Chrome will fire an event called `beforeinstallprompt` that we should use it to show the prompt to our user. Keep an eye on different browsers and check the latest news to see if they support this event or similar events.

Although Safari does not support the automatic Add to Home Screen prompt or `beforeinstsallprompt` event, the manually add to home screen is shown by tapping the share button, even though it behaves a bit differently compared with other browsers. I hope that by the time you read this book, an automatic version of this feature will be supported by Safari and all other browsers.

Note   Chrome 67 and earlier showed an "Add to Home Screen" banner. It was removed in Chrome 68 and a dialog will be shown if it is listened to `beforeinstallprompt` and the user taps on an element that has a proper gesture event.

Handling Installation Event (Deferring the Prompt)

As we have seen, when all the criteria are met, beforeinstallprompt event fires on the window object. It is crucial to listen to this event to indicate when the app is installable, and we need to act accordingly on the web app to show an appropriate UI to notify our user that they are able to install this app on their home screen.

While add to home screen is our main goal, this event can be used for other purposes also, such as the following:

1. Sending user choice to our analytics system.

2. Defer displaying the notification until we ensure that's the best time to show in which user will tap or click.

In order to save the event that has been fired, we need to write the code as the following:

```
let deferredPrompt;

window.addEventListener('beforeinstallprompt', event => {
  // Prevent automatically showing the prompt if browser still supports it
  event.preventDefault();
  // Stash the event so it can be triggered later.
  deferredPrompt = event;
  // This is time to update UI, notify the user they can install app to
  home screen
  const button = document.getElementById('add-to-home-screen-button');
  button.style.display = 'block';

  button.addEventListner('click', () => {
    if (deferredPrompt) {
      // will show prompt
      deferredPrompt.prompt();

      // Wait for the user to respond to the prompt
      deferredPrompt.userChoice.then(choiceResult => {
        // outcome is either "accepted" or "dismissed"
        if (choiceResult.outcome === 'accepted') {
          // User accepted the A2HS prompt
          // send data to analytics
```

```
            // do whatever you want
        } else {
            // User dismissed the A2HS prompt
            // send data to analytics
            // do whatever you want
        }
          // we don't need this event anymore
        deferredPrompt = null;
        // delete or hide this button as it's not needed anymore
        button.style.display = 'none';
      });
    }
  });
});
```

It's only possible to call prompt() on the deferred event once. If the user dismisses it, we need to wait until the browsers trigger beforeinstallprompt event on the next page navigation.

The Mini-Info Bar

The mini-info bar is an interim experience for Chrome on Android at the time of writing this book; it is moving toward creating a consistent experience across all platforms that includes an install button into the omnibox as shown in Figure 6-3.

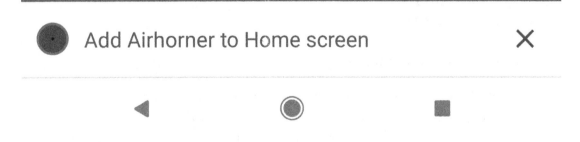

Figure 6-3. *The mini-info bar in Google Chrome on Android*[4]

---

[4]https://developers.google.com/web/updates/2018/06/a2hs-updates

This is Chrome UI component and we are not able to control it. Once it has been dismissed by user, it will not appear again until a sufficient amount of time. Regardless of preventDefault() on the beforeinstallprompt event, if the website meets all the criteria above, this mini-bar will appear.

This experimental functionality may be controllable or completely eradicated in the future.

Implementing Functionality into Angular App

Let's now implement the code above in our Angular sample project. Start off by creating a service called AddToHomeScreenService and import it to CoreModule.

This service will hold the prompt event and will share this event according to the modules.

```
@Injectable({
  providedIn: 'root'
})
export class AddToHomeScreenService {
  public deferredPromptFired$ = new BehaviorSubject<boolean>(false);
  public deferredPrompt;

  get deferredPromptFired() {
    this.deferredPromptFired$.next(!!this.deferredPrompt);
    return this.deferredPromptFired$;
  }

  public showPrompt() {
    if (this.deferredPrompt) {
      // will show prompt
      this.deferredPrompt.prompt();

      // Wait for the user to respond to the prompt
      this.deferredPrompt.userChoice.then(choiceResult => {
        // outcome is either "accepted" or "dismissed"
        if (choiceResult.outcome === 'accepted') {
          // User accepted the A2HS prompt
          // send data to analytics
```

```
          // do whatever you want
          this.sendToAnalytics(choiceResult.userChoice);
        } else {
          // User dismissed the A2HS prompt
          // send data to analytics
          // do whatever you want
          this.sendToAnalytics(choiceResult.userChoice);
        }

        // we don't need this event anymore
        this.deferredPrompt = null;
        this.deferredPromptFired$.next(false);
      });
    }
  }

  public sendToAnalytics(userChoice) {
    // for example, send data to Google Analytics
    console.log(userChoice);
  }
}
```

In the app.component.ts file, by adding @HostListener, we will listen to for a beforeinstallprompt event and by injecting AddToHomeScreenService, we have access to the deferredPrompt, which helps to keep our event object.

```
export class AppComponent implements OnInit {
  joke$: Observable<string>;

  @HostListener('window:beforeinstallprompt', ['$event'])
  onEventFire(e) {
    this.a2hs.deferredPrompt = e;
  }

  constructor(
 private db: DataService,
 private a2hs: AddToHomeScreenService
) {}
```

```
ngOnInit() {
  this.joke$ = this.db.getRandomDadJoke();
}
}
```

Next, I decided to show a notification box to my user on the notes list page. I think this is the best place to ask if the user would like to install the app since they have already benefited from the app, and it's likely that they will accept the prompt. So, it's good practice not to bother a user with an unwanted prompt or notification and ask them, instead, when it makes sense.

AddToHomeScreenService was injected to NotesListComponent and UI has been created accordingly.

```
export class NotesListComponent implements OnInit {
    isAddToHomeScreenEnabled$;

        constructor(private db: DataService,
        private a2hs: AddToHomeScreenService) {}

        ngOnInit() {
          // this.notes$ = this.db.getNotes();
          this.notes$ = this.db.initializeNotes();
          this.isDbLoading$ = this.db.isLoading$;
          this.isAddToHomeScreenEnabled$ = this.a2hs.deferredPromptFired;
        }
}
```

And in the notes-list.component.html file, at the top of the page, I will add a simple card to ask the user if they like to interact with prompt as soon as it it's ready.

```
<mat-card *ngIf="isAddToHomeScreenEnabled$ | async">
  <mat-card-subtitle>Add To Home Screen</mat-card-subtitle>
  <mat-card-content>
    Do you know you can install this app on your homescreen?
    <button mat-raised-button color="primary" (click)="showPrompt()">Show
    me</button>
  </mat-card-content>
</mat-card>
```

```
<div *ngIf="notes$ | async as notes; else notFound">
  <app-note-card *ngFor="let note of notes" [note]="note"
[loading]="isDbLoading$ | async" [routerLink]="['/notes', note.id]">
  </app-note-card>
</div>
<ng-template #notFound>
  <mat-card>
    <mat-card-title>
      Either you have no notes
    </mat-card-title>
  </mat-card>
</ng-template>
```

Put all of it together and build an application for production and then deploy to Firebase.

Adding to Home Screen on Mobile and Desktop

Now that we have implemented all the criteria, it's time to test it on the mobile and desktop. Since Google Chrome has the best support for installing an app, you may ask what actually Google Chrome does when a user accepts the prompt?

Chrome handles most of the heavy lifting for us:

1. **Mobile**:

   Chrome will generate a WebAPK,[5] which results in better integrated experiences for the users.

2. **Desktop**:

   Your app is installed and will run in an app window[6] on both Mac and Windows machines.

Note   To test install flow for Desktop PWA on Mac, you'll need to enable the #enable-desktop-pwas flag in Google Chrome. It may be the default in the future or when you are reading this book.

---

[5]https://developers.google.com/web/fundamentals/integration/webapks
[6]https://developers.google.com/web/progressive-web-apps/desktop#app-window

Let's see this in action on a Mac and Android phone, as shown in Figure 6-4.

Figure 6-4. *Notification is shown once beforeinstallprompt in Chrome on Android and Mac was fired*

When you click on the button to show the prompt, a browser dialog prompt will appear (see Figure 6-5).

Figure 6-5. *Prompt Dialog in Chrome on Mac*

Once you click on Install, the app will have installed in Chrome Apps folder and will be ready to be served as a standalone app (see Figure 6-6). This feature is also available on Windows 10.

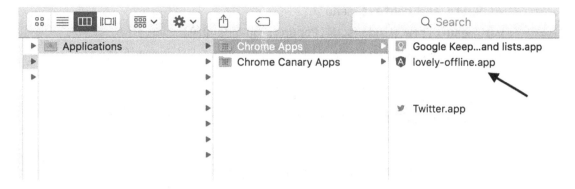

Figure 6-6. *PWA was installed in Chrome apps on Mac*

Microsoft Windows[7]

PWA in Edge is a first-class citizen. Once PWA was distributed through the Microsoft Store, the entire Windows 10 install base of 600+ million active monthly users are your potential app audience!

Interestingly, when PWAs are in Windows 10, they run as Universal Windows Platforms apps and will gain the following technical advantages:

- Standalone window

- Independent process from browser (isolated cache, less overhead)

- No storage quota (for IndexedDB, local storage, etc.)

- Offline and background processes Access to native Windows Runtime (WinRT) APIs via JavaScript

- Appearance in "app" contexts such as the Windows Start menu and Cortana search results

One of the greatest features is the ability to access WinRT APIs. It's just a matter of identifying what you need to use, obtaining the requisite permissions, and employing feature detection to call that API on supported environments (see Figure 6-7). Let's look at one example:

```
if (window.Windows && Windows.UI.Popups) {
    document.addEventListener('contextmenu', function (e) {
```

---

[7]https://docs.microsoft.com/en-us/microsoft-edge/progressive-web-apps

```
// Build the context menu
var menu = new Windows.UI.Popups.PopupMenu();
menu.commands.append(new Windows.UI.Popups.UICommand("Option 1",
null, 1));
menu.commands.append(new Windows.UI.Popups.UICommandSeparator);
menu.commands.append(new Windows.UI.Popups.UICommand("Option 2",
null, 2));

// Convert from webpage to WinRT coordinates
function pageToWinRT(pageX, pageY) {
    var zoomFactor = document.documentElement.msContentZoomFactor;
    return {
        x: (pageX - window.pageXOffset) * zoomFactor,
        y: (pageY - window.pageYOffset) * zoomFactor
    };
}

// When the menu is invoked, execute the requested command
menu.showAsync(pageToWinRT(e.pageX, e.pageY)).done(function
(invokedCommand) {
    if (invokedCommand !== null) {
        switch (invokedCommand.id) {
            case 1:
                console.log('Option 1 selected');
                // Invoke code for option 1
                break;
            case 2:
                console.log('Option 2 selected');
                // Invoke code for option 2
                break;
            default:
                break;
        }
```

```
        } else {
            // The command is null if no command was invoked.
            console.log("Context menu dismissed");
        }
    });
}, false);
}
```

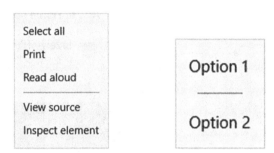

Figure 6-7. *Context menu on Microsoft Edge and Windows App*

Android and Chrome

Flow is similar for Chrome in Android. beforeinstallprompt event is triggered. Once we tap on the button that we implemented, the dialog will be shown (see Figure 6-8).

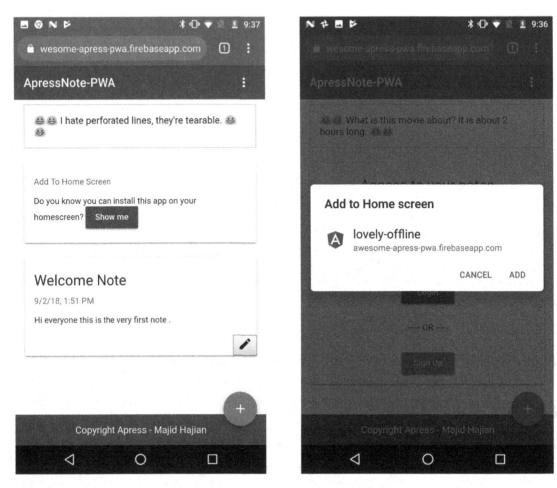

Figure 6-8. *Install app notification to user and add to home screen dialog*

As soon as the user accepts it to install, App icon and short_name will have been placed just next to other native apps icons in the home screen as shown in Figure 6-9.

Note   Samsung internet browser behavior is similar to Chrome but reacts slightly differently.

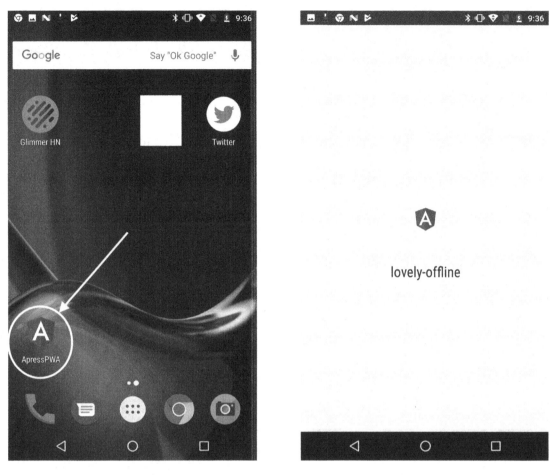

Figure 6-9. *App installed on home screen and once tapped to open, splash screen with configured background and icons is shown*

When you tap to open the app, no browser chrome (navigation buttons, address bar, menu options, etc.) are visible with the fullscreen option, and you'll notice that the status bar on the top adopts the `theme_color,` which we have configured in our app (see Figure 6-10).

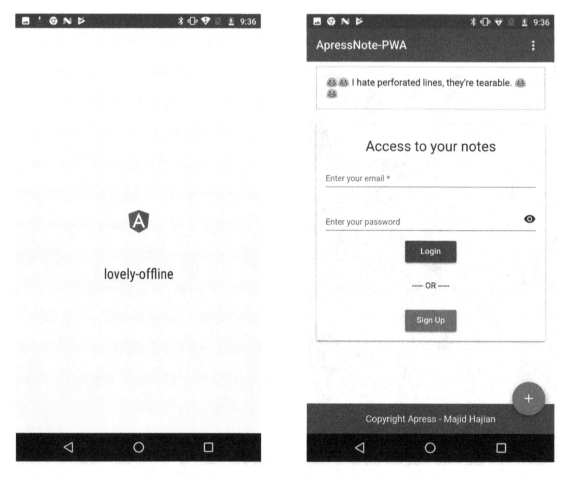

Figure 6-10. *PWA looks similar to native app once it opens*

Manually Adding to Home Screen

Dialog prompt is not guaranteed to always be triggered. So, there are possibilities to manually add a PWA to the home screen. This feature is also available on Safari iOS.

In Chrome, if you click on menu context menu on the top-right side of the browser, you'll see the menu options where you can find add to home screen, tap on it, and a prompt dialog UI appears.

In Safari, the add to home screen feature is hidden under the share button. You should explicitly hit share and then you'll find add to home screen as shown in Figure 6-11. However, Safari doesn't exactly follow the Web App Manifest spec and may be changed in the future – hopefully by the time you are reading the book.

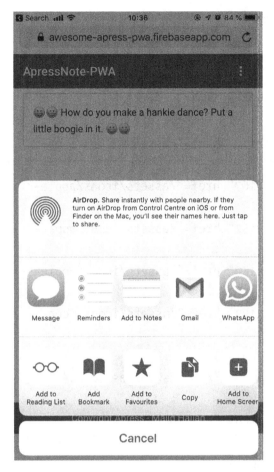
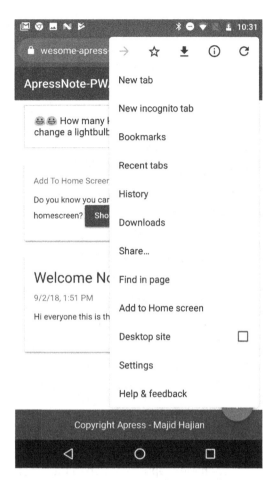

Figure 6-11. *Add to Home Screen buttons are available on Safari and Chrome*

Further Enhancement

There are a few tags available to refine UI in for Apple and Microsoft where web manifest
is not supported. I add them to index.html between head tag. Even though it's a minor
improvement, we still progressively enhance our user experience, which is our goal in PWA.

```
<!-- Enhancement for Safari-->
<meta name="apple-mobile-web-app-capable" content="yes">
<meta name="apple-mobile-web-app-status-bar-style" content="default">
<meta name="apple-mobile-web-app-title" content="ApressNote">
```

```
<link rel="apple-touch-startup-image" href="/assets/icons/icon-512x512.
png">
<link rel="apple-touch-icon" sizes="57x57" href="/assets/icons/icon-
96x96.png">
<link rel="apple-touch-icon" sizes="76x76" href="/assets/icons/icon-
72x72.png">
<link rel="apple-touch-icon" sizes="114x114" href="/assets/icons/icon-
114x114.png">
<link rel="apple-touch-icon" sizes="167x167" href="/assets/icons/apple-
icon-384x384.png">
<link rel="apple-touch-icon" sizes="152x152" href="/assets/icons/apple-
icon-152x152.png">
<link rel="apple-touch-icon" sizes="180x180" href="/assets/icons/apple-
icon-384x384.png">
<link rel="apple-touch-icon" sizes="192x192" href="/assets/icons/icon-
192x192.png">
<!-- Tile icon for Win8 (144x144 + tile color) -->
<meta name="msapplication-TileImage" content="/assets/images/icons/icon-
144x144.png">
<meta name="msapplication-TileColor" content="#3372DF">
<meta name="msapplication-starturl" content="/">
<meta name="application-name" content="ApressPWA">

<!-- Mobile specific browser color -->
<meta name="theme-color" content="#3f51b5">
```

apple-mobile-web-app-capable: behaves similarly to display fullscreen mode if set to yes. We determine whether a web page is displayed in fullscreen mode using the **window.navigator.standalone** in Safari.

apple-mobile-web-app-status-bar-style: this meta tag has no effect unless you first specify fullscreen mode as described in *apple-apple-mobile-web-app-capable*. If content is set to default, the status bar appears normal. If set to black, the status bar has a black background. If set to black-translucent, the status bar is black and translucent. If set to default or black, the web content is displayed below the status bar. If set to black-translucent, the web content is displayed on the entire screen, partially obscured by the status bar. The default value is default.

apple-touch-startup-image: specifies a launch screen image that is displayed while your web application launches. By default, a screenshot of the web application the last time it was launched is used.

apple-mobile-web-app-title: specifies a web application title for the launch icon. By default, the <title> tag is used.

apple-touch-icon:[8] specifies an icon to represent your web application or web page that user may want to add to the home screen. These links, represented by an icon, are called Web Clips.

application-name:[9] the default name displayed with the pinned sites tile (or icon).

msapplication-starturl: the root URL of the pinned site similar to start_url in web manifest.

msapplication-TileColor: sets the background color for a live tile.

msapplication-TileImage: specifies a URI for the desired image in the background image for live tile.

While you can add all of the enhancements manually yourself, there is a library from Google Chrome Team that can help you mitigate this issue automatically.

PWACompat Library[10]

PWAcompat is a library that brings the Web App Manifest to noncompliant browsers for better PWAs; you can use the PWACompat library where we will fill the gap for wider support in most browsers through legacy HTML tags for icons and theming. Basically, you just need to include the library script in your page and you are done!

```
<link rel="manifest" href="manifest.json" />
<script async src="https://cdn.jsdelivr.net/npm/pwacompat@2.0.7/pwacompat.
min.js"></script>
```

What actually this library does is to update your page and also the following:

- Create meta icon tags for all icons in the manifest (e.g., for a favicon, older browsers)

---

[8]https://developer.apple.com/library/archive/documentation/AppleApplications/Reference/SafariWebContent/ConfiguringWebApplications/ConfiguringWebApplications.html

[9]https://technet.microsoft.com/en-us/windows/dn255024(v=vs.60), to find out more about window site metadata.

[10]https://github.com/GoogleChromeLabs/pwacompat

- Create fallback meta tags for various browsers (e.g., iOS, WebKit/ Chromium forks etc.) describing how a PWA should open

- Sets the theme color based on the manifest

For Safari, PWACompat also:

- Sets apple-mobile-web-app-capable (opening without a browser chrome) for display modes standalone, fullscreen, or minimal-ui

- Creates apple-touch-icon images, adding the manifest background to transparent icons: otherwise, iOS renders transparency as black

- Creates dynamic splash images, closely matching the splash images generated for Chromium-based browsers

For PWAs on Windows with access to UWP APIs:

- Sets the title bar color

Keep an eye on the library to see the latest version and features.

Summary

Advanced caching and the add to home screen have been implemented. We are one step closer to the native app counterparts. In the next chapter, we are going to boost Angular performance and work on App Shell to take our application to the next level.

CHAPTER 7

App Shell and Angular Performance

No one likes to wait for long to see that an application is loading. In fact, statistics show that if the initial rendering takes more than three seconds, it's very likely that a user leaves our app. One of the main fundamentals of PWAs is to be fast. In native apps, the user usually is presented a splash screen and after a reasonable amount of time will see the main content and skeleton. On the other hand, there will be white screen until bootstrapping is finished, especially a single page app.

In this chapter, we will review the app shell model to understand what it is and how it works. Then, we will set up Angular CLI to help us generate our Angular App Shell. Finally, we are going to step beyond the app shell and optimize our Angular app to achieve better performance.

The App Shell Model

This model has been introduced in order to build a PWA that, reliably, instantly loads and boosts perceived startup performance for the user similar to what they see in native applications.

The app "shell" is the minimal HTML, CSS, and JavaScript that are required for the user interface in order to see something meaningful when they load the application. We can think of what they should see above the fold content or the main skeleton as quickly as possible. It can be cached offline and should be instantly loaded and must have reliable performance to the user on repeat visits. In other words, an application shell is not loaded from the network every time a user visits the app.

© Majid Hajian 2019
M. Hajian, *Progressive Web Apps with Angular*, https://doi.org/10.1007/978-1-4842-4448-7_7

You may ask, what about the content? Content, in this case, is requested from the network if necessary. This architecture may not work for all scenarios and applications; however, it's has been the go-to-approach for Angular app, which is mostly considered a single-page application.

As seen in Figures 7-1 and 7-2, an application shell is similar to the native app skeleton that is necessary to boot up the app and show the initial UI to user; however, it doesn't contain the data. So, we can simply bundle it up and publish it to the app store. This architecture not only help to simulate a native-like app and load it fast, but also, from an economical perspective, will save data as we have cached them and will reload caches on repeated visits.

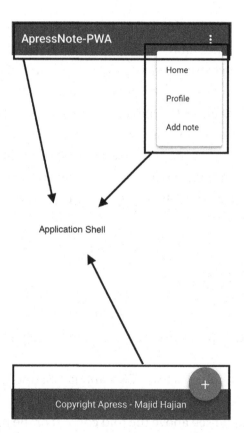

Figure 7-1. *Application shell*

Figure 7-2. Dynamic content

In Chapter 4, we technically cached our application shell and managed to even cache part of our dynamic content in Chapter 5, which also boosted our user experience.

Angular App Shell

An app shell concept in Angular consists of two meanings: "pre-caching app's UI" and "pre-rendering of the UI during build-time." In general, using both cache and pre-rendering UIs together can create an Angular App Shell.

Although we have cached our static assets, which include application shell requirements, it is not shown to the user until Angular is bootstrapped. The time that we have shown meaningful content to our user is when JavaScript files have been parsed and executed; thus the Angular App has been bootstrapped. As we know, we reference our JavaScript files in index.html; therefore, the user hits this file first before even the files are downloaded.

In low-performance apps and especially on the first-time visit, there is a time between seeing app content and a blank screen, which is basically our index.html and does not have any elements.

Angular CLI has a built-in functionality that helps us to generate our app shell at build time automatically. Before we go further, let's see what index.html contains after building for prod in /dist folder. Open your project and build for prod or if you have cloned the repository for this book, simply change your directory to chapter07 and then to 02-app-shell; finally, run the following command:

npm run build:prod

If we compare index.html from src folder and dist folder, we notice that we only see JS files and CSS files injected into this file.

```
<!doctype html>
<html lang="en">

<head>
  ...
  <link rel="stylesheet" href="styles.c418d0a7774195ac83e5.css">
</head>

<body>
  <app-root></app-root>
  <noscript>Please enable JavaScript to continue using this application.
  </noscript>
  <script type="text/javascript" src="runtime.3d4490af672566f1a0de.js">
  </script>
  <script type="text/javascript" src="polyfills.c53b1132b0de9f2601bd.js">
  </script>
  <script type="text/javascript" src="main.a136972022b8598085fb.js">
  </script>
</body>

</html>
```

I would like to measure the app startup performance after build. You can either run ng serve --prod or after build run a local server to run the app. If you are still in project repository for this book, simply run npm run prod then follow these steps:

1. Open a new browser, possibly incognito where we ensure there is no cache.

2. Open DevTools in Chrome and select tab performance.

3. Open capture setting and select Fast 3G for Network and 4x Slowdown for CPU; this is typically when we want to simulate throttling for a mobile (Figure 7-3).

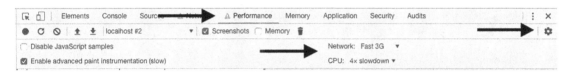

Figure 7-3. *Open capture setting and select Fast 3G and 4x slowdown*

4. Click on record and hit enter to load the website or simply reload the page by hitting the reload icon in performance tab.

As you can see in Figure 7-4, the browser is rendering the page at about 2000 ms while the first paint attempt has started around 500 ms, but since there is no content and nothing to show, it remains blank.

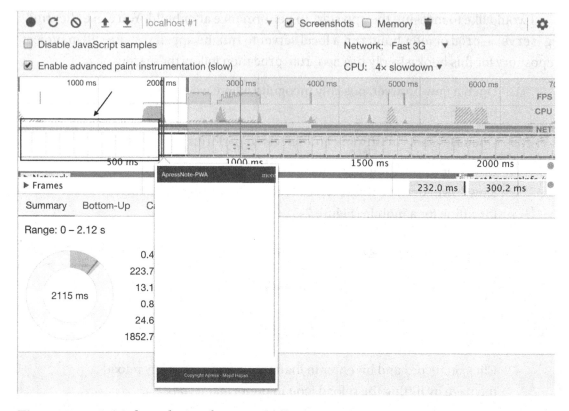

Figure 7-4. Initial rendering for app shell after Angular is bootstrapped around 2 seconds

Angular App Shell and Angular Universal

Angular Universal generates static application pages on the server through a process called server-side rendering (SSR). When Universal is integrated with your app, it can pre-generate pages as HTML files that can be served later.

Having looked at the application structure, `app.component.ts` has the main skeleton, which includes a header and footer.

```
template: `
<div class="appress-pwa-note">
  <app-header></app-header>
  <div class="main">
    <div *ngIf="joke$ | async as joke" class="joke">
    {{ joke }}
    </div>
```

```
    <router-outlet></router-outlet>
  </div>
  <app-footer></app-footer>
</div>
`
 ,
```

It seems that if we can pre-render this component, we can have an app shell before bootstrapping Angular. As you see in the component template, it has <router-outlet> that is going to be replaced with content; thus, we need to specify what we want to put in place of the router outlet.

This is where we are using Angular Universal by running simple commands via Angular CLI to generate an app-shell at build time and output in index.html. We define the route we would like to pre-render and then we are good to go. Hence, we are going to scaffold for an Angular Universal to gain pre-rendering capabilities. Angular CLI will be a built-in command that will help us to achieve our goal painlessly. Simply run the following command:

```
ng generate app-shell --client-project <my-app> --universal-project
<server-app>
```

- Angular CLI generates App Shell.

- --universal-project specifies which Angular Universal application we want to use for pre-rendering.

- --client-project specifies the client project that we would like to use for pre-rendering.

- Optionally, you can use --route to specify what route name should be used for generating App Shell. The default value is shell.

Since Angular CLI 6+ can handle multiple client projects, it's important to find the correct app. If you don't know your client project name, look inside the angular.json CLI configuration file.

Here is the command output:

```
CREATE src/main.server.ts (220 bytes)
CREATE src/app/app.server.module.ts (590 bytes)
CREATE src/tsconfig.server.json (219 bytes)
CREATE src/app/app-shell/app-shell.component.css (0 bytes)
```

```
CREATE src/app/app-shell/app-shell.component.html (28 bytes)
CREATE src/app/app-shell/app-shell.component.spec.ts (643 bytes)
CREATE src/app/app-shell/app-shell.component.ts (280 bytes)
UPDATE package.json (1822 bytes)
UPDATE angular.json (5045 bytes)
UPDATE src/main.ts (656 bytes)
UPDATE src/app/app.module.ts (1504 bytes)
```

If you want to do the process manually or if you wonder how it works under the hood. I will break the code down.

Main.`server.ts` has been created to bootstrap the `app-server-module`:

```
import { enableProdMode } from '@angular/core';

import { environment } from './environments/environment';

if (environment.production) {
  enableProdMode();
}

export { AppServerModule } from './app/app.server.module';
```

`app-server.module.ts` with only one route `shell` where it's being replaced with `router-outlet`

```
import { NgModule } from '@angular/core';
import { ServerModule } from '@angular/platform-server';

import { AppModule } from './app.module';
import { AppComponent } from './app.component';
import { Routes, RouterModule } from '@angular/router';
import { AppShellComponent } from './app-shell/app-shell.component';

const routes: Routes = [ { path: 'shell', component: AppShellComponent }];

@NgModule({
  imports: [
    AppModule,
    ServerModule,
    RouterModule.forRoot(routes),
  ],
```

```
  bootstrap: [AppComponent],
  declarations: [AppShellComponent],
})
export class AppServerModule {}
```

app-shell.component where we can add what we need to show for pre-rendering; in this case, I will add a simple loading message.

```
// app-shell.component.html
<div class="loading" style="text-align:center; padding:3rem">
  loading... will be sevring you very very soon
</div>`
```

```
// app-shell.component.ts
@Component({
  selector: 'app-app-shell',
  templateUrl: './app-shell.component.html',
  styleUrls: ['./app-shell.component.css']
})
export class AppShellComponent implements OnInit {
  constructor() { }
  ngOnInit() {
  }
}
```

tsconfig-server.json will have all requirements for server-side rendering an Angular app.

```
{
  "extends": "./tsconfig.app.json",
  "compilerOptions": {
    "outDir": "../out-tsc/app-server",
    "baseUrl": "."
  },
  "angularCompilerOptions": {
    "entryModule": "app/app.server.module#AppServerModule"
  }
}
```

And platform-server module has been added to package.json:

```
"@angular/platform-server": "^7.0.1",
```

In app.module.ts, BrowserModule has configured in order to transition from a server-rendered app, if one is present on the page.

```
BrowserModule.withServerTransition({ appId: 'serverApp' }),
```

Besides all the other changes, there are new configurations in angular.json file where we have two new targets:

```
"server": {
        "builder": "@angular-devkit/build-angular:server",
        "options": {
          "outputPath": "dist/lovely-offline-server",
          "main": "src/main.server.ts",
          "tsConfig": "src/tsconfig.server.json"
        },
        "configurations": {
          "production": {
            "fileReplacements": [
              {
                "replace": "src/environments/environment.ts",
                "with": "src/environments/environment.prod.ts"
              }
            ]
          }
        }
    },
    "app-shell": {
      "builder": "@angular-devkit/build-angular:app-shell",
      "options": {
        "browserTarget": "lovely-offline:build",
        "serverTarget": "lovely-offline:server",
        "route": "shell" // where we define our route
      },
```

```
    "configurations": {
      "production": {
        "browserTarget": "lovely-offline:build:production"
      }
    }
  }
}
```

As you have seen, `app-shell` component was linked to `/shell` route but only in the `Angular Universal` application. This special route is an internal Angular CLI mechanism in order to generate App Shell. It will replace `router-outlet` tag and the user will not able to navigate to it.

Generating the App Shell in Production

So, everything seems ready and has been set up properly. Let's now build with the app shell target.

To trigger a production build, all you need to do is run one of the below commands:

```
ng run <project-name>:app-shell:production
ng run <project-name>:app-shell --configuration production
```

Therefore, in the project, run the following command:

```
ng run lovely-offline:app-shell:production
```

This command will target the client app named `lovely-offline` and the target build, which is `app-shell`. Angular CLI starts building and bundling and once it's done, output is ready in `dist` folder. Let's take a look at `index.html` now.

```
<app-root _nghost-sc0="" ng-version="7.0.1">
    <div _ngcontent-sc0="" class="appress-pwa-note">
      <app-header _ngcontent-sc0="" _nghost-sc1="">
        <mat-toolbar _ngcontent-sc1="" class="mat-toolbar mat-primary mat-
        toolbar-single-row" color="primary"
          ng-reflect-color="primary"><span _ngcontent-sc1="" tabindex="0"
          ng-reflect-router-link="/">ApressNote-PWA</span><span
            _ngcontent-sc1="" class="space-between"></span><button _
          ngcontent-sc1="" aria-haspopup="true"
```

```
            mat-icon-button="" class="mat-icon-button _mat-animation-
            noopable"
            ng-reflect-_deprecated-mat-menu-trigger-for="[object
            Object]"><span class="mat-button-wrapper">
              <mat-icon _ngcontent-sc1="" class="mat-icon material-icons"
              role="img" aria-hidden="true">more_vert</mat-icon>
            </span>
            <div class="mat-button-ripple mat-ripple mat-button-ripple-
            round" matripple="" ng-reflect-centered="true"
              ng-reflect-disabled="false" ng-reflect-trigger="[object
              Object]"></div>
            <div class="mat-button-focus-overlay"></div>
          </button></mat-toolbar>
        <mat-menu _ngcontent-sc1="" x-position="before" class="ng-tns-c6-0">
          <!---->
        </mat-menu>
      </app-header>
      <div _ngcontent-sc0="" class="main">
        <!--bindings={
  "ng-reflect-ng-if": "How many kids with ADD does it"
}-->
        <div _ngcontent-sc0="" class="joke ng-star-inserted"> How many kids
        with ADD does it take to change a
          lightbulb? Let's go ride bikes! </div>
        <router-outlet _ngcontent-sc0=""></router-outlet>
        <app-app-shell _nghost-sc7="" class="ng-star-inserted">
          <div _ngcontent-sc7="" class="loading" style="text-align:center;
          padding:3rem"> loading... will be sevring
            you very very soon
          </div>`
        </app-app-shell>
      </div>
      <app-footer _ngcontent-sc0="" _nghost-sc2="">
        <footer _ngcontent-sc2="">
          <div _ngcontent-sc2="" class="copyright">Copyright Apress - Majid
          Hajian</div>
```

```
      </footer>
      <div _ngcontent-sc2="" class="addNote"><button _ngcontent-sc2=""
      mat-fab="" class="mat-fab mat-accent _mat-animation-noopable"
          tabindex="0" ng-reflect-router-link="/notes/add"><span
          class="mat-button-wrapper">
            <mat-icon _ngcontent-sc2="" class="mat-icon material-icons"
            role="img" aria-hidden="true">add circle</mat-icon>
          </span>
          <div class="mat-button-ripple mat-ripple mat-button-ripple-
          round" matripple="" ng-reflect-centered="false"
            ng-reflect-disabled="false" ng-reflect-trigger="[object
            Object]"></div>
          <div class="mat-button-focus-overlay"></div>
        </button></div>
      </app-footer>
    </div>
  </app-root>
```

It looks very different from what we had before. Angular CLI has generated a shell based on /shell route, which has a footer and header, including a joke section.

In addition to HTML, you see that all CSS based on these components have also been generated and added to <head> </head>.

I will add a npm script to build App Shell and measure the performance again.

```
"build:prod:shell": "ng run lovely-offline:app-shell:production",
```

And

```
"prod": "npm run build:prod:shell && cd dist && http-server -p 4200 -c-1",
```

Run the local server by hitting

```
npm run prod
```

If you are running your own project, make sure you have http-server installed and you change the directory to /dist and run http-server -p 4200 c-1.

After the server is ready, navigate to localhost:4200 in Chrome and do the same performance profiling as we did before App Shell implementation.

The result may differ from app to app and where you run the test, but the main point is that Angular App Shell could potentially enhance start up load time. As you see in Figure 7-5, we managed to render our application shell to the user at around 100 ms and as soon as Angular is bootstrapped dynamic content, it will be loaded.

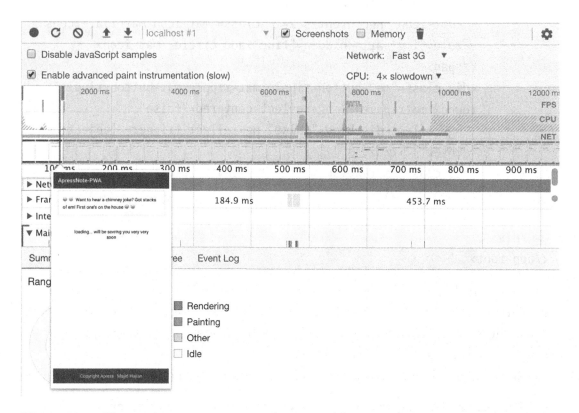

Figure 7-5. *First paint starts at around 100 ms after we implement Angular App Shell*

Measuring App Shell Performance via webpagetest.org

Although we have run a local test with our local server via the Chrome Performance tab in DevTools, it's not very precise. Webpagetest.org is a tool that we can use to measure a website's performance and generate details about the test, including many features that are useful when it comes to web app optimization.

Let's run a test for our app on Firebase before we deploy new App Shell implementation.

Open webpagetest website and go to simple testing tab. Enter your website name and select "**Mobile regular 3G**" (see Figure 7-6). Select both "Include repeat view" and "run lighthouse audit." You can run more tests with different settings. Finally, start the test.

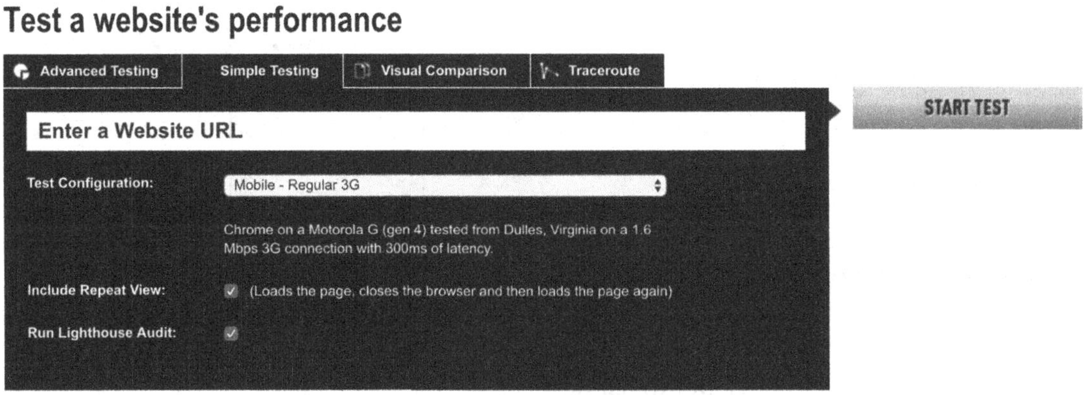

Test a website's performance

Figure 7-6. *Simple testing setting on webpagetest.org*

Once a result is ready, we see that before App Shell optimization, the time to interact is around 7.8 seconds and the browser starts rendering around 6.9 seconds, which is somehow expected due to bootstrapping Angular (see Figure 7-7). To see more details, check out this link:

https://www.webpagetest.org/result/181030_ZA_ff4f3780bea8eb430be1171a5297ae35/

Performance Results (Median Run)

	Load Time	First Byte	Start Render	User Time	Speed Index	First Interactive (beta)	Document Complete			Fully Loaded			Cost
							Time	Requests	Bytes In	Time	Requests	Bytes In	
First View (Run 1)	8.423s	1.710s	6.912s	4.517s	7.438s	7.814s	8.423s	11	399 KB	8.423s	17	435 KB	$---
Repeat View (Run 2)	3.960s	3.039s	2.381s	0.942s	2.664s	> 2.570s	3.960s	0	0 KB	3.960s	2	134 KB	

Plot Full Results

Figure 7-7. *Webpagetest result before App Shell and more optimizations, run on Mobile Regular 3G network*

I will deploy the app to Firebase with App Shell implementation. Once deployment is done, navigate to the website and see the source via Chrome. You'll see that the App Shell and inline styles are already in the source. Open webpagetest.org and run the exact same test again.

As soon as the result is ready, a significant improvement is seen. The time to interact has reduced to 5.9 seconds and the start render time dropped at least 2 seconds compared to the previous test. You see that a simple model in the app could have a notable impact on user experience (see Figure 7-8).

Performance Results (Median Run)

	Load Time	First Byte	Start Render	User Time	Speed Index	First Interactive (beta)	Document Complete			Fully Loaded			
							Time	Requests	Bytes In	Time	Requests	Bytes In	Cost
First View (Run 2)	6.789s	1.464s	4.254s	3.886s	5.017s	> 5.952s	6.789s	11	402 KB	6.789s	17	438 KB	$----
Repeat View (Run 3)	4.556s	3.090s	1.729s	1.373s	2.191s	> 2.992s	4.556s	1	133 KB	4.556s	2	134 KB	

Plot Full Results

Figure 7-8. *Webpagetest result after App Shell, run on Mobile Regular 3G network*

To see more details, check out this link:

```
https://www.webpagetest.org/result/181031_KE_538b7df1cabf6cbe4a3565a3f6c42fc6/
```

Measuring App Shell Performance via Audit tab in Chrome DevTools

While webpagetest.org is able to run a test application via Lighthouse, I would like to run the measure with my web app running on Chrome DevTools on my machine. Keep in mind, the more tests you do, the better. So, don't give up, and run more tests on different tools.

Simply open your Chrome DevTools while the web app on Firebase is loading. Go to Audit tab as you are familiar with, and select the Performance check box as well as Progressive Web App. Make sure *Simulated Fast 3G, 4x CPU Slowdown* is chosen for throttling and then hit the "Run Audit" button. I will do this test before and after I deploy the app with App Shell implementation. You can see the result in Figures 7-9 through 7-12.

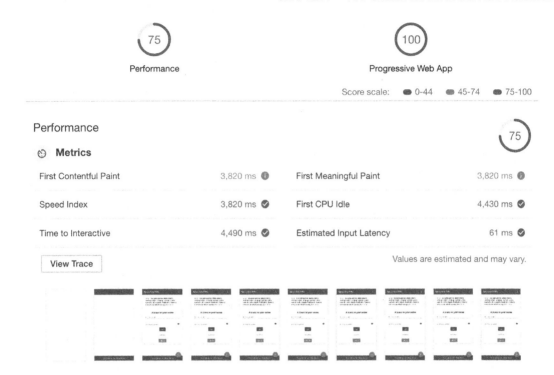

Figure 7-9. *Audit website in Chrome audit tab to check performance score before deploying App Shell implementation on simulated mobile fast 3G*

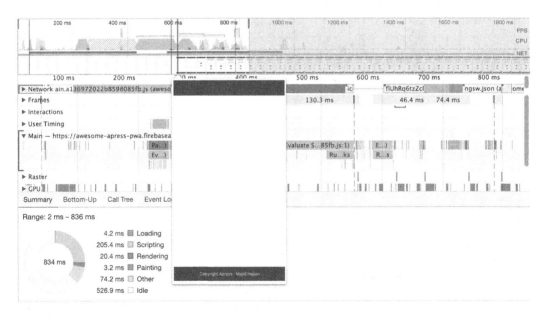

Figure 7-10. *Performance tab before deploying App Shell implementation, tested on good internet connection, and initial rendering is around 700 ms*

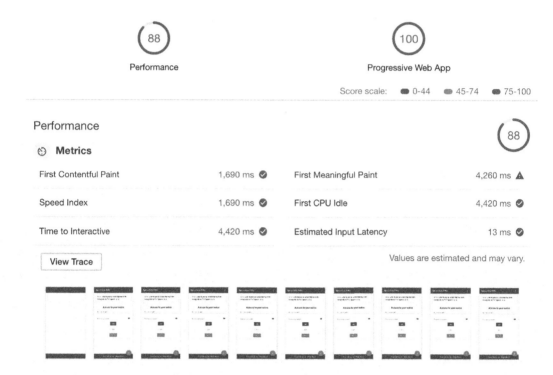

Figure 7-11. *Audit website in Chrome audit tab to check performance score after deploying App Shell implementation on simulated mobile fast 3G*

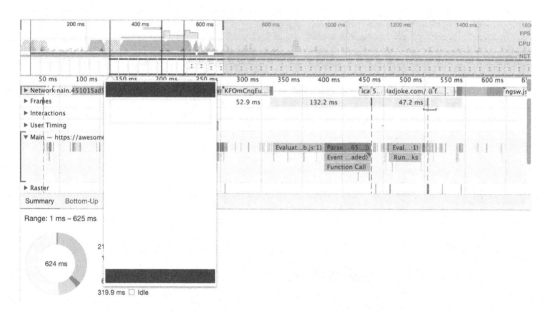

Figure 7-12. *performance tab after deploying App Shell implementation, tested on good internet connection, initial rendering is around 150 ms*

As we have seen, in this particular app, the App Shell has represented a huge improvement to the typical time to the first paint of a full SPA, which could sometimes keep a user waiting for a few noticeable seconds.

Although, App Shell model is one way to improve a startup load, it's not the only thing that we can do in our applications. There are even more optimizations that we can do in a web app, especially in an Angular application, in order to boost the performance.

Beyond the App Shell, Further Optimizations

As we know, web apps are still fighting with native apps in terms of performance perception; thus, each blink of an eye is going to be important. There are an infinite number of tips and tricks that we can try to do in the app to eke out another few milliseconds.

In general, performance in Angular is mostly divided into two sections:

1. Runtime performance, which targets best practices to improve mostly change detection, rendering related optimizations.

2. Network performance, which targets best practices to enhance the load time of our application, including latency and bandwidth reduction.

There are common best practices that are known in web development and overlap both sections. However, in this section, my focus point is network performance and faster load time. I will review some of the most important tips that we can do in order to improve loading speed.

Analyze Bundle Sizes and Lazy Load Module

No doubt that the less JavaScript code in the bundle size, the better for downloading and parsing. Angular CLI uses Webpack to bundle the app. By passing `--stats-json` in `build` command, Angular CLI will generate a JSON file that contains all bundle information and we simply can analyze it.

Just follow the steps below:

1. Install the tool with `npm install webpack-bundle-analyzer -D`

2. Add `--stats-json` to build script in `packge.json`

   `"build:prod": "ng build --prod `**`--stats-json`**`",`

3. Add new script to `package.json` file

   `"analyzer": "webpack-bundle-analyzer dist/stats.json"`

4. Build and then run `npm run analyzer`

Once build is done, there will be a `stats.json` file in the `/dist` folder that contains all information about the project bundles. You'll be redirected to the browser as soon as you run the npm command, and you'll see how the app stats look like as shown in Figure 7-13.

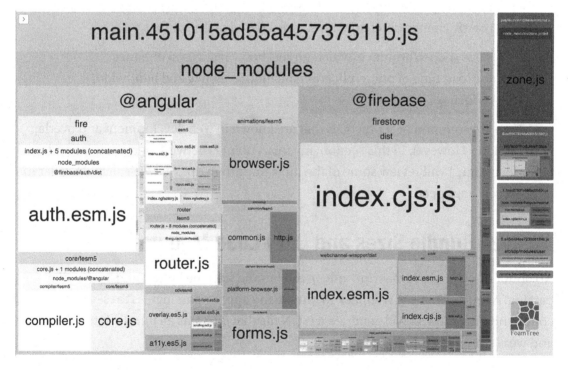

Figure 7-13. *Analysis of the project app; lazy loaded modules are shown to the right of the picture*

One way of splitting code to decease the bundle size is to use lazy loading in Angular. Lazy loading gives you an ability to optimize your application load time by splitting the application to feature modules and loading them on demand.

```
{
  path: 'user',
  loadChildren: './modules/user/user.module#UserModule'
},
{
  path: 'notes',
  loadChildren: './modules/notes/notes.module#NotesModule',
  canLoad: [AuthGuard]
}
```

We can even prevent whole modules from being loaded based on some condition. For example, in the project application, we have prevented loading the whole module by adding canLoad guard, if it's necessary based on the rule in the guard.

The analysis may differ from app to app and it's based on how you architect your app.

Waterfall View from Web Page Test

Waterfall view reveals many helpful loading details that can be used for tracking down bottlenecks: for instance, things that block rendering, or requests that can be eliminated or deferred. An overview of how long that takes from initial a request until is done. Useful information about http handshaking and etc. For example, Figure 7-14 shows that the project app renders blocks by loading Google fonts, or it delays painting around 450 ms because the browser is parsing CSS.

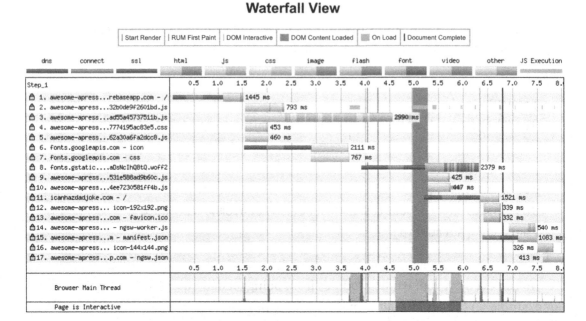

Figure 7-14. *The app waterfall view from webpagetest.org*

Reduce Render Blocking CSS

It is a common mistake that is seen in many applications in which they will load a lot of CSS while it's not necessary for the content that are can be seen in the screen or so-called above-the-fold-content.

Generally speaking, we should determine what is crucial for the app skeleton, app shell, and for the initial load and add them to style.css. We should try to minimize the footprint of our initial style file.

Additionally, we should import shared styles in lazy loaded modules. Sometimes we even need to import styles to only those lazy loaded modules that need a particular style. For example, imagine that we have a chart module that has been loaded lazily. If this module needs a specific styling, we should only import that to this where it will be loaded on demand.

In a real example, think of our app, since we are pre-rendering and app shell and Angular CLI will inject all essential styling to index.html. It may make sense to remove Angular Material theme CSS file and our main style.scss file into AppComponent, because basically the whole application needs those styles and we can simply pre-render and inject that styling into index.html head, which will result removing the style.css bundle file that blocks the render.

```
// Angular.json
"styles": [
            {
              "input": "node_modules/@angular/material/prebuilt-themes/
              indigo-pink.css"
            },
            "src/styles.scss"
          ],

// remove these files and it looks like
"styles": [],
```

And then import them to AppComponent:

```
//app.component.ts
@Component({
  selector: 'app-root',
  template: `
  <div class="appress-pwa-note">
    <app-header></app-header>
    <div class="main">
      <div *ngIf="joke$ | async as joke" class="joke">
      {{ joke }}
      </div>
      <router-outlet></router-outlet>
    </div>
    <app-footer></app-footer>
  </div>
  `,
  styleUrls: [
    '../../node_modules/@angular/material/prebuilt-themes/indigo-pink.css',
    '../../styles.scss'
  ]
})
```

Now, if you build the application and then check /dist/index.html, you'll see that all stylings have been added to the head and there is no more css file as before.

Once more, this is just an example that I want to show how you can think of optimizing your app; and it may make sense for our Note app but doesn't seem a good option for your next project. Keep in mind, you should evaluate the app performance after each change and see if there is an improvement.

Optimize Fonts

It's very likely that you are using fonts in web applications these days, especially external fonts such as Google fonts. While we add the style link to the head of the page, it should be taken into consideration that these fonts will block rendering. That means rendering will hold off until these styles are downloaded and rendered. It is important to slim down the initial need for fonts and load the reset of them on demand.

Self-Hosting Fonts

Using a web font face block means that the browser decides what to do if it takes a long time for that web font to fetch. Some browsers will wait anywhere up to three seconds for this before falling back to a system font, and they'll eventually swap it out to the font once it's downloaded.

We are trying to avoid invisible text, so thanks to new feature called font-display, this helps to decide how web fonts will render or fall back based on how long it takes for them to swap.

Swap gives the font face a zero-second block period and an infinite swap period. In other words, the browser will render text pretty quickly with a fallback font if downloading takes time. Once the web font is ready, it is going to swap. This feature has a good browser support.[1]

```
@font-face {
  font-family: YouFont;
  font-style: normal;
  font-display: swap;
  font-weight: 400;
```

---

[1]https://caniuse.com/#search=font-display

```
src: local(yo-font Regular'), local(YouFont -Regular'),
    /* Chrome 26+, Opera 23+, Firefox 39+ */
    url(you-font -v12-latin-regular.woff2') format('woff2'),
      /* Chrome 6+, Firefox 3.6+, IE 9+, Safari 5.1+ */
    url(you-font -v12-latin-regular.woff') format('woff');
}
```

In case of Note app, it makes sense to show our user their notes as quickly as possible and then move on, and transition over to the web font once it is ready. Keep in mind that we still get a **FOUT**[2] (flash of unstyled text).

CDN-Based Fonts

Clearly, we are using Google web fonts in the Note app. There are many different approaches to optimize these types of fonts. On way is to asynchronously add them to UI, which helps to avoid block rendering. There are tools and libraries that we can use to lazy load fonts, but perhaps one of the most well-known libraries is Web Font loader.[3]

However, I have decided to load my fonts differently in my Angular project in order to unveil two attributes that help loading JavaScript files while they don't block rendering. I have created a JavaScript file named lazy-fonts.js and added it to /src and will add the following code, which basically adds a script tag to the head.

```
(function(d) {
  var x = d.createElement('link');
  var y = d.getElementsByTagName('script')[0];
  x.rel = 'stylesheet';
  x.href = 'https://fonts.googleapis.com/icon?family=Material+Icons';
  y.parentNode.insertBefore(x, y);
  })(document);

(function(d) {
  var x = d.createElement('link');
  var y = d.getElementsByTagName('script')[0];
```

---

[2]https://en.wikipedia.org/wiki/Flash_of_unstyled_content
[3]https://github.com/typekit/webfontloader

```
  x.rel = 'stylesheet';
  x.href = 'https://fonts.googleapis.com/css?family=Roboto:300,400,500';
  y.parentNode.insertBefore(x, y);
})(document);
```

I will also delete the fonts tags between <head> in the index.html file in the Application and will reference this file right before </body>. Last but not least, I will add this file into my assets array in Angular configuration file, which tells Angular CLI to copy this file from the src to dist folder root.

```
// angular.json
"assets": [
            "src/favicon.ico",
            "src/assets",
            "src/manifest.json",
            "src/lazy-fonts.js"
          ],
```

and

```
// index.html
<script type="text/javascript" src="lazy-fonts.js"></script>
</body>
```

Modern browsers have a couple of additional options to keep the scripts from blocking the page-rendering process. The two main features are the following:

- **defer attribute**: tells browser to continue rendering while the resource is being downloaded but to not execute this JS resource until it's finished rendering HTML. In other words, the browser will wait for the script to execute until rendering is completely done. For angular-cli app, currently there is no way to add this automatically during the build, so you have to do it manually after the build.

- **async attribute**: tells browsers that continuing rendering while the script resource is also being downloaded will only pause parsing from HTML to execute the script. This is useful when you need the script to be executed as soon as possible but not block rendering from your application shell. The best example is to use it with Google analytics scripts, which are usually independent of any other scripts.

So, based on the definition I would like to add async to my script file.

```
// index.html
<script type="text/javascript" src="lazy-fonts.js" async></script>
</body>
```

This will help to render HTML without being blocked by the script, which will also add the fonts to the app.

Browser Resource Hinting

You might have heard of preload, prefetch, and preconnect. Eventually, these enable web developers to optimize delivery of the resources, reduce round-trips, and fetch resources faster than it's requested.

- **Preload**: is a new standard to of how to gain more control on how resources should be fetched for current navigation. This directive is defined within a <link> element, <link rel="preload">. This allows the browser to set priority to prefetch even before the resource is reached. See Figure 7-15 for browser support.

  ```
  <link rel="preload" href="https://example.com/fonts/font.
  woff" as="font" crossorigin>
  ```

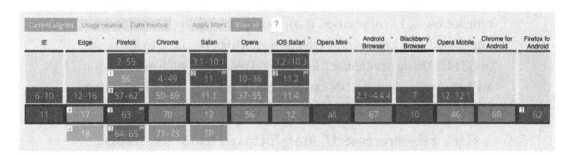

Figure 7-15. *Preload browser support as of writing this book*

- **Prefetch**: is set as a low priority resource hint that informs the browser to fetch that particular resource in the background when the browser is idle. We use prefetch for those resources that may be needed later: for example, prefetch pictures that will need to be shown on the second navigation on the website. Element is defined similar to preload. See Figure 7-16 for browser support.

```
<link rel="prefetch" href="/uploads/images/pic.png">
```

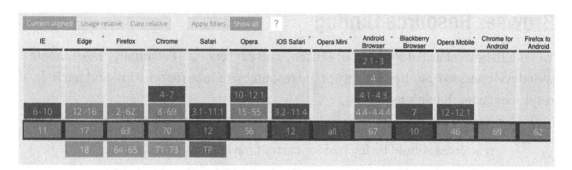

Figure 7-16. *Prefetch brower support as of writing this book*

- **Preconnect**: this allows the browser to set up early connection before an HTTP request is actually sent to the server, including DNS lookups, TLS negotiations, and TCP handshakes. One of the benefits of having this resource hint is to eliminate roundtrip latency and save time for users. In some cases, it could improve up to 400 ms for the initial load. The tag is similar to preload, which is added to the head in HTML. Using preconnect for external resources such as fonts that are being served via a CDN can potentially boost loading time. See Figure 7-17 for browser support.

```
<link rel="preconnect" href="https://fonts.googleapis.
com"crossorigin="anonymous">
```

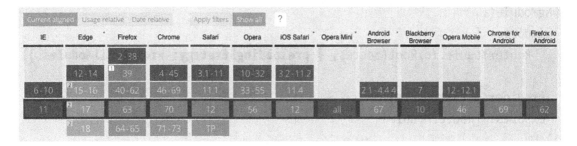

Figure 7-17. *Preconnect browser support as of writing this book*

Since we are using Google fonts in PWA Note project, adding resources hits `preconnect` and `preload` and may help loading performance. Open `src/index.html` and add the following codes:

```
<head>
  <link rel="preconnect" href="https://fonts.googleapis.com"
  crossorigin="anonymous">
  <link rel="preconnect" href="https://fonts.gstatic.com"
  crossorigin="anonymous">
  <link rel="preload" href="https://fonts.googleapis.com/
  icon?family=Material+Icons" as="style">
  <link rel="preload" href="https://fonts.googleapis.com/
  css?family=Roboto:300,400,500" as="style">
  <link rel="preload" href="lazy-fonts.js" as="script">
```

Once we build and deploy to Firebase, we can run another test to measure performance after adding these tags. You may not see a huge improvement, but even 100 ms counts. Remember, we strive to reduce milliseconds.

Preload Angular Lazy Loaded Modules

Angular enables us to preload all lazy loaded modules. This feature is inherited from Angular Router module where we are able to change the preloading strategy.

While you are able to write a custom provider to define a preloading strategy, I use `PreloadAllModules`, which is in Angular Router module already. Open `app-routing. module.ts` and add a second argument to `forRoot` on `RouterModule`.

```
@NgModule({
  imports: [
    RouterModule.forRoot(routes, { preloadingStrategy: PreloadAllModules })
  ],
  providers: [AuthGuard],
  exports: [RouterModule]
})
export class AppRoutingModule {}
```

This allows the browser to prefetch and cache these modules even before they are on demand; thus, subsequent navigations are instant while the initial load is as small as possible. This might be especially useful when our lazy load modules are pretty big in size. Keep in mind that preloading will not affect the initial load performance.

HTTP/2 Server Push[4]

HTTP/2 (h2) Server Push is one of the performance features included in version 2 of the HTTP protocol.

As long as all the URLs are delivered over the same hostname and protocol, the web server is allowed to "push" contents to the client ahead of time even if the client has not requested them.

Having push resources compete with the delivery of the HTML can impact page load times. This can be avoided by limiting the amount and size of what is pushed.

Firebase allows us to push content to the client by configuring `firebase.json` located in the root of our project. The rule looks like the code below:

```
"hosting": {
  "headers": [
    {
      "source": "/",
      "headers": [
        {
          "key": "Link",
```

---

[4]https://en.wikipedia.org/wiki/HTTP/2_Server_Push

```
         "value": "</lazy-fonts.js>;rel=preload;as=script,</css/any-
         file.css>;rel=preload;as=style"
      }
    ]
  }
 ],
}
```

Although this feature sounds promising, do not try to overuse it.

Summary

App Shell pattern is a great way to boost initial load speed, and we have seen that Angular CLI by utilizing Angular Universal will generate a proper app shell for any Angular project as long as it is well architected.

We optimize our application for enhancing performance in a network level to build a blazing fast application. Although I have covered the main important topics in performance and optimizations, you are not limited and should take things a step further and refine even more. Things like Google Closure Compiler, Tree-shaking, Build-optimizer flag, Ivy Render Engine, Cache-control header, Gzip compression, Header compression in HTTP/2, Compressing images, Change Detection optimization, Pure pipes and memorization, are just examples of how far you can get and how fast the application can be.

As I mentioned, progressive enhancement is one of the most important keys in building PWAs. So, implement features with feature-detecting in browsers, always keep all of your users in mind, iteratively enhance your app performance, and give your users the best integration and interaction experience regardless of what browser they are using.

In the next chapter, we shift our attention to engaging part of a PWA and will see how we can send push notifications to our users.

CHAPTER 8

Push Notifications

There are different ways to keep your user engaged and up to date such as by email, in-app notifications, and push notifications! Native mobile apps have been engaging their users by push notifications for a long time. This feature was not supported on the web until PWAs were born. Thanks to new standard APIs such as Notification API and Push API, which are built on top of Service Worker, it's possible to send push notifications to web users.

In this chapter, you'll discover the basics of push notifications and will build a working example for the existing application, PWA Note. You'll see how we write a Firebase Cloud Function in order to send push notifications from a server. All in all, after this chapter, you should be able to run your own server for sending push notifications and implement this feature in Angular in no time.

Introduction to Push Notifications

Most modern web applications will keep their users updated and communicate through different channels such as their social medias, emails, and in-app notifications. While all of these channels are great, they don't always grab their users' attention, especially when the user navigates away from the app.

Traditionally, native applications had this amazing ability, push notification, until PWAs were born. That's why PWAs are a game changer. A notification is a message that can be shown on the user's device and is triggered either locally by Web Notifications API[1] or can be pushed from the server to the user when the app is not even running, thanks to Service Worker.

---

[1] https://www.w3.org/TR/notifications/

© Majid Hajian 2019

M. Hajian, *Progressive Web Apps with Angular*, https://doi.org/10.1007/978-1-4842-4448-7_8

Web Notifications

The notification API allows a web page to control the display of system notifications to the user. Since this message is shown outside of the top-level browsing context viewport, it can be displayed to the user even if the user switches tabs. The best part is that this API is designed to be compatible with existing notification systems across different platforms. On supported platforms, the user needs to grant the current origin permission to display system notifications. Generally, it can be done by calling the `Notification.requestPermission()` method (Figure 8-1).

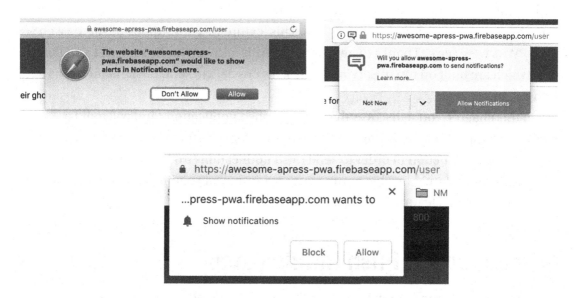

Figure 8-1. *Permission popup for web notifications in different browsers*

Once permission is granted, on the web page, we just need to instantiate `Notification` constructor with an appropriate title and options (see Figure 8-2).

```
new Notification("New Email Received", { icon: "mail.png" })
```

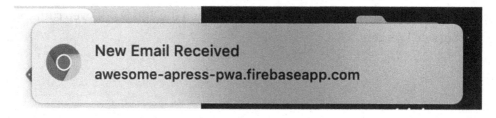

Figure 8-2. *Simple notification received in Chrome browser*

This is pretty great. It would be nice if we can involve Service Worker, too. When showing a notification is handled by Service Worker, it's called "Persistent notifications," since Service Worker remains persistent in the background of the app whether it's running or not.

Almost all of the code is going to be the same as before; the only difference is that we just need to call showNotification method on sw object.

```
nagivator.serviceWorker.ready.then(sw =>{
    sw.showNotification('title', { icon: "main.png"})
})
```

You'll find out more about possible options for the notifications in this chapter.

Push Notifications

Undoubtedly, one of the most powerful and incredible ways to engage with our user is push notifications, where they extend the app beyond the browser. There are several pieces that come together to make push notifications work. One of the main pieces is Push API that enables web developers to do this similarly to native apps technology, which is called Push Messaging.

In a few steps, I'll try to simplify the push notification architecture:

1. After the user grants permission, the app asks a web push service for a PushSubscription object. Keep in mind that each browser has its own implementation of a push service.

2. The web push service returns the PushSubscription object. Here is when you can save this object in your database in order to reuse it for pushing notifications.

3. In our app, we define which action requires a push notification. Therefore, the app back end will handle sending push notifications based on the subscription details.

4. Finally, once the web push service sends the notification, Service Worker will receive the notification and show it.

There are different events for push notification in Service Worker such as push and notificationclick events.

Note   In Service Worker, you can listen to push and other events related to push
notifications such as notificationclick

Looking at Figure 8-3, you'll see how it works visually.

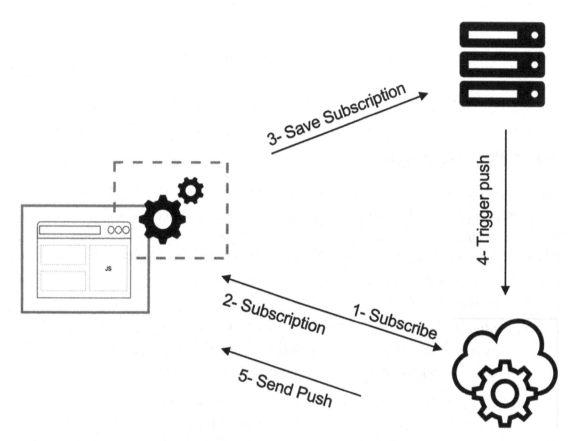

Figure 8-3. *Push notification process*

Requesting for a subscription object without identifying the app itself in the web
push server, potentially, will expose a lot of risks and vulnerabilities. The solution is to
use Voluntary Application Server Identification (VAPID) keys, also known as application
server keys. This ensures that the server will know who is requesting the push and
who will receive it. This is considered a security precaution to make sure nothing goes
maliciously wrong between the application and the server.

The process is pretty simple:

1. Your application server creates a public/private key pair. Public key is used as a unique server identifier for subscribing the user to notifications sent by that server, and the private key is used by the application server to sign messages, before sending them to the Push Service for delivery.

   There are different ways to generate public/private keys. For instance,

   a. You can use *web-push-codelab.glitch.me* and generate keys. Then store the keys safely, especially private key (it should be hidden to public) and use it when it's needed.

   b. There is npm package called web-push that we can use to both generate private/public keys. Also, it can be used to push a notification in the app back-end server.

   To generate with web push library:

   ```
   npm install web-push -g
   ```

   Once package is installed, run the following command to generate key pair:

   ```
   web-push generate-vapid-keys --json
   ```

   Using this command, here is what a VAPID key pair looks like:

   ```
   {
     "publicKey":"ByP9KTS5K7ZLBx- _x3qf5F4_hf2WrL2qEaOqKb-
   aCJbcxEvyn62GDTyOK7TfmOKSPqp8vQFODaG8hpSBknz iEFo",
     "privateKey":"fGcS9j-KgY29NM7myQXXoGcO-fGcSsA_fGODaG8h"
   }
   ```

2. The public key is given to your web app. When the user elects to receive pushes, add the public key to the subscribe() call's options object. Later in this chapter, we need the public key to pass into the requestSubscription method and Angular Service Worker will handle the permission request.

The subscribe method on PushManager needs
ApplicationSeverKey as UInt8Array,[2] which is handled by
Angular Service Worker under the hood.

3. When your app back end sends a push message, include a signed
    JSON web token along with the public key.

Note   If you have cloned the project source, go to https://github.com/mhadaily/
awesome-apress-pwa/tree/master/chapter08/01-push-notification. To generate
vapid pair keys, run npm install first and then npm run vapid.

Browser Supports

At the time of writing this book, the Push API is supported by the major browsers Firefox,
Chrome, Opera, and Microsoft Edge. Safari doesn't support Push API. However, if you
would like to target Safari, too, there is a recommendation on the Apple Developer's
website on how to send push notifications for websites. You can find this document on
developer.apple.com/notifications/safari-push-notifications for more information. Keep
in mind that this solution is not related to Safari on iOS.

Now that you know how push notifications work, it's time to start implementing
Angular Service Worker to handle push notifications in our application.

Push Notification in Angular

Angular Service Worker provides SwPush service, which has different methods and
properties to facilitate push notification implementation. While we can use the Angular
way, it's not obligatory to use it in order to subscribe and unsubscribe because those
methods are basically just syntax sugar on top of native pushManager object methods.
However, in this section, I will keep using the Angular way.

Since we have already installed Angular Service Worker, we now are able to
inject SwPush service. First, we should allow our user to subscribe for receiving push

---

[2]If you like to know more, check urlB64ToUint8Array() function here: https://github.com/
GoogleChromeLabs/web-push-codelab/blob/master/app/scripts/main.js

notification. In order to do that, the user should grant a permission to subscribe to notifications. Let's change the app UI to let the user enable notification.

I will add a button in the menu that when the user clicks, it triggers request permission. Since we do care about our user experience, I'll add another button for when the user likes to unsubscribe from a push notification.

```
<button mat-menu-item (click)="requestPermission()"
*ngIf="!(subscription$ | async) && (user$ | async) && isEnabled">
  <mat-icon>notifications_on</mat-icon>
  <span>Enable alerts</span>
</button>
<button mat-menu-item (click)="requestUnsubscribe()"
*ngIf="subscription$ | async">
  <mat-icon>notifications_off</mat-icon>
  <span>Disabled alerts</span>
</button>
```

We are progressively building our application; therefore, we should make sure that this feature is available for those who have Service Worker registered and pushManager object is available in the Service Worker registration. As you see, we hide the *Enable Alerts* button when there is already a subscription enabled and Service Worker is enabled.

requestPermission and requestUnsubscribe methods are defined in the HeaderComponent class.

```
export class HeaderComponent {
  private readonly VAPID_PUBLIC_KEY = 'YOUR VAPID PUBLIC KEY';

  public user$ = this.auth.user$;
  public subscription$ = this.swPush.subscription;
  public isEnabled = this.swPush.isEnabled;

  constructor(
      private auth: AuthService, private swPush: SwPush,
      private snackBar: SnackBarService, private dataService: DataService,
    private router: Router
) { }
```

```
requestPermission() {
  this.swPush
    .requestSubscription({
      serverPublicKey: this.VAPID_PUBLIC_KEY
    })
    .then(async (sub: PushSubscription) => {
      const subJSON = sub.toJSON();
      await this.dataService.addPushSubscription(subJSON);
      return this.snackBar.open('You are subscribed now!');
    })
    .catch(e => {
      console.error(e);
      this.snackBar.open('Subscription failed');
    });
}

requestUnsubscribe() {
  this.swPush
    .unsubscribe()
    .then(() => {
      this.snackBar.open('You are unsubscribed');
    })
    .catch(e => {
      console.error(e);
      this.snackBar.open('unsubscribe failed');
    });
}
}
```

Let's break down the code.

SwPush subscription property is an observable that is associated to the Service Worker get subscription method or if there is not, the subscription is null.

In requestPermission method, the user is asked for permission by calling requestSubscription on swPush service. We should pass our VAPID public key as serverPublicKey to this method.

```
this.swPush
  .requestSubscription({
    serverPublicKey: this.VAPID_PUBLIC_KEY
  })
```

This method returns a Promise that contains PushSubscription. The push notification object has the following methods and properties:

```
interface PushSubscription {
    readonly endpoint: string;
    readonly expirationTime: number | null;
    readonly options: PushSubscriptionOptions;
    getKey(name: PushEncryptionKeyName): ArrayBuffer | null;
    toJSON(): PushSubscriptionJSON;
    unsubscribe(): Promise<boolean>;
}
```

As a result, we are going to call toJSON()[3] function to receive the PushSubscriptionJSON object, which includes essential properties for sending notifications where we send it to the back end and store it our database.

```
interface PushSubscriptionJSON {
    endpoint?: string;
    expirationTime?: number | null;
    keys?: Record<string, string>;
}
```

I have created a simple method in the data service to store push subscription data in the database.

```
const subJSON = sub.toJSON();
 await this.dataService.addPushSubscription(subJSON);
```

By passing subscription JSON object to the addPushSUbscription method, I will store this object to another collection called subscription for the active user in Firestore. Our user may have more than one subscription based on different

---

[3]Standard serializer – returns a JSON representation of the subscription properties.

browsers and devices. So, it's important to store all subscription for this user and send notifications to all of the devices that are registered to receive notifications.

```
addPushSubscription(sub: PushSubscriptionJSON):
Promise<DocumentReference> {
  const { keys, endpoint, expirationTime } = sub;
  return this.afDb
    .collection(this.USERS_COLLECTION)
    .doc(this.auth.id)
    .collection(this.SUBSCRIPTION_COLLECTION)
    .add({ keys, endpoint, expirationTime });
}
```

We have implemented another button to allow our user to opt out from receiving notifications if they are willing to. Therefore, the requestUnsubscribe method will call unsubscribe() method on swPush that returns a Promise and once resolved, the user will be unsubscribed.

```
requestUnsubscribe() {
  this.swPush
    .unsubscribe()
    .then(() => {
      this.snackBar.open('You are unsubscribed');
    })
    .catch(e => {
      console.error(e);
      this.snackBar.open('unsubscribe failed');
    });
}
```

Now we have implemented the basics of our needs, let's build an application for a production and run server. Navigate to Chrome browser and under the menu, click on enable alerts (see Figure 8-4).

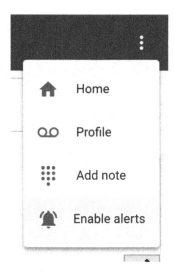

Figure 8-4. *Enable alerts buttons when Service Worker is enabled and there is no notification subscription*

Once clicked, you should be able to see a permission popup (see Figures 8-5 and 8-6). What you'll see is a native browser UI, and it may differ from browser to browser on different platforms. However, you'll have two options – "allow" and "block" – where you can grant sufficient permission for receiving notifications. Once either of these options is chosen, this modal will not get triggered anymore.

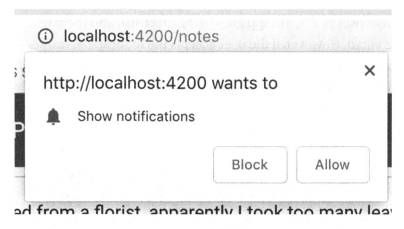

Figure 8-5. *Notification request popup in Chrome*

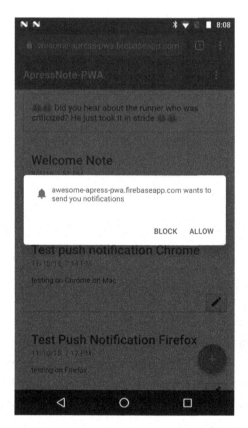

Figure 8-6. *Notification request modal on Chrome, Android*

If the user chooses Block, the app goes to the block list, and there will not be any subscription granted. However, if the user accepts the request, the browser will generate a push notification subscription for this user on the device, and therefore the request permission will successfully be evaluated, and then the push subscription will be passed to then(). To covert the result to JSON format, we call toJSON() and then we send it over to the back end in order to store it to the database (see Figure 8-7).

Figure 8-7. *Snack bar message when user accepts the request and it's stored in database*

You may now notice that enable alerts under the menu has become disable alerts as soon as permission is granted, and the subscription object returns from the push server (see Figures 8-8 and 8-9).

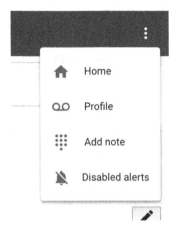

Figure 8-8. *If there is an active subscription, disable alerts is displayed and lets the user unsubscribe from the subscription*

This is a good practice to give our user the ability to opt out from receiving notifications.

Figure 8-9. *Snack bar message when user unsubscription is successful*

Having looked at the database, the user subscription has been added to the subscriptions collection for the current user. We are now ready to push notifications to our users based on their subscription information in our database.

Let's have a look at the subscription object in JSON format (see Figure 8-10).

```
{
    "endpoint": "UNIQUE URL",
    "expirationTime": null,
    "keys": {  "p256dh": "KEY",  "auth": "KEY" }
}
```

To understand better how Push Notifications works in general, I will uncover push notification object properties:

- **endpoint:** This contains a unique URL from Browser Push Service used by the application back end to send push notifications to this subscription.

- **expirationTime:** Some messages are time sensitive and don't need to be sent if a certain time interval has passed: for instance, if message has an authentication code that expires at a certain time.

- **p256dh:** This is an encryption key that our back end will use to encrypt the message, before sending it to the Push Service.

- **auth:** This is an authentication secret, which is one of the inputs of the message content encryption process.

All of the information is essential to be able to send push notifications to this user.

Figure 8-10. *JSON format of subscription object stored for the active user in the app. For instance, this user has more than one subscription, and we may want to send push notifications to all of them*

Showing Again the Allow/Block Notifications Popup

While testing locally, you may hit the Block button accidentally or deliberately, and the permission popup will never display anymore. Instead, if you click on the subscription button, the Promise is going to be rejected and the catch block in our code will be triggered (see Figure 8-11).

Figure 8-11. Permission denied in console and snack bar message to show subscription fail where it is triggered in Catch block in the Request Permission Block

To fix this issue, we should remove the app from the block list in the browser. For instance, in Chrome:

1. Go to `chrome://settings/content/notifications`.

2. Scroll down to the Block list where all the websites that are blocked from emitting push notifications are located.

3. Delete localhost or your app URL from the Block list.

The popup should now appear again, and if we click on the Allow option, a Push Subscription object will be generated.

Sending Push Notifications

A user's subscriptions object has been stored in the database. It means we are able to push a notification to the user even if there is more than one subscription.

In order to send a push notification, we are going to write a simple Firebase Cloud Function to save the note into the database and once it's saved, send a notification to the user with a note ID that says the note has been synced with an appropriate ID retrieved from the database. This is just an example; you may want to send notifications for different purposes, and after this section, you should be able to do that in no time.

Note   Although sending push notifications is one of the best ways to engage with the user, sending too many unwanted and unnecessary notifications may have the opposite impact and makes the user frustrated and annoyed. Thus, it is our responsibility to respect a user's privacy and experiences.

In the app, we are going to define a new method in DataService that will accept a note object and post it to the endpoint that is created by Firebase Cloud Function. It will then replace the addNote() method.

```
// DataService
  protected readonly SAVE_NOTE_ENDPOINT =
    'https://us-central1-awesome-apress-pwa.cloudfunctions.net/saveNote';

  saveNoteFromCloudFunction(
    note: Note
  ): Observable<{ success: boolean; data: Note }> {
    return this.http.post<{ success: boolean; data: Note }>(
      this.SAVE_NOTE_ENDPOINT,
      {
        user: this.auth.id,
        data: {
          ...note,
          created_at: this.timestamp,
          updated_at: this.timestamp
        }
      }
    );
  }
```

Now we will write the function and as soon as we deploy, the saveNote endpoint will be provided by Firebase.

Firebase Cloud Function

In Chapter 2 we prepared a project that was ready for defining functions. Node.js engine had been set to 8, which is the latest and most up-to-date version of Node in Firebase as of writing this book.

We are going to use Firebase SDK for the Cloud Function setup with Firestore.

```
const admin = require('firebase-admin');
const functions = require('firebase-functions');
const webpush = require('web-push');
```

```javascript
const cors = require('cors')({
  origin: true
});

const serviceAccount = require('./awesome-apress-pwa-firebase-adminsdk-
l9fnh-6b35c787b9.json');

admin.initializeApp({
  credential: admin.credential.cert(serviceAccount),
  databaseURL: 'https://awesome-apress-pwa.firebaseio.com'
});

const sendNotification = (noteId, subscriptions) => {
  webpush.setVapidDetails(
    'mailto:me@majidhajian.com',
    'VAPID PUBLIC KEY',
    'VAPID PRIVATE KEY
  );

  const pushPayload = {
    notification: {
      title: 'WebPush: New Note',
      body: `Note ${noteId} has been synced!`,
      icon: 'https://placekitten.com/200/139',
      badge: 'https://placekitten.com/50/50',
      dir: 'ltr',
      lang: 'en',
      renotify: false,
      requireInteraction: false,
      timestamp: new Date().getTime(),
      silent: false,
      tag: 'saveNote',
      vibrate: [100, 50, 100],
      data: {
        noteID: noteId,
        dateOfArrival: Date.now(),
        primaryKey: 1
      },
```

```
      actions: [
        {
          action: 'open',
          title: 'Open Note', icon: 'images/checkmark.png'
        },
        {
          action: 'cancel',
          title: 'Close', icon: 'images/checkmark.png'
        }
      ]
    }
  };

  if (subscriptions) {
    setTimeout(() => {
      subscriptions.forEach(pushConfig => {
        webpush
          .sendNotification(pushConfig.data(), JSON.stringify(pushPayload))
          .then(_ => console.log('message has been sent'))
          .catch(err => {
            console.log(`PushError ${err}`);
            // Check for "410 - Gone" status and delete it
            if (err.statusCode === 410) {
              pushConfig.ref.delete();
            }
          });
      });
    }, 3000);
  }
};

exports.saveNote = functions.https.onRequest((request, response) => {
  const { user, data } = request.body;
  cors(request, response, async () => {
    return admin
      .firestore()
```

```
      .collection(`users/${user}/notes`)
      .add(data)
      .then(async noteDoc => {
        const note = await noteDoc.get();
        const data = note.data();
        data.id = note.id;

        const subscriptions = await admin
          .firestore()
          .collection(`users/${user}/subscriptions`)
          .get();

        sendNotification(note.id, subscriptions);

        return response.status(201).json({
          succcess: true,
          data
        });
      })
      .catch(err => {
        console.log(err);
        response.status(500).json({
          error: err,
          succcess: false
        });
      });
  });
});
```

Note   We have used Node.js for this example, but you are able to use other
languages such as Python, Java, and Go. Feel free to choose what you like. To find
out more, you can check the Firebase documentation website.

Let's break down the code.

1. We have imported libraries required for the functions. As you see,
   I am using web-push library for sending notifications.

```
const admin = require('firebase-admin');
const functions = require('firebase-functions');
const webpush = require('web-push'); // to send Push Notification
const cors = require('cors')({ // to solve CORS issue we use this
library
  origin: true
});
```

The webpush library will then do the following steps:

- the payload of the message is going to be encrypted using the
  p256dh public key and the auth authentication secret

- the encrypted payload is then going to be signed using the VAPID
  private key

- the message is then going to be sent to the Firebase Cloud
  Messaging endpoint specified in the endpoint property of the
  subscription object

2. To Initialize the app, you need to pass the essential credential
   and database URL. When you get this credential, you should go
   to *Firebase console, settings* and then *Service accounts* tab. Select
   Admin SDK language, in this case Node.js, then click on *Generate
   new private key*. A JSON file is downloaded that contains all
   necessary credentials. It's important to keep this information safe
   and never reveal publicly. For example, my JSON file has been
   added to .gitignore

```
const serviceAccount = require('./awesome-apress-pwa-firebase-
adminsdk-l9fnh-6b35c787b9.json');

admin.initializeApp({
  credential: admin.credential.cert(serviceAccount),
  databaseURL: 'https://awesome-apress-pwa.firebaseio.com'
});
```

3. **saveNote** function will save a note to the database and then we retrieve a user's subscriptions from the database and will send push notifications to the user. You may want to implement a different logic to send push notifications in your application. However, sending a notification itself is the same as it's described in the following. As mentioned, this endpoint will be used in DataService.

4. **sendNotification**: this function is pretty self-explanatory.

   a. Set VAPID details by calling webpush.setValidDetails(), and you need to pass an email, public and private VAPID keys.

   b. Send a notification by calling webpush.sendNotification(). This function accepts two arguments: subscription config, which we have stored in the database for the user, followed by the push payload. It returns a Promise. If the notification is sent successfully, Promise will resolve. Basically, this means the subscription configs are still valid. However, if is an error in subscription config like when a user unsubscribes, sending a notification to that particular endpoint rejects and the status code will be 410, meaning this endpoint is gone. Therefore, Promise rejects. Catch block is where we clean up our database by removing dead subscription configs.

```
// Check for "410 - Gone" status and delete it
        if (err.statusCode === 410) {
          pushConfig.ref.delete();
        }
```

IPush Message Body

Angular Service Worker needs specific formats to show the push notification correctly. As seen, in the example code above, it's a root object that has only one property, which is notification. In this property, we are going to define our push message configurations.

Let's break them down:

Remember ServiceWorkerRegistration.showNotification(title, [options]), here are the properties for options, passing to showNotification() in Service Worker:

- **title**: The title that must be shown within the notification. This tag is used in Angular Service Worker to pass as a first argument in the showNotification function. The rest of properties are passed as one object called options in the second argument of show Notification functions.

- **body**: A string representing extra content to display within the notification

- **icon**: The URL of an image to be used as an icon by the notification

- **badge**: The URL of an image to represent the notification when there is not enough space to display the notification itself. For example, the Android Notification Bar, on Android devices.

- **dir**: The direction of the notification; it can be auto, ltr, or rtl

- **lang**: Specify the language used within the notification

- **image**: The URL of an image to be displayed in the notification.

- **renotify**: A Boolean that indicates whether to suppress vibrations and audible alerts when reusing a tag value. The default is false. If you set renotify: true on a notification without a tag, you'll get the following error:

  ```
  TypeError: Failed to execute 'showNotification' on
  'ServiceWorkerRegistration':
   Notifications which set the renotify flag must specify a
  non-empty tag
  ```

- **requireInteraction**: Indicates that on devices with sufficiently large screens, a notification should remain active until the user clicks or dismisses it. If this value is absent or false, the desktop version of Chrome will auto-minimize notifications after approximately 20 seconds. The default value is false.

- **silent**: This option allows you to show a new notification but prevents the default behavior of vibration, sound, and turning on the device's display. If you define both silent and renotify, silent will take precedence.

- **tag**: A string ID that "groups" notifications together, providing an easy way to determine how multiple notifications are displayed to the user.

- **vibrate**: A vibration pattern to run with the display of the notification. A vibration pattern can be an array with as few as one member. Android devices respect this option.

- **timestamp**: Show the timestamp of the notification.

- **data**: Any data type that we want to be associated with the notification.

- **actions**: An array of actions to display in the notification. The members of the array should be an object literal. It may contain the following values:

  - **action**: a user action to be displayed on the notification.

  - **title**: text to be shown to the user.

  - **icon**: the URL of an icon to display with the action.

Appropriate responses are built using `event.action` within the `notificationclick` event.

Note   Silent push notifications are now encompassed in the Budget API,[4] which is a new API designed to allow developers to perform limited background work without notifying the user, such as a silent push or performing a background fetch.

These comprehensive options perform differently in each platform. As of writing this book, Chrome, in particular on Android, has implemented all of these options. It's likely that if browsers don't support one or more of these options, they will be ignored.

After sending push notifications, all users' browsers that have a subscription will show the notification in the notification center (see Figure 8-12 and 8-13).

---

[4]https://developers.google.com/web/updates/2017/06/budget-api

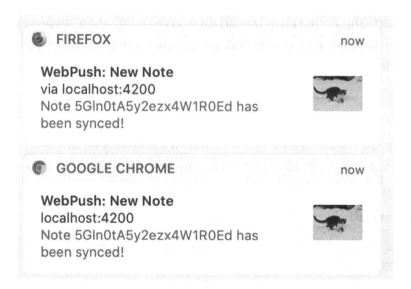

Figure 8-12. *Notification shown on Mac, both Chrome and Firefox*

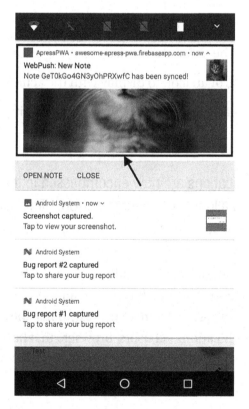

Figure 8-13. *Notifications in Android*

Listen to Messages in Angular

SwPush service provides an Observable that allows us to listen to each message. We may need to perform a different action based on what we receive.

```
// header.componetnt.ts

constructor(
    private auth: AuthService,
    private swPush: SwPush,
    private snackBar: SnackBarService,
    private dataService: DataService,
    private router: Router
) {

  this.swPush.messages.subscribe((msg: { notification: object }) =>
    this.handlePushMessage(msg)
  );

}
```

We listen and do what we want. For instance, in this case, we just need to show the notification body to a user in the snack bar.

```
handlePushMessage({ notification }) {
  this.snackBar.open(`Push Notification: ${notification.body}`);
}
```

This is already existing, but what if the user clicks on notification? Let's explore this in the next section.

Notification Actions and Handling Notification Click Events

In Service Worker, like when we listen to install or push event, we can also listen to a notificationclick event. And because we have implemented actions on notification options, we will know what the user clicked on, an action or anywhere else. This makes the app very flexible on what we want to do based on the user choice. This feature was not available in Angular Service Worker until version 7.1, which has introduced a new Observable on SwPush Service called notificationClicks. There are limitations for the current implementation, which is, as these events processed in the app, so it should be opened in the browser.

```
// header.componetnt.ts
constructor(
    private auth: AuthService,
    private swPush: SwPush,
    private snackBar: SnackBarService,
    private dataService: DataService,
    private router: Router
) {
    this.swPush.messages.subscribe((msg: { notification: object }) =>
        this.handlePushMessage(msg)
    );

    this.swPush.notificationClicks.subscribe(options =>
        this.handlePushNotificationClick(options)
    );
}
```

The options that are passed have two properties: action, which is selected by the choice of the user when he or she clicked on the notification action; and notification, which are all of the notification properties that been pushed to the user.

```
handlePushNotificationClick({ action, notification }) {
    switch (action) {
        case 'open': {
            this.router.navigate(['notes', notification.data.noteID, {
            queryParams: { pushNotification: true } }]);
            break;
        }
        case 'cancel': {
            this.snackBar.dismiss();
        }
            // or anything else
    }
}
```

As an example, in `data` property, we have defined `nodeID;` and we have implemented that when a user clicks on `open` action, we redirect our application to the detailed note view.

It might be a good idea to add some indicator that you can measure how many users click on the notification. For instance, you can send some analytics or add a `queryParams`.

Note   Remember, though, `actions` are not supported in all browsers. So, have a backup for your app in case you face an `undefined` due to lack of browser support.

Deploy to Firebase

It seems we have implemented our needs for the application PWA Note. I will deploy the application to Firebase as always by running the following command:

```
npm run deploy
```

Summary

In this chapter, we explored another native-like feature and are now one step closer toward building a PWA that resembles a native app.

In the next chapter, I am going to shift your focus back to persistent data. Although we have cached dynamic data on runtime, there are different solutions and architectures that you can use in your application to help persist data in the user browsers and synchronize it back to the server when necessary. This gives our user a powerful capability to work fully offline with our application and helps us to build a much faster, reliable, and performant application.

CHAPTER 9

Resilient Angular App and Offline Browsing

One important aspect of PWAs is the concept of building an app that can be served offline. Up until this point of the book, we have made an application and enabled offline capabilities. We have seen the power of Service Worker, which has done most of the heavy lifting when it comes to storing static assets and dynamic content by leveraging Cache API. All in all, the achievement is significant compared to a traditional web application.

However, there is still room for improvement. Let's imagine that you are building an application that communicates through REST API. Although Service Worker is facilitating to cache content and serve faster, it doesn't help with a poor internet connection as soon as the network first strategy must be applied, and the respond and request have a long latency. Or what should we do with the application state or the app data set?

In PWA Note app, users' experience is most likely disrupted because we keep them waiting until sending a message to the server is successfully completed if they have a poor internet connection. in fact, a delay of more than 10 seconds will often make users leave a site instantly. Slowness and lack of acceptable user experience could abruptly affect your business if it relies on the app.

In this chapter, I am going to explorer an approach that provides a consistent user experience whether the users' devices have no connectively, limited connectivity, or great connectively. This model reduces latency down to zero as it provides access to content stored directly on the device and synchronizes data in all users' devices over HTTP.

© Majid Hajian 2019
M. Hajian, *Progressive Web Apps with Angular*, https://doi.org/10.1007/978-1-4842-4448-7_9

Offline Storage

Before HTML5, application data had to be stored in cookies, included in every server request while it was limited up to 4 KB. Web Storage is not only more secure but also capable of storing large amounts of data locally without affecting website performance. It is per origin and all pages, from the same origin, can store and access the same data. The two mechanisms within web storages are as follows:

- **sessionStorage** maintains a separate storage area for each given origin that's available for the duration of the page session (as long as the browser is open, including page reloads and restores).

- **localStorage** does the same thing but persists even when the browser is closed and reopened.

There are two downsides to this API:

1. You need to serialize and deserialize data when you want to store (only strings).

2. API is synchronous, which means it blocks the application and has no Web Worker support.

Due to these issues, we shift our focus to other options in order to achieve better performance and support in Web Worker.

- **WebSQL** is asynchronous (callback-based); however, it also has no Web Worker support and was rejected by Firefox and Edge but is in Chrome and Safari. It's also depreciated.

- **File System API** is asynchronous too (callback-based) and does work in Web Workers and Windows (albeit with a synchronous API). Unfortunately, it doesn't have much interest outside of Chrome and is sandboxed (meaning you don't get native file access).

- **File API** is being improved over in the File and Directory Entries API and File API specs. A File API library exists and for file saving, I've been using FileSaver.js as a stopgap. The writable-files proposal may eventually give us a better standards-track solution for seamless, local file interaction.

- **IndexedDB** is a key-value pair NoSQL database and supports large scale storage (up to 20%–50% of hard drive capacity) and supports many data types like number, string, JSON, blob, and so on. As it is asynchronous, it can be used everywhere including Web Workers and is widely supported in the browsers.

- **Cache API** provides a storage mechanism for Request / Response object pairs that are cached, for example, as part of the Service Worker life cycle. Note that the Cache interface is exposed to window scopes as well as workers.

As we have seen, it seems the best options are IndexedDB[1] and Cache API. A combination of both APIs makes it much more reliable and provides a better user experience. We have used Cache API to store URL addressable resources such as static files and request and respond from REST APIs. There are no hard rules how to use and architect your application to leverage these APIs. Some applications might be sufficiently simple that they can just use the Cache API alone, while others may find it valuable to partially cache their JSON payloads in IDB so that in browsers without Cache API support, you still get the benefit of some local caching during the session.

Note   IndexedDB API is powerful but may seem too complicated for simple cases. I recommend trying libraries such as LocalForage, Dexie.js, zangoDB, PouchDB, LoxiJs, JsStore, IDB, LokiJs that help to wrap IndexedDB APIs, which make it more programmer friendly. Also, this API was buggy and slow in Safari 10; therefore some of these libraries implemented a fall back to WebSQL in Safari as opposed to indexedDB to gain a better performance. Although this issue was resolved and IndexedDB is stable in all major browsers, if your apps target older browsers for some certain reasons, you may need to use suggested libraries: for example, Localforage

---

[1]https://developer.mozilla.org/en/docs/Web/API/IndexedDB_API

Even though there is no specific architecture, it's recommended that

- For the network resources necessary to load your app while offline, use the Cache.

- For all other data, use IndexedDB, for instance, application state and data set are the best candidates to be stored in IndexedDB.

Offline First Approach

A common way to build a web application is to be a consumer of a back-end server to store and retrieve data for persistency (Figure 9-1).

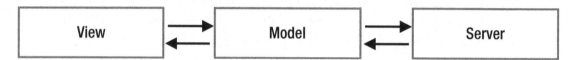

Figure 9-1. *Data-binding ways in traditional web applications*

One issue with this approach is that a flaky or nonexistent internet connection may interrupt the user experience and lead to unreliable performance. To fix that, we have used Service Worker and will leverage other storage techniques to substantially improve the user experience in all situations, including a perfect wireless environment.

In this approach (shown in Figure 9-2), the user interacts with the cache constantly where it's stored in the client device; therefore, there will be zero latency.

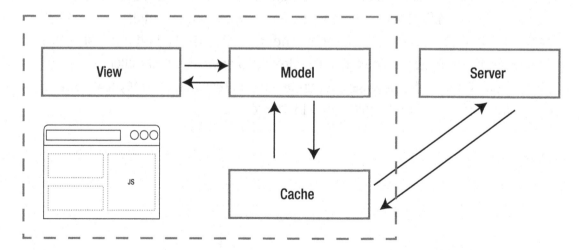

Figure 9-2. *Offline first approach, 4-way data binding*

Service Worker can intercept request between the client and server if needed. We can even think of how to synchronize our data with the server.

Note   Thanks to Background Sync event in Service Worker, it's easily possible to resolve synchronization. I will explore the `sync` event in Chapter 14 when we are implementing Workbox because this feature is not available in Angular Service Worker as of now (Angular 7.1).

I am going to step forward and tweak this model a bit more. What if we can implement a logic that can sync data from and to a server whether the user is online or offline; and therefore, that server can manipulate data and do necessary adjustments afterward (see Figures 9-3 and 9-4). Think how much this approach can improve a user's experience.

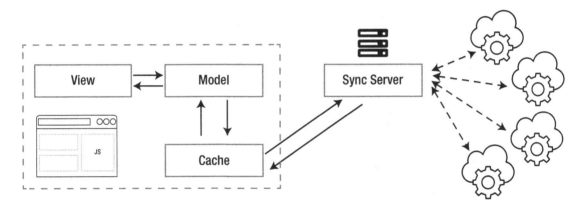

Figure 9-3. *Offline first approach with syncing in mind*

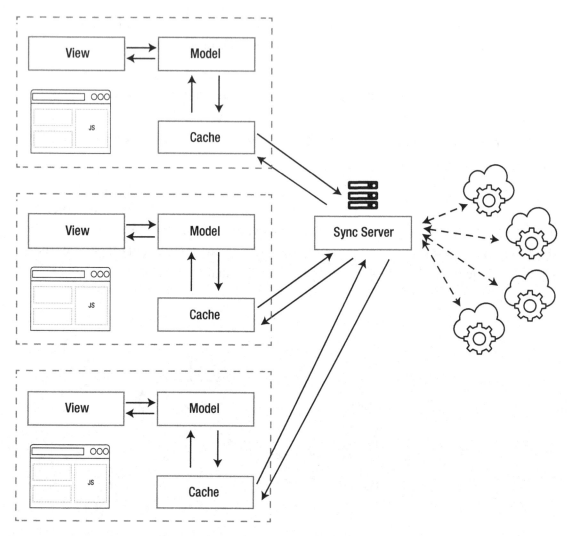

Figure 9-4. *Data can be distributed and synchronized through all user's devices from/to sync server*

Let's experiment with the offline first database approach in PWA Note application and see how it works in action.

Implement Offline First Approach with Sync Server

We have figured out that IndexedDB is what we need to use in a client app. The next hurdle is figuring out how to store and sync the app's data and state. Offline syncing is a bit more challenging than it looks. I believe one of the best solutions to overcome this obstacle is to use PouchDB.[2] Keep in mind, you are not limited to this solution, and you may need to either implement your own logic for your application or use another third party.[3] All in all, the goal is to implement offline first cache for storing data and sync back to the server accordingly.

Note   PouchDB is an open source JavaScript database inspired by Apache CouchDB[4] that is designed to run well within the browser. PouchDB was created to help web developers build applications that work as well offline as they do online. It enables applications to store data locally while offline, then synchronize it with CouchDB and compatible servers when the application is back online, keeping the user's data in sync no matter where they next log in.

You can use PouchDB without the sync feature too, but for the sake of offline capability, I enable the sync and offline features in PouchDB.

First, we need to install pouchdb:

```
npm install pouchdb
```

The pouchdb-browser preset contains the version of PouchDB that is designed for the browser. In particular, it ships with the IndexedDB and WebSQL adapters as its default adapters. It also contains the replication, HTTP, and map/reduce plugins. Use this preset if you only want to use PouchDB in the browser, and don't want to use it in Node. js. (e.g., to avoid installing LevelDB.)

Therefore, instead of pouchdb, I install pouchdb-browser alternately:

```
npm install pouchdb-browser
```

Carry on and create a new service in Angular by running:

```
ng g s modules/core/offline-db
```

To create a remote sync database server, for simplicity, I install pouchdb-server.[5]

```
npm install -g pouchdb-server
```

---

[2]https://pouchdb.com

[3]Hoodie is another example; you can find more about it on https://hood.ie.

[4]http://couchdb.apache.org

[5]PouchDB can sync back data to any services that speak to the CouchDB replication protocol. For examples, CouchDB, IBM Cloudant, Couchbase.

Run the PouchDB server:

```
pouchdb-server --port 5984
```

If you clone the project repository and want to see the example codes, first install npm packages and then npm run pouchdb-server

In OfflineDbService, we need to instantiate PouchDB. To sync, the simplest case is unidirectional replication, meaning you just want one database to mirror its changes to a second one. Writes to the second database, however, will not propagate back to the master database; however, we need bidirectional replication to make things easier for your poor, tired fingers; PouchDB has a shortcut API.

```
import PouchDB from 'pouchdb-browser';


  constructor() {
// create new local database
    this._DB = new PouchDB(this.DB_NAME);
// shortcut API for bidirectional replication
    this._DB.sync(this.REMOTE_DB, {
      live: true,
      retry: true
    });
  }
```

Note   If you see an error due to undefined global object in console, please add (window as any).global = window; at the bottom of Polyfills.ts.[6]

Database has been instantiated successfully; therefore, CRUD operations need to be implemented.

```
public get(id: string) {
    return this._DB.get(id);
  }
```

---

[6]This is a known issue with pouchdb 7 and Angular 6 and 7 as of the writing of this book.

```
public async delete(id) {
  const doc = await this.get(id);
  const deleteResult = this._DB.remove(doc);
  return deleteResult;
}

public add(note: any) {
  return this._DB.post({
    ...note,
    created_at: this.timestamp,
    updated_at: this.timestamp
  });
}

public async edit(document: any) {
  const result = await this.get(document._id);
  document._rev = result._rev;
  return this._DB.put({
    ...document,
    updated_at: this.timestamp
  });
}
```

To retrieve all notes from the database, I define another function getAll where I will call this method on loading application to show notes to my user.

```
public async getAll(page?: number) {
    const doc = await this._DB.allDocs({
      include_docs: true,
      limit: 40,
      skip: page || 0
    });
    this._allDocs = doc.rows.map(row => row.doc);
    // Handle database change on documents
    this.listenToDBChange();
    return this._allDocs;
}
```

PouchDB provides a changes() method that is an event emitter and will emit a 'change' event on each document change, a 'complete' event when all the changes have been processed, and an 'error' event when an error occurs. Calling cancel() will automatically unsubscribe all event listeners.

```
listenToDBChange() {
  if (this.listener) {
    return;
  }

  this.listener = this._DB
    .changes({ live: true, since: 'now', include_docs: true })
    .on('change', change => {
      this.onDBChange(change);
    });
}
```

From now on, we have a listener that can detect each document change and manipulate the data accordingly. For instance, in onDBChange method in the OfflineDbService, I have implemented a very simple logic to detect what types of change have happened to the document and run a logic based on that.

```
private onDBChange(change) {
  this.ngZone.run(() => {
    const index = this._allDocs.findIndex(row => row._id === change.id);

    if (change.deleted) {
      this._allDocs.splice(index, 1);
      return;
    }

    if (index > -1) {
      // doc is updated
      this._allDocs[index] = change.doc;
    } else {
      // new doc
```

```
      this._allDocs.unshift(change.doc);
    }
  });
}
```

Altogether, the `OfflineDBServer` looks like the following:

```
export class OfflineDbService {
  private readonly LOCAL_DB_NAME = 'apress_pwa_note';
  private readonly DB_NAME = `${this.LOCAL_DB_NAME}_${this.auth.id}`;
  private readonly REMOTE_DB = `http://localhost:5984/${this.DB_NAME}`;
  private _DB: PouchDB.Database;
  private listener = null;
  private _allDocs: any[];

  get timestamp() {
    return;
  }

  constructor(private auth: AuthService, private ngZone: NgZone) {
    this._DB = new PouchDB(this.DB_NAME);
    this._DB.sync(this.REMOTE_DB, {
      live: true,
      retry: true
    });
  }

  listenToDBChange() {
    if (this.listener) {
      return;
    }

    this.listener = this._DB
      .changes({ live: true, since: 'now', include_docs: true })
      .on('change', change => {
        this.onDBChange(change);
      });
  }
```

```
private onDBChange(change) {
  console.log('>>>>>> DBChange', change);
  this.ngZone.run(() => {
    const index = this._allDocs.findIndex(row => row._id === change.id);

    if (change.deleted) {
      this._allDocs.splice(index, 1);
      return;
    }

    if (index > -1) {
      // doc is updated
      this._allDocs[index] = change.doc;
    } else {
      // new doc
      this._allDocs.unshift(change.doc);
    }
  });
}

public async getAll(page?: number) {
  const doc = await this._DB.allDocs({
    include_docs: true,
    limit: 40,
    skip: page || 0
  });
  this._allDocs = doc.rows.map(row => row.doc);
  // Handle database change on documents
  this.listenToDBChange();
  return this._allDocs;
}

public get(id: string) {
  return this._DB.get(id);
}
```

```
public async delete(id) {
  const doc = await this.get(id);
  const deleteResult = this._DB.remove(doc);
  return deleteResult;
}

public add(note: any) {
  return this._DB.post({
    ...note,
    created_at: this.timestamp,
    updated_at: this.timestamp
  });
}

public async edit(document: any) {
  const result = await this.get(document._id);
  document._rev = result._rev;
  return this._DB.put({
    ...document,
    updated_at: this.timestamp
  });
}
}
```

Now I need to change all components and replace DataService with OfflineDbService. To begin, NotesListComponent:

```
constructor(
    private offlineDB: OfflineDbService,
  ) {}

  ngOnInit() {
// here is we call getAll() and consequesntly subscribe to change listerner
    this.offlineDB.getAll().then(allDoc => {
      this.notes = allDoc;
    });
  }
```

onSaveNote() on NotesAddComponent is updated to

```
constructor(
    private router: Router,
    private offlineDB: OfflineDbService,
    private snackBar: SnackBarService
) {}

  onSaveNote(values) {
    this.loading$.next(true);
// Notice we add everything to local DB
    this.offlineDB.add(values).then(
      doc => {
        this.router.navigate(['/notes']);
        this.snackBar.open(`LOCAL: ${doc.id} has been succeffully saved`);
        this.loading$.next(false);
      },
      e => {
        this.loading$.next(false);
        this.errorMessages$.next('something is wrong when adding to DB');
      }
    );
  }
```

And here is the same change to NoteDetailsComponent where we have Edit, Get, Delete operations.

```
constructor(
    private offlineDB: OfflineDbService,
    private route: ActivatedRoute,
    private snackBar: SnackBarService,
    private router: Router
) {}

  ngOnInit() {
    const id = this.route.snapshot.paramMap.get('id');
    this.id = id;
    this.getNote(id);
  }
```

```
  getNote(id) {
// get note from offline DB
    this.offlineDB.get(id).then(note => {
      this.note = note;
    });
  }

  delete() {
    if (confirm('Are you sure?')) {
// delete note from offline DB
      this.offlineDB
        .delete(this.id)
        .then(() => {
          this.router.navigate(['/notes']);
          this.snackBar.open(`${this.id} successfully was deleted`);
        })
        .catch(e => {
          this.snackBar.open('Unable to delete this note');
        });
    }
  }

  edit() {
    this.isEdit = !this.isEdit;
  }

  saveNote(values) {
// edit in offline DB
    this.offlineDB
      .edit(values)
      .then(() => {
        this.getNote(values._id);
        this.snackBar.open('Successfully done');
        this.edit();
      })
```

```
    .catch(e => {
      this.snackBar.open('Unable to edit this note');
      this.edit();
    });
}
```

It's time to test the application, and we don't necessarily need Service Worker; therefore, we can simply run my application in development mode locally. So, run npm start and then navigate to localhost:4200 to see the application. Try to add a new note and observe the console messages (see Figure 9-5).

```
>>>>>> DBChange                                    offline-db.service.ts:40
{id: "231410f4-d1ee-4c2b-8b91-2b4ad59d03c7", changes: Array(1), doc: {...},
seq: 50} ℹ
  ▼ changes: Array(1)
    ▼ 0:
        rev: "6-0d28d9f1273b5c0da17c50789d3a3668"
      ▶ __proto__: Object
      length: 1
    ▶ __proto__: Array(0)
  ▼ doc:
      content: "YES! "
      created_at: 1543075531140
      title: "Welcome to PouchDB world"
      _id: "231410f4-d1ee-4c2b-8b91-2b4ad59d03c7"
      _rev: "6-0d28d9f1273b5c0da17c50789d3a3668"
    ▶ __proto__: Object
    id: "231410f4-d1ee-4c2b-8b91-2b4ad59d03c7"
    seq: 50
  ▶ __proto__: Object
```

Figure 9-5. *Change object is emitted for each change on database*

As you have been shown in Figure 9-5, each document has an _id and _rev property that is being added automatically. The change object contains all the necessary information that we can use in our app logic to manipulate the data.

> **Note**   The `rev` field in the response indicates a revision of the document. Each document has a field by the name `_rev`. Every time a document is updated, the `_rev` field of the document is changed. Each revision points to its previous revision. PouchDB maintains a history of each document (much like git). `_rev` allows PouchDB and CouchDB to elegantly handle conflicts, among its other benefits.

Open two different browsers on your computer, for instance, Chrome and Firefox and open the app on each. First, you'll notice that you will have the exact same notes on both browsers. Now add a new note in one browser, and check the other one (see Figure 9-6); you'll notice the new note will appear quickly in another browser where the app is open.

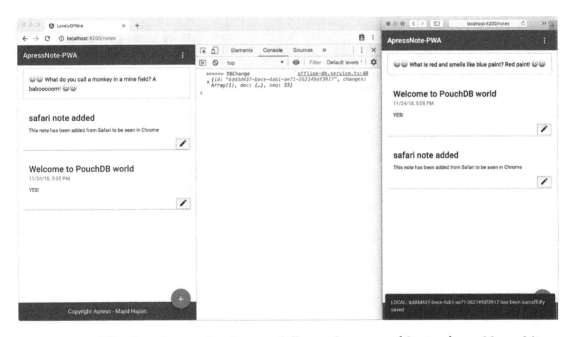

Figure 9-6.   *The App is running in two different browsers (devices), and by adding a note from one, as soon as it's added to sync server, a change will get emitted and immediately the note will appear in another browser (device)*

So far so good; you'll notice that there will be zero latency to show or add a note, since the content is going to be added to the cache first and then will be synced back with the server. Therefore, our user will not notice the latency between the cache and server.

What if our user goes offline? Let's test it out. We'll disconnect the network by checking offline in Chrome and then will try to delete a note from Safari where it's online still and add a note from Chrome browser, which is offline (see Figures 9-7 and 9-8).

Note   PouchDB has two types of data: documents and attachments.

Documents   As in CouchDB, the documents you store must be serializable as JSON.

Attachments   PouchDB also supports attachments, which are the most efficient way to store binary data. Attachments may either be supplied as base64-encoded strings or as Blob objects.

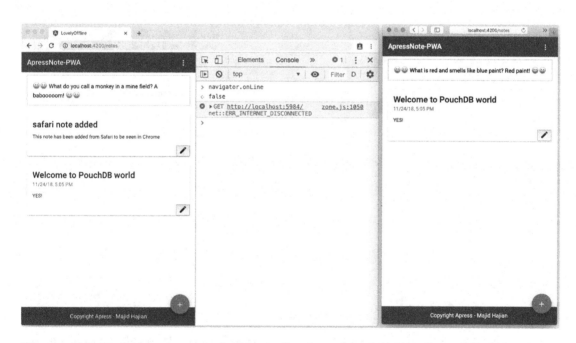

Figure 9-7.   *Deleting one note from another browser that is online will reflect on the remote database, but since another browser is offline, it will not receive the update*

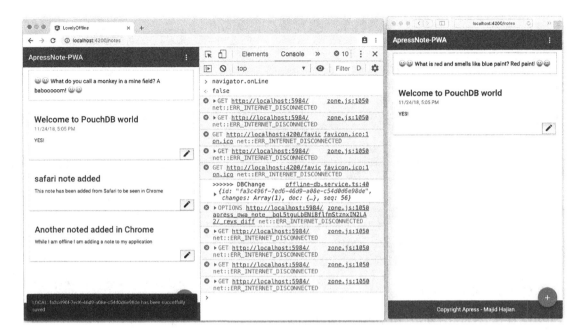

Figure 9-8. *Add a note in a browser (device) even when the user is offline. App allows the user to add this note; however, it does not reflect on the remote database until the user comes back online.*

Once I am done, I will make the Chrome network online again and will wait a bit. You'll see after a few seconds that the app in both browsers will be synced successfully (see Figure 9-9).

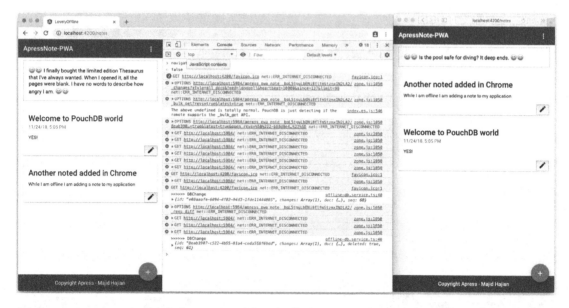

Figure 9-9. *App in both browsers (devices) is synced when user comes back online*

There has been no interruption in the user experience, and there has been fast performance and reliable data and synchronization – isn't it amazing?

As said, PouchDB is one way to the implement offline first approach. Depending on your application and requirements, you may use different libraries or even your own implementation where you use IndexedDB APIs directly.

Implement Persistent Data with Angular Firebase

Cloud Firestore supports offline data persistence. This feature caches a copy of the Cloud Firestore data that your app is actively using, so your app can access the data when the device is offline. You can write, read, listen to, and query the cached data. When the device comes back online, Cloud Firestore synchronizes any local changes made by your app to the data stored remotely in Cloud Firestore.

Offline persistence is an experimental feature that is supported only by the Chrome, Safari, and Firefox web browsers.

To enable offline persistence, enablePersistence() must be called while importing AngularFirestoreModule into your @NgModule:

```
@NgModule({
  declarations: [AppComponent, LoadingComponent],
  imports: [
    CoreModule,
    LayoutModule,
    BrowserModule.withServerTransition({ appId: 'serverApp' }),
    HttpClientModule,
    AppRoutingModule,
    AngularFireModule.initializeApp(environment.firebase),
    AngularFirestoreModule.enablePersistence(),
    // AngularFirestoreModule, // needed for database features
    AngularFireAuthModule, // needed for auth features,
    BrowserAnimationsModule, // needed for animation
    ServiceWorkerModule.register('ngsw-worker.js', {
      enabled: environment.production
    }),
    RouterModule
  ],
  providers: [],
  bootstrap: [AppComponent]
})
export class AppModule {}
```

If a user opens multiple browser tabs that point to the same Cloud Firestore database, and offline persistence is enabled, Cloud Firestore will work correctly only in the first tab. However, As of September 2018, experimental multi-tab is available for you to play with. You just need to pass {experimentalTabSynchronization: true} to enbalePersistence() function such as:

AngularFirestoreModule.enablePersistence({experimentalTabSynchronization: true})

Next, we need to make sure we are using Angular Firestore APIs.

For instance, in `NotesListComponent`, use `getNotes()` method instead of `initializedNotes()`

```
ngOnInit() {
        this.notes$ = this.db.getNotes();
            // this.notes$ = this.db.initializeNotes();
}
```

In `NoteDetailsComponent`, use `getNote()` method instead of `getNoteFromDirectApi()`:

```
  ngOnInit() {
    const id = this.route.snapshot.paramMap.get('id');
    this.id = id;
    this.note$ = this.data.getNote(id);
    // this.note$ = this.data.getNoteFromDirectApi(id);
  }
```

And in `NotesAddComponent`, call the `addNote()` method on `DataService`.

```
onSaveNote(values) {
    this.data.addNote(values).then(
      doc => {
        this.snackBar.open(`LOCAL: ${doc.id} has been succeffully saved`);
      },
      e => {
        this.errorMessages$.next('something is wrong when adding to DB');
      }
    );
    this.router.navigate(['/notes']);
  }
```

Run the application and disconnect from the network. You can add a note even though you are offline; and as soon as you come back online, the data will sync back to Firestore.

We can go ahead and deploy the app to Firebase by running:

```
npm run deploy
```

User Interface Considerations

Imagine that our application works even when users are offline. Users will continue adding content and modify more and more. Users usually do not notice that the data is not synced due to slowness or no internet connection. In this case, there are several UI considerations that can be done in the app to show some signals to the users as to whether they are offline or online:

1. Change the header and footer color to some other colors that indicate they are offline; for instance, in the Note app, we can gray out the blue header when the user is offline.

2. Show a notification or a popup when the user is offline; for instance, when the user is adding a note in Note PWA app, we can show a message that you are offline, but we will sync back data to server as soon as you are online.

3. Display an icon or other indication that clearly shows even though a note has been added, it's not synced with the server yet and only exists on the user local device.

4. Resolve conflicts based on user decision; for instance, a user may edit a note in different devices at once when all devices are offline, and when all devices come online again, there might be conflicts between each revision. In this case, it's a good practice to show our user a notification and tell them that there are different revisions based on their edit; therefore, they can select which update is the one that needs to be applied.

These are just a few ideas. You may have better ideas based on your app. It is important to enhance the UIs along with adding more functionalities and features to boost the user experience.

Last but not least, by listening for a change event on navigator.connection, we can react to proper logic based on the change accordingly. As an example, take a look at the function below where we can find out more about the network information:

```
constructor(
  private auth: AuthService,
  private swPush: SwPush,
```

```
    private snackBar: SnackBarService,
    private dataService: DataService,
    private router: Router
  ) {
    (<any>navigator).connection.addEventListener('change', this.
    onConnectionChange);
  }

  onConnectionChange() {
    const { downlink, effectiveType, type } = (<any>navigator).connection;

    console.log(`Effective network connection type: ${effectiveType}`);
    console.log(`Downlink Speed/bandwidth estimate: ${downlink}Mb/s`);
    console.log(
      `type of connection is ${type} but could be of bluetooth, cellular,
      ethernet, none, wifi, wimax, other, unknown`
    );

    if (/\slow-2g|2g|3g/.test((<any>navigator).connection.effectiveType)) {
      this.snackBar.open(`You connection is slow!`);
    } else {
      this.snackBar.open(`Connection is fast!`);
    }
  }
}
```

As you see, you can write your own logic based on how the network information changes.

Note   If you want to see and run all the examples and codes on your machine, simply clone https://github.com/mhadaily/awesome-apress-pwa.git, then go to chapter09. For pouchdb implementation, you'll find 01-pouchdb; go to folder and install all packages first by running npm install and then run both app and pouchdb-server by running npm start and npm run pouchdb-server respectively. For Firestore implementation, go to 02-firebase-presistent-db, run npm install and npm start respectively.

Summary

One main aspect of PWAs is to enhance the user experience. Providing an offline experience – whether with a flaky connection in transport or being offline in the airplane – is invaluable to boost user satisfaction and improve the app's performance.

To support a meaningful experience in an offline case, not only we should cache our static assets and requests and responses, but also storing data on the client side seems essential. By rethinking how to architect an application in the front end and make it offline – first by leveraging browser offline storage, like IndexedDB, with one of the libraries available (PouchDB), the app has been moved to the next level.

CHAPTER 10

Debugging and Measurement Tools

As developers, we work with debugging tools on a daily basis, and we cannot think of coding without them. For developing a PWA, we may need more tools to help us inspect our code, find bugs, run, simulate offline mode, and test Service Worker. To progressively enhance our application, measuring different aspects such as performance and PWA criteria, and engagement by tracking, seem crucial, too.

In this chapter, I will explorer a lot of tools that will help us to inspect, debug and develop, and measure a PWA more easily and pleasantly. Although you may find many of these tools familiar, I still would like to have all of them in one chapter where you can refer to it anytime you like.

Debugging

First things first, let's start by looking into debugging possibilities.

NGSW Debug

Angular Service Worker has a specific URL in order to check the state of `ngsw`. To get access to it, you should navigate to `/ngsw/state` to your website base URL.

© Majid Hajian 2019
M. Hajian, *Progressive Web Apps with Angular*, https://doi.org/10.1007/978-1-4842-4448-7_10

For instance, if you are running your production app on your local machine, you should be able to navigate to `https://localhost:3000/ngsw/state` and see the information, which looks like the following:

```
NGSW Debug Info:

Driver state: NORMAL ((nominal))
Latest manifest hash: b15d32a87eae976c0909801e2b8962df20a7deec
Last update check: 13s304u

=== Version b15d32a87eae976c0909801e2b8962df20a7deec ===

Clients: 9d63b22a-f76b-f642-aab4-e6c8e627f66a, 20e02d5b-746e-8e48-b04e-
232d3a43e760, 40ccc813-b89f-5643-8e67-a6e93b688ee9


=== Idle Task Queue ===
Last update tick: 13s647u
Last update run: 8s646u
Task queue:

Debug log:
[13s638u] Error(Response not Ok (fetchAndCacheOnce): request for https://
fonts.googleapis.com/icon?family=Material+Icons returned response 0 ,
fetchAndCacheOnce/<@https://awesome-apress-pwa.firebaseapp.com/ngsw-worker.
js:589:31
fulfilled@https://awesome-apress-pwa.firebaseapp.com/ngsw-worker.js:312:52
) while running idle task revalidate(ngsw:b15d32a87eae976c0909801
e2b8962df20a7deec:assets, assets): https://fonts.googleapis.com/
icon?family=Material+Icons
```

This state may help you to find useful information that makes debugging easier.

Web App Manifest

A web manifest allows you to control how your app behaves when launched and displayed to the user. Along with Service Worker, it offers users the Add to Homescreen option. In Chapter 6, we looked into the web app manifest in depth.

Chrome DevTools

Once Chrome DevTools are Opened, go to the *Application* panel and click on *Manifest* to inspect it (see Figure 10-1).

- To look at the manifest source, click the link below the App Manifest label.

- Press the **Add to homescreen** button to simulate an Add to Homescreen event. On the Chrome Desktop, it triggers the browser to add the app to the shelf. On mobile, it prompts the user to install the app (add the icon to the home screen).

- The Identity and Presentation sections just display fields from the manifest source in a more user-friendly display.

- The Icons section displays every icon that you've specified.

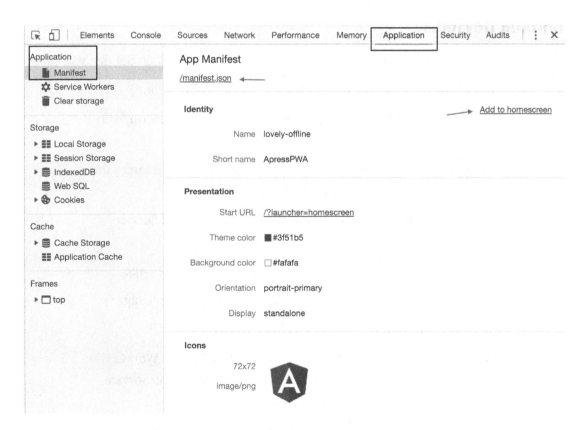

Figure 10-1. Manifest inspector in Chrome

Online Validators

It is easy to find many websites and online tools that can also validate a web app manifest, for instance, `manifest-validator.appspot.com`.

Online Generators

Sometimes generating web app manifests might be time consuming or monotonous. Hence, online generators come in handy, for example, `tomitm.github.io/appmanifest`.

Service Workers

Service Workers give developers the amazing ability to intercept network requests and create a truly offline-first web app. In Chapters 4 and 5, we introduced the Service Worker via Angular Service Worker.

Chrome DevTools

Open DevTools and go to Application Panel (see Figure 10-2). Click on Service Workers.

- The **Offline** puts the website in the corresponding tab offline.

- The **Update on reload** forces the Service Worker to update on every page load.

- The **Bypass for network** bypasses the Service Worker and forces the browser to go to the network for requested resources.

- The **Update** performs a one-time update of the specified Service Worker.

- The **Push** emulates a push notification with a specific message.

- The **Sync** emulates a background sync event with a specific tag.

- The **Unregister** unregisters the specified Service Worker.

- The **Source** tells you when the currently running Service Worker was installed. If you click on the click, it will redirect you to the Service Worker source under the **Sources** panel.

- The **Status** tells you the status of the Service Worker. Since Service Workers are designed to be stopped and started by the browser at any time, we can explicitly stop the Service Worker using the stop button, which will simulate it to reveal bugs due to faulty assumptions about persistent global states.

- The **Clients** tells you the origin that the Service Worker is scoped to.

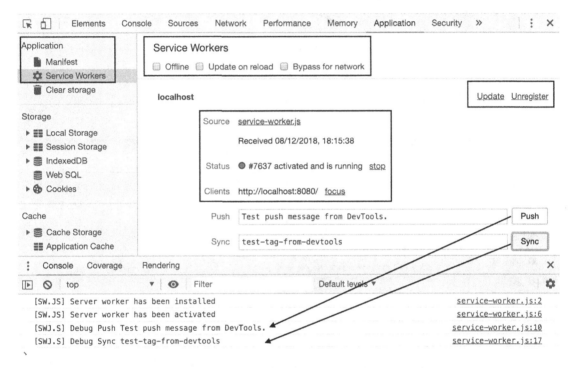

Figure 10-2. *Service Worker debugger in Chrome DevTools*

Firefox DevTools

The about:debugging page provides an interface for interacting with Service Workers. There are several different ways to open about:debugging; however, I will encourage you to open debugger by simply entering the command in the Firefox address bar.

You'll see a few options such as push, debug, and unregister, which are similar to a Chrome expect push emulate push event without a payload (see Figure 10-3).

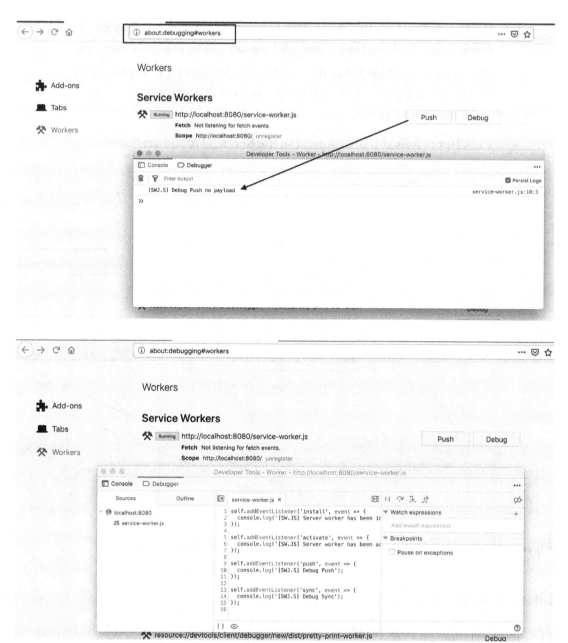

Figure 10-3. *Service Worker debugger in Firefox DevTools*

Service Worker Mock

Pinterest engineers have developed a set of tools to work with Service Worker. *Service Worker Mock* is a library that creates an environment with the following properties that make it easy to turn a Node.js environment into a faux Service Worker environment and will be helpful when you need to write integration tests.

```
const env = {
  // Environment polyfills
  skipWaiting: Function,
  caches: CacheStorage,
  clients: Clients,
  registration: ServiceWorkerRegistration,
  addEventListener: Function,
  Request: constructor Function,
  Response: constructor Function,
  URL: constructor Function,

  // Test helpers
  listeners: Object,
  trigger: Function,
  snapshot: Function,
};
```

The Service Worker mock is best used by applying its result to the global scope, then calling **require(':/service-worker.js')** with the path to your Service Worker file. The file will use the global mocks for things like adding event listeners. Let's write a simple test:

```
// service-worker.js
const TESTCACHE = 'TESTCACHE';
const TESTCACHE_URLS = [
  'index.html',
  './' // Alias for index.html
];

self.addEventListener('install', event => {
  console.log('[SW.JS] Server worker has been installed');
  event.waitUntil(
```

```
    caches
      .open(TESTCACHE)
      .then(cache => cache.addAll(TESTCACHE_URLS))
      .then(self.skipWaiting())
  );
});

// The activate handler takes care of cleaning up old caches.
self.addEventListener('activate', event => {
  console.log('[SW.JS] Server worker has been activated');
  const currentCaches = [TESTCACHE];
  event.waitUntil(
    caches
      .keys()
      .then(cacheNames => cacheNames.filter(cacheName => !currentCaches.
      includes(cacheName)))
      .then(cachesToDelete => {
        return Promise.all(cachesToDelete.map(cacheToDelete => caches.
        delete(cacheToDelete)));
      })
      .then(() => self.clients.claim())
  );
});

self.addEventListener('push', event => {
  console.log(
    '[SWJ.S] Debug Push',
    event.data ? event.data.text() : 'no payload'
  );
});

self.addEventListener('sync', event => {
  console.log('[SWJ.S] Debug Sync', event.tag);
});
```

I will write my test using the Jest framework and service-worker-mock library.

```
// service-worker.test.js
const makeServiceWorkerEnv = require('service-worker-mock');
const makeFetchMock = require('service-worker-mock/fetch');

describe('Service worker', () => {
  beforeEach(() => {
    Object.assign(
      global,
      makeServiceWorkerEnv(),
      makeFetchMock()
      // If you're using sinon ur similar you'd probably use below instead
         of makeFetchMock
      // fetch: sinon.stub().returns(Promise.resolve())
    );
    jest.resetModules();
  });

  it('should add listeners', () => {
    require('./service-worker.js');
    expect(self.listeners['install']).toBeDefined();
    expect(self.listeners['activate']).toBeDefined();
    expect(self.listeners['push']).toBeDefined();
    expect(self.listeners['sync']).toBeDefined();
    expect(self.listeners['fetch']).toBeUndefined();
  });

  it('should delete old caches on activate', async () => {
    require('./service-worker.js');
    // Create old cache
    await self.caches.open('OLD_CACHE');
    expect(self.snapshot().caches.OLD_CACHE).toBeDefined();
    // Activate and verify old cache is removed
    await self.trigger('activate');
    expect(self.snapshot().caches.OLD_CACHE).toBeUndefined();
  });
});
```

Run Jest or npm test.

```
PASS  ./service-worker.test.js
  Service worker
    ✓ should add listeners (7ms)
    ✓ should delete old caches on activate (15ms)

  console.log service-worker.js:19
    [SW.JS] Server worker has been activated

Test Suites: 1 passed, 1 total
Tests:       2 passed, 2 total
Snapshots:   0 total
Time:        0.77s, estimated 1s
Ran all test suites.
```

Note   Clone https://github.com/mhadaily/awesome-apress-pwa.git and go to the Chapter10 directory and see samples. npm test will run the test.

Storage

You might already be familiar with many types of web storage. A web storage's standard such as Local Storage, Session Storage, IndexedDB (have extensively used it), Web SQL, and Cookies are found in all major browsers. I am especially interested in IndexedDB, which can generally be used in Service Worker.

Chrome DevTools

In DevTools, navigate to the Application tab (see Figure 10-4). Select IndexedDB.

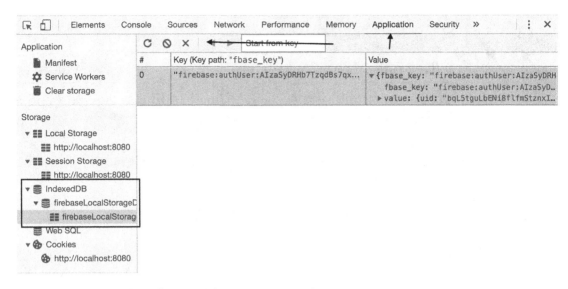

Figure 10-4. *IndexedDB in Chrome DevTools*

By right-clicking on the object store, you can find a clear action and by clicking on the database name, you will find delete and refresh database buttons where you can delete or refresh the database respectively (see Figure 10-5).

Figure 10-5. *Clear, refresh, delete IndexedDB in Chrome DevTools/*

You can clear and refresh the object store by the little action buttons on top of the object store's list UI. You are also able to delete selected data. You may find the refresh and delete action by right-clicking on each piece of data (see Figure 10-6).

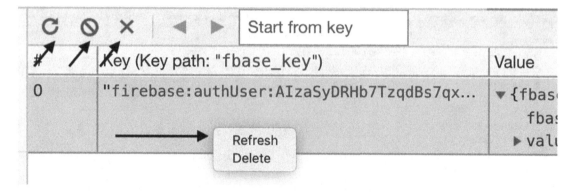

Figure 10-6. Clear, refresh, delete IndexedDB on Object store

Firefox DevTools

When you open Firefox DevTools, you may not see the storage panel by default. You should enable it from the setting as seen in Figure 10-7.

Figure 10-7. Enable storage from DevTools Setting in Firefox

Once enabled, Click on Storage panel and you'll find IndexedDB as seen in Figure 10-8.

Figure 10-8. Storage panel in Firefox DevTools

Cache

The Cache Storage pane provides a read-only list of resources that have been cached using the Cache API.

Chrome DevTools

Note that the first time you open a cache and add a resource to it, DevTools might not detect the change. Reload the page and you should see the cache. If you've got two or more caches open, you'll see them listed below the Cache Storage Cache Storage drop-down (see Figure 10-9).

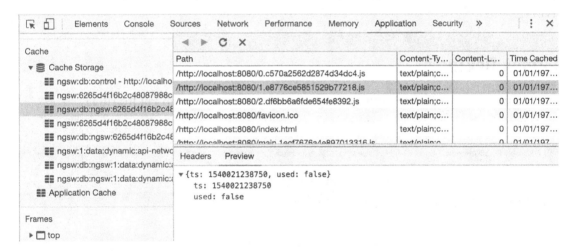

Figure 10-9. *Cache Storage in Chrome DevTools*

When loading resources cached by Service Workers Cache Storage using the Cache API, the Network panel of the DevTools shows it as coming from Service Worker (see Figure 10-10).

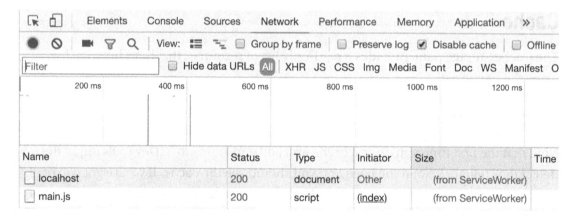

Figure 10-10. *Network request in Chrome DevTools Cache Storage from Service Worker*

Firefox DevTools

Caches name are available under storage Cache as you can see in Figure 10-11.

Figure 10-11. *Cache Storage in Firefox DevTools*

When loading resources cached by Service Workers Cache Storage using the Cache API, Firefox shows it is cached in the Network panel (see Figure 10-12).

Status	Method	File	Domain	Cause	Type	Transferred	Size	o r
304	GET	/	localhost:8080	document	html	cached	663 B	→
304	GET	main.js	localhost:8080	script	js	cached	0 B	

Figure 10-12. *Network request in Firefox DevTools Cache Storage from Service Worker*

Simulate Offline Behavior

To verify everything works as planned while our application is offline, we need to make sure we are able to simulate no connectivity.

Chrome and Firefox provide a handy feature that we can leverage to mock the offline mode.

Chrome

In addition to the Offline check box in Service Worker under the Application panel, we are able to use the offline check box under the Network panel (see Figure 10-13).

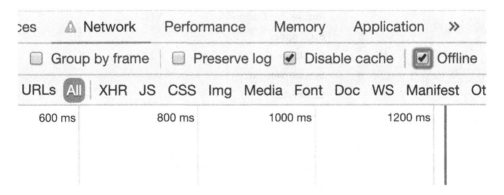

Figure 10-13. *Offline mode under Network panel in Chrome DevTools*

Firefox

In order to enable offline mode in Firefox, click on the menu icon and then click **Developer** ➤ **Work Offline** (see Figure 10-14).

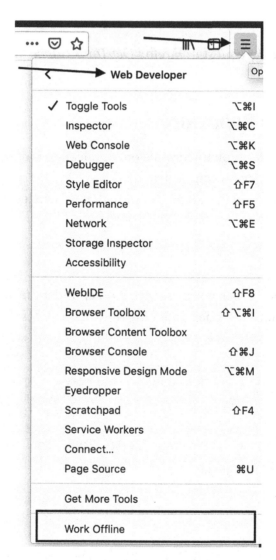

Figure 10-14. *Offline mode Firefox*

Sometimes the offline simulator doesn't do the proper job, and you may need to actually turn off your internet and reconnect again. For example, at the time I am writing this book, when you work with background sync in Service Worker, you may need to really turn off your internet connection.

Simulate Different Network Conditions

There are also many parts of the world where 3G and 2G speeds are the norm. Also, we are constantly moving between various states of connectivity. To verify that our app works well for these consumers, we need to test our application in different network connections and devices.

In both Chrome and Firefox, we have a throttling option that you can find in Figures 10-15 and 10-16.

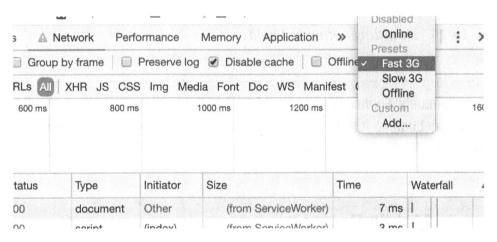

Figure 10-15.   *Throttling option in Chrome under Network Tab; you are able to add custom profile as you wish*

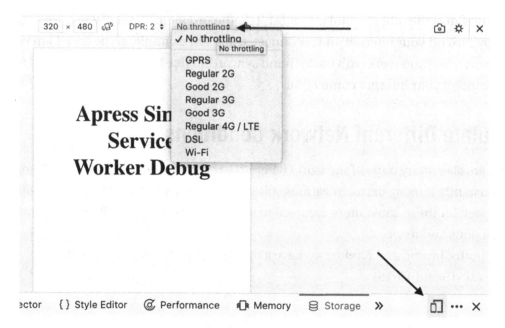

Figure 10-16. *Throttling option in Firefox*

Note   Ultimately, Service Worker is a plain JavaScript file, where you can use all JavaScript debugging features such as Debugger or break point to inspect code inside Service Worker.

Simulate Mobile Devices

You can run your PWA on a real device while it's connected to your browser via USB, or you can run an emulator and perform your test and inspect what you are looking for.

Remote Debugging and Measuring

To connect your Android device to Chrome, you can follow the instructions on this link: https://goo.gl/syNfSR; and to connect to Firefox, you can find instructions on this link: https://goo.gl/P7gFNE.

Emulators

To set up and run the iOS simulator, follow this link: `https://goo.gl/ymihLs`. And for Android, follow the instructions on this link: `https://goo.gl/EGPpxx`.

Online Tools

BrowserStack is a cross-browser testing tool. With it you can test your website across browsers on multiple operating systems and mobile devices without individual virtual machines, devices, or emulators. BrowserStack also offers remote testing on physical devices, so if you find yourself needing to test your website performance on many devices, it can be a helpful time-saver.

Measurement

It is always important to measure our application for different aspects such as speed, performance, or user experience in order to deliver a quality application progressively. In this section, I will explorer possibilities that help us to get better insight about out application, which allows us to continuously refine our application.

Audit

As seen in previous chapters, the Audit panel in Chrome DevTools, which is powered by Lighthouse, is one of the best tools that we can use to perform auditing on our application. It has different options including performance and PWA (see Figure 10-17).

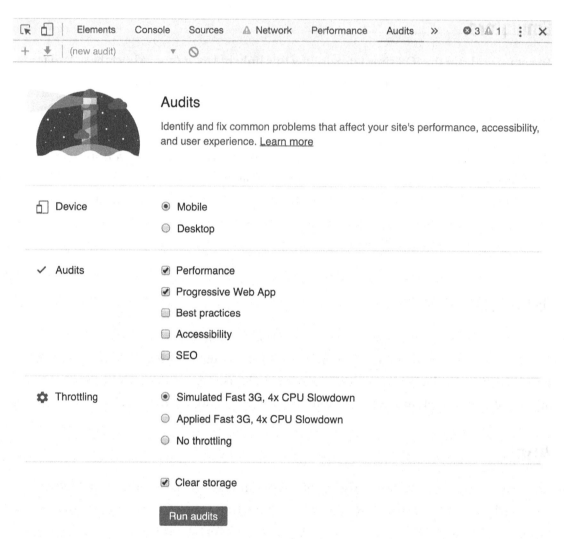

Figure 10-17. Lighthouse in Chrome DevTools Audit tab where different audits can be selected and performed

It is likely that we will automate our audit test or add that to the CD/CI[1] pipeline. Lighthouse[2] is also available as the Node command-line tool and can also be used as a Node module programmatically.

---

[1]Continuous Delivery, Continuous Integration.

[2]https://developers.google.com/web/tools/lighthouse

To run Lighthouse in the command line, do the following:

1. Make sure Chrome for Desktop and Node is installed.

2. Install Lighthouse.

```
npm install -g lighthouse
```

to run an audit

```
lighthouse <url>
```

for example

```
lighthouse https://awesome-apress-pwa.firebaseapp.com --view
```

You can see more options by running

```
lighthouse --help
```

Let's take a look at how we can add Lighthouse programmatically.

Lighthouse with Chrome Launcher

We will write an example that will run `chrome-launcher` and perform Lighthouse audits. This test is helpful when you run a test for your application, especially if you want to run multiple automated tests.

```
// lighthouse-chrome-launcher.js
const lighthouse = require('lighthouse');
const chromeLauncher = require('chrome-launcher');

function launchChromeAndRunLighthouse(url, opts, config = null) {
  return chromeLauncher
    .launch({ chromeFlags: opts.chromeFlags })
    .then(chrome => {
      opts.port = chrome.port;
      return lighthouse(url, opts, config).then(results => {
        // use results.lhr for the JS-consumeable output
        // https://github.com/GoogleChrome/lighthouse/blob/master/types/
           lhr.d.ts
        // use results.report for the HTML/JSON/CSV output as a string
```

```
      // use results.artifacts for the trace/screenshots/other specific
         case you need (rarer)
      return chrome.kill().then(() => results.lhr);
    });
  });
}

const opts = {
  chromeFlags: ['--show-paint-rects'],
  onlyCategories: ['performance', 'pwa'] // you can leave it empty for all
audits
};

// Usage:
launchChromeAndRunLighthouse(
  'https://awesome-apress-pwa.firebaseapp.com',
  opts
).then(results => {
  // Use results!
  console.log({
    pwa: results.categories.pwa.score,
    performance: results.categories.performance.score
  });
});
```

When you run this file, you'll get the result, and you can add your logic based on the scores.

```
node lighthouse-chrome-launcher.js
```

You'll see

```
{ pwa: 1, performance: 0. 95 }
```

For instance, if a particular page has lower score than 0.5 in PWA, you can exit build and ask to improve that page.

Lighthouse with Puppeteer[3]

Puppeteer is a Node library that provides a high-level API to control Chrome or Chromium over a DevTools Protocol. Puppeteer runs headless by default but can be configured to run full (non-headless) Chrome or Chromium. Lighthouse and Puppeteer is an excellent combination to run audits in our CD/CI where we cannot use the Chrome launcher.

```
// lighthouse-puppeteer.js
const puppeteer = require('puppeteer');
const lighthouse = require('lighthouse');
const { URL } = require('url');
const run = async url => {
  // Use Puppeteer to launch headful Chrome and don't use its default
    800x600 viewport.
  const browser = await puppeteer.launch({
    headless: true,
    defaultViewport: null
  });
  browser.on('targetchanged', async target => {
    const page = await target.page();
    function addStyleContent(content) {
      const style = document.createElement('style');
      style.type = 'text/css';
      style.appendChild(document.createTextNode(content));
      document.head.appendChild(style);
    }
    const css = '* {color: red}';
    if (page && page.url() === url) {
      const client = await page.target().createCDPSession();
      await client.send('Runtime.evaluate', {
        expression: `(${addStyleContent.toString()})('${css}')`
      });
    }
```

---

[3]Headless Chrome Node API https://pptr.dev.

```
  });
  const { lhr } = await lighthouse(
    url,
    {
      port: new URL(browser.wsEndpoint()).port,
      output: 'json',
      logLevel: 'error',
      chromeFlags: ['--show-paint-rects'],
      onlyCategories: ['performance', 'pwa']
    },
    {
      extends: 'lighthouse:default'
    }
  );
  await browser.close();
  return {
    pwa: lhr.categories.pwa.score,
    performance: lhr.categories.performance.score
  };
};
```

run('https://awesome-apress-pwa.firebaseapp.com').then(res => console.log(res));

Then you can run this file:

node lighthouse-puppeteer.js

And you'll see

{ pwa: 1, performance: 0.96 }

Analytics

PWAs allows applications to offer functionality that weren't possible before: for instance, adding offline behavior to a page or allowing users to launch a website from the home screen.

Generally, there are three events that we are interested in:

- Add to home screen: This will allow us to understand how users are reacting to the browser prompt and based on users' choices, we can know how valuable the service is being to the users.

- Run from home screen: Adding an icon to the home screen is just the first step. It would be beneficial to understand how adding our service to the home screen affects user engagement.

- Offline pageviews frequency: This allows us to track how many users are accessing the service while offline.

Tracking Home Screen Prompts

We are going to use beforeinstallprompt event to track how many users are being asked to add a website to their home screen and what will be their decision and based on that, we will send information to our tracking system: for instance, Google Analytics.

Open AddToHomeScreenService

```
public showPrompt() {
    if (this.deferredPrompt) {
      // will show prompt
      this.deferredPrompt.prompt();

      // Wait for the user to respond to the prompt
      this.deferredPrompt.userChoice.then(choiceResult => {
        // outcome is either "accepted" or "dismissed"
        if (choiceResult.outcome === 'accepted') {
          // User accepted the A2HS prompt
          // send data to analytics
          // do whatever you want
          this.sendToAnalytics(choiceResult.userChoice);
        } else {
```

```
        // User dismissed the A2HS prompt
        // send data to analytics
        // do whatever you want
        this.sendToAnalytics(choiceResult.userChoice);
      }

      // we don't need this event anymore
      this.deferredPrompt = null;
      this.deferredPromptFired$.next(false);
    });
  }
}

public sendToAnalytics (userChoice) {
  // for example, send data to Google Analytics, you can create another
    service
  // or you may use a library to send this event to Google Analytics
  // ga('send', 'event', 'A2H', userChoice);
  console.log(userChoice);
  this.deferredPromptFired$.next(false);
}
```

Tracking Sessions from the Home Screen

One of the most reliable ways to track sessions being started from the home screen is to add a custom query param to start_url on our application manifest. For instance, if you are using Google Analytics, you can add custom campaigns parameters.[4]

Generally, there are five parameters that you can add to your URLs:

> utm_source: Identify the advertiser, site, publication, etc., that is sending traffic to your property: for example, google, newsletter4, billboard.

> utm_medium: The advertising or marketing medium: for example, cpc, banner, email newsletter.

---

[4]https://support.google.com/analytics/answer/1033863?hl=en

utm_campaign: The individual campaign name, slogan, promo code, etc., for a product.

utm_term: Identify paid search keywords. If you're manually tagging paid keyword campaigns, you should also use utm_term to specify the keyword.

utm_content: Used to differentiate similar content or links within the same ad. For example, if you have two call-to-action links within the same email message, you can use utm_content and set different values for each so you can tell which version is more effective.

As an example:

```
// manifest.json
{ ...
  "background_color": "#fafafa",
  "display": "standalone",
  "scope": "/",
  "//": "Append tracking parameters to start_url",
  "start_url": "/?utm_source=homescreen",
  "icons": [
    {
      "src": "assets/icons/icon-72x72.png",
      "sizes": "72x72",
      "type": "image/png"
    },
...
}
```

To see the Campaigns reports:

1. Sign in to Google Analytics.

2. Navigate to your view.

3. Open Reports.

4. Select Acquisition ➤ Campaigns.

You may user other tracking systems as needed to create your desirables using the same mechanism.

Track Offline Pageviews

At the time of writing this book, there is no implemented solution in Angular Service Worker.

Workbox is providing support for offline pageview tracking. In Chapters 13 and 14, we will implement this module and see how it works.

Online Tools

webpagetest.org is a go-to tool when it comes to measuring performance. You will find in-depth documentation here: sites.google.com/a/webpagetest.org/docs.

web.dev/measure is a new tool from Google that helps developers like you learn and apply the web's modern capabilities to your own sites and apps.

Real Device

Last but not least, never forget real-device testing and measure your application performance and behavior on an average device or on your top-visited devices based on your analytics system. It's imperative to have an overview on a real device to see that app in the real world.

Summary

In this chapter, we talked about the handiest tools to debug and measure a PWA. However, things will not always go so well. In the next chapter, I will reveal possibilities to show that id your application and Service Worker go wrong, you will still be able to survive.

CHAPTER 11

Safety Service Worker

Service Workers are indeed powerful, and the Angular Service Worker is no exception. They do complex and advanced jobs for building a web application. However, based on my experience building PWAs over the years, things are not always going in a way that we like. It may happen that the Service Worker acts in unforeseen ways, and it may interrupt the user experience or even make our app completely useless and unreachable.

Getting rid of a Service Worker is not as easy as it looks when you have registered a Service Worker in the browser. Knowing how to unregister a service worker from a client can leave your site in a suspended state of failure, which may lead to a frustrating experience for your users.

A simple example is when you have registered a Service Worker and want to remove a registered Service Worker file; therefore, a browser will not find the Service Worker file any more, and the old Service Worker will stay on the browser until a new Service Worker file gets registered. You will see that this mistake can have a disruptive impact on your clients.

Luckily, Angular Service Worker contains several solutions such as Fail-safe, which is a self-destructing way to unregister itself from the browser. In this chapter, I am going to show you different mechanisms – a so-called "kill switch" – in addition to Angular solutions where you can kill off or unregister your Service Worker, clean the cache, and more, in order to avoid serving disruptive web applications to the user. You can use these methods while you are debugging or even when you feel you need to get rid of the PWA feature for your application.

Fail-safe

Angular provides a simple solution to deactivate the Service Worker. As we have seen in previous chapters, ngsw-config.json (ngsw.json after build in dist folder) is the manifest where we define our Service Worker rules and logic.

© Majid Hajian 2019

M. Hajian, *Progressive Web Apps with Angular*, https://doi.org/10.1007/978-1-4842-4448-7_11

Angular Service Worker tries to fetch the ngsw manifest on app initialization and when it checks for new updates on navigation requests, by executing the fetchLatestManifest method. Let's take a look at the method closely:

```
fetchLatestManifest(ignoreOfflineError = false) {
    return __awaiter$5(this, void 0, void 0, function* () {
        const res = yield this.safeFetch(this.adapter.
        newRequest('ngsw.json?ngsw-cache-bust=' + Math.random()));
        if (!res.ok) {
            if (res.status === 404) {
                yield this.deleteAllCaches();
                yield this.scope.registration.unregister();
            }
            else if (res.status === 504 && ignoreOfflineError) {
                return null;
            }
            throw new Error(`Manifest fetch failed! (status: ${res.
            status})`);
        }
        this.lastUpdateCheck = this.adapter.time;
        return res.json();
    });
}
```

As seen in the snippet, Angular tries to fetch with a random cache-bust query param where it makes sure that the file was not cached and is fresh.

If this file doesn't exist or basically the response status code is 404, Angular Service Worker will first delete all caches and then unregister the current SW registration.

Thus, if in your application something went wrong, you can simply **rename or remove** ngsw.json file, which essentially removes all caches; de-registers itself; or, in other words, self-destructs itself.

```
rm dist/ngsw.json
```

Here is a function where it handles deleting all caches:

```
deleteAllCaches() {
    return __awaiter$5(this, void 0, void 0, function* () {
        yield (yield this.scope.caches.keys())
            .filter(key => key.startsWith('ngsw:'))
            .reduce((previous, key) => __awaiter$5(this, void 0,
            void 0, function* () {
            yield Promise.all([
                previous,
                this.scope.caches.delete(key),
            ]);
        }), Promise.resolve());
    });
}
```

Note that if you turn "serviceWorker" to false in angular.json, ngsw.json will not be generated; therefore, this mechanism will work too.

Safety Worker

The Angular Service Worker package contains a simple no-op[1] Service Worker script that can replace ngsw-worker.js:

```
self.addEventListener('install', event => { self.skipWaiting(); });
```

```
self.addEventListener('activate', event => {
  event.waitUntil(self.clients.claim());
  self.registration.unregister().then(
      () => { console.log('NGSW Safety Worker - unregistered old service
      worker');      });
});
```

---

[1] A no op (or no-op), for no operation, is a computer instruction that takes up a small amount of space but specifies no operation. Here it refers to a simple Service Worker that doesn't do anything expect that it just registers itself, or we may delete just caches in an active event or unregister if necessary.

Let's break down this script:

1. It listens to install even and forces to skip waiting in order to immediately install.

2. It listens to activate event:

   a. Make sure all clients (tabs, for instances) are claimed in order to use the latest installed Service Worker. The `claim()` method of the clients allows an active service worker to set itself as the controller for all clients within its scope. This triggers a "`controllerchange`" event on `navigator.serviceWorker` in any clients that become controlled by this Service Worker.

   b. It will unregister itself immediately.

In order to unregister your current Service Worker, copy the file content into `ngsw-worker.js` or any Service Worker name that was registered and is in use.

```
cp dist/satefy-worker.js dist/ngsw-worker.js
```

This script can be used both to deactivate Angular Service Worker as well as any other Service Worker that might have been served on the website.

Extended Safety Worker

However, in most cases a simple no-op Service Worker will work. In some cases, we may need to delete all caches or force a user's tab (each client of the website) to be refreshed in order to receive the latest update. For instance, when you redirect your website to a new origin (domain), your Service Worker may abruptly misbehave.

So, how to solve this?

1. To remove all caches:

```
caches.keys().then(cacheNames => {
    return Promise.all(
      cacheNames.map(cacheName => caches.delete(cacheName))
    );
})
```

If you want to just filter the Angular cache name and delete them:

```
caches.keys().then(cacheNames => {
    return Promise.all(
      cacheNames
        .filter(key => key.startsWith('ngsw:'))
        .map(cacheName => caches.delete(cacheName))
    );
  })
```

2. To Refresh all Windows type clients (tabs):

   a. Get a list of all window clients (tabs).

   b. Each client exposes a method called navigatem which allow us to redirect the client to another page.

   c. We navigate each client to itself in order to force it to reload the page!

   ```
   self.clients.matchAll({ type: 'window' })
   .then(clients => {
       for (const client of clients) {
         client.navigate(client.url);
       }
     });
   ```

Put them all together:

```
self.addEventListener('install', event => {
  self.skipWaiting();
});

self.addEventListener('activate', event => {
  event.waitUntil(self.clients.claim());

  self.registration.unregister().then(async () => {
    console.log('NGSW Safety Worker - unregistered old service
    worker');
```

```
    // Get all cache keys
    const cacheNames = await caches.keys();
    // If you want to delete Only Angular Caches
    const AngularCaches = cacheNames.filter(key => key.
    startsWith('ngsw:'));
    // Delete all caches
    await Promise.all(AngularCaches.map(cacheName => caches.
    delete(cacheName)));

    // Grab a list of all tabs
    const clients = await self.clients.matchAll({ type: 'window'
  });
    // Reload pages
    for (const client of clients) {
      client.navigate(client.url);
    }
  });
  });
```

Summary

Although our goal is to develop, build, and deploy an application that works, bugs are unavoidable. In this chapter, we made a backup plan – a so-called "kill switch" – ready for cases in which we need to get rid of a buggy Service Worker until we can debug and fix the problem. Angular, in particular, provides several methods that makes sure our application works flawlessly as much as possible: such as fail-safe and safety-worker script mechanisms.

We have also extended the no-op Service Worker script and learned how to unregister Service Worker, claims for all clients, clean up caches, and reload pages if necessary. I hope you never get to use these methods and that everything goes well; however, you now know what to do if something unexpectedly goes wrong.

CHAPTER 12

Modern Web APIs

What if I tell you that you can build a web app, connect to a device that supports Bluetooth Low Energy, and have control over it from your web application? What if a user's login credentials are kept in the browsers safely, and when users access the website, they are automatically signed in? What if a login to a web application needs a device connected via USB to authenticate a user? What if I can access share options on a native platform via a JavaScript API within our browser? I know what you might be thinking now; but even though these all sounded like dreams 10 years ago, today most of them are achievable or at least close to becoming realities.

For the past decade, much of the web has evolved significantly. New web APIs allow developers to connect web applications to hardware via Bluetooth and USB. Online payment has never been easier than it is today. Single sign-on and password-less solutions have brought a much better user experience with minimal effort. Developing a cross-platform via the same API across all devices and operating systems was very difficult whereas, today, it's such a pleasant way to develop and build a web application – especially Progressive Web Apps (PWAs) since a lot of new APIs have been standardized that provide a high-level JavaScript API in our browsers to gain access to underlying low-level APIs of the platform.

In this chapter, I have chosen a few new technologies and APIs to explore and integrate with PWA note apps such as Credential Management, Payment Request, Geolocation, Media Streams, Web Bluetooth, and Web USB. I will ensure that the fundamentals of these APIs will be covered. However, you may need to develop additional ones for your applications based on your needs and requirements.

Additionally, I would suggest keeping an eye on Web Share, Web VR/AR, Background fetch, Accessibility improvement, Web Assembly, and many more new standards that are either under development or under consideration and will empower the web, especially by building a PWA.

289

© Majid Hajian 2019
M. Hajian, *Progressive Web Apps with Angular*, https://doi.org/10.1007/978-1-4842-4448-7_12

Credential Management

The Credential management API is a Promised-based standard browser API that facilitates seamless sign-ins across devices by providing an interface between the website and the browser. This API allows the user to sign in with one tab via an account chooser and helps to store credentials in the browsers by which can be synced across devices. This helps that user who has signed in to one browser already – he or she can then stay logged in to all other devices as well if they use the same browser.

This API not only works with native-browser password management, but it can also provide information about credentials from a federated identity provider. What it means is this: any entity that a website trusts to correctly authenticate a user and provide an API for that purpose can be a provider in this API to store the credential and retrieve it if necessary. For example, Google Account, GitHub, Twitter, Facebook, or OpenID Connect are examples of a federated identity provider framework.

Keep in mind that this API will only work when the origin is secure; in other words, similar to PWA, your website must run on HTTPS.

Let's start implementing in an Angular project and see how it works.

First, we will create a service called `CredentialManagementService`, and we import to my `CoreModule`.

```
declare const PasswordCredential: any;
declare const FederatedCredential: any;
declare const navigator: any;
declare const window: any;

@Injectable({
  providedIn: 'root'
})
export class CredentialManagementService {
  isCredentialManagementSupported: boolean;

  constructor(private snackBar: SnackBarService) {
    if (window.PasswordCredential || window.FederatedCredential) {
      this.isCredentialManagementSupported = true;
    } else {
```

```
    this.isCredentialManagementSupported = false;
    console.log('Credential Management API is not supported in this
    browser');
  }
}
```

async store({ username, password }) {
```
  if (this.isCredentialManagementSupported) {
    // You can either pass the passwordCredentialData as below
    // or simply pass down your HTMLFormElement. A reference to an
        HTMLFormElement with appropriate input fields.
    // The form should, at the very least, contain an id and password.
    // It could also require a CSRF token.
    /*
      <form id="form" method="post">
        <input type="text" name="id" autocomplete="username" />
        <input type="password" name="password" autocomplete="current-
        password" />
        <input type="hidden" name="csrf_token" value="*****" />
      </form>
      <script>
          const form = document.querySelector('#form');
          const credential = new PasswordCredential(form);
    // if you have a federated provider
     const cred = new FederatedCredential({
       id: id,
       name: name,
       provider: 'https://account.google.com',
       iconURL: iconUrl
          });
      <script>
    */
```

```
      // Create credential object synchronously.
      const credential = new PasswordCredential({
        id: username,
        password: password
        // name: name,
        // iconURL: iconUrl
      });
      const isStored = await navigator.credentials.store(credential);
      if (isStored) {
        this.snackBar.open('You password and username saved in your browser');
      }
    }
  }

  async get() {
    if (this.isCredentialManagementSupported) {
      return navigator.credentials.get({
        password: true,
        mediation: 'silent'
        // federated: {
        //   providers: ['https://accounts.google.com']
        // },
      });
    }
  }

  preventSilentAccess() {
    if (this.isCredentialManagementSupported) {
      navigator.credentials.preventSilentAccess();
    }
  }
}
```

This service has three methods that are basically wrappers around the main credential API methods to check if the API is available in the browser or not. Let's break the service down:

1. A **feature detection** when service is initialized to ensure this API is available.

   `if `**`(window.PasswordCredential || window.FederatedCredential)`**` {}`

2. **store** method:

   A) Accepts username and password, and therefore we can create a password credential where it'll be ready to store in credentials. `PasswordCredential` constructor accepts both `HTMLFormElement` and an object of essential fields. If you want to pass in the `HTMLFormElement`, make sure your form contains at least an ID and Password as well as CSRF token. In the method, the call constructor with ID, which is a username and password. `name` and `iconURL`, are names of the user that is signing in and the user's avatar image, respectively and optionally. Keep in mind that we run this code if the feature is available; otherwise we let the user work with the application normally.

   Since we are building a PWA, it is always important to provide an alternative for those users whose browser of choice doesn't support features that are being used.

   B) If you are going to use third-party login, you must call `FederatedCredential` constructor with an `id` as well as `provider` endpoint.

   C) Credentials API is available on navigator, the store function is Promised-based and by calling that, we can save user credentials in the browser.

   D) Finally, we show a message to the user in order to inform them that we store their password in the browser.

3. get method:

   After feature detection is checked, we call `get` on `navigation.` `credentials` by passing in the configuration such as `password,` `mediation.` `Mediation` defines how we want to tell the browser to show the account chooser to user, which has three values:

optional, required, and silent. When mediation is optional,
the user is explicitly shown an account chooser to sign in after a
navigator.credentials.preventSilentAccess() was called.
This is normally to ensure automatic sign-in doesn't happen after
the user chooses to sign out or unregister.

Once navigator.credentials.get() resolves, it returns either
an undefined or a credential object. To determine whether it
is a PasswordCredential or a FederatedCredential, simply look
at the type property of the object, which will be either password
or federated. If the type is federated, the provider property is a
string that represents the identity provider.

4. preventSilentAccess method:

We call preventSilentAccess() on navigator.credentials.
This will ensure the auto sign-in will not happen until next time
the user enables auto sign-in. To resume auto sign-in, a user can
choose to intentionally sign in by choosing the account they wish
to sign in with, from the account chooser. Then the user is always
signed back in until they explicitly sign out.

To continue with UserContainerComponent, we will first inject this service, then will
define my autoSignIn method and will call that on ngOnInit. On both the signup and
login methods, we will call the store method from the credential service to save and
update the user credential.

Finally, when a user logs out, we need to call preventSilentAccess(). This is what it
looks like:

```
constructor(
  private credentialManagement: CredentialManagementService,
  private fb: FormBuilder,
  private auth: AuthService,
  private snackBar: SnackBarService
) {}

ngOnInit() {
  this.createLoginForm();
  if (!this.auth.authenticated) {
```

```
    this.autoSignIn();
  }
}

private async autoSignIn() {
  const credential = await this.credentialManagement.get();

  if (credential && credential.type === 'password') {
    const { password, id, type } = credential;
    const isLogin = await this._loginFirebase({ password, email: id });
    if (isLogin) {
    // make sure to show a proper message to the user
      this.snackBar.open(`Signed in by ${id} automatically!`);
    }
  }
}

public signUp() {
  this.checkFormValidity(async () => {
    const signup = await this.auth.signUpFirebase(this.loginForm.value);
    const isLogin = await this.auth.authenticateUser(signup);
    if (isLogin) {
      const { email, password } = this.loginForm.value;
      this.credentialManagement.store({ username: email, password });
    }
  });
}

public login() {
  this.checkFormValidity(async () => {
    const { email, password } = this.loginForm.value;
    const isLogin = this._loginFirebase({ email, password });
    if (isLogin) {
      this.credentialManagement.store({ username: email, password });
    }
  });
}
```

```
public logOut() {
  this.auth
    .logOutFirebase()
    .then(() => {
      this.auth.authErrorMessages$.next(null);
      this.auth.isLoading$.next(false);
      this.auth.user$.next(null);
      // prevent auto signin until next time user login explicity
      // or allow us for auto sign in
      this.credentialManagement.preventSilentAccess();
    })
    .catch(e => {
      console.error(e);
      this.auth.isLoading$.next(false);
      this.auth.authErrorMessages$.next(
        'Something is wrong when signing out!'
      );
    });
}
```

Note   Clone https://github.com/mhadaily/awesome-apress-pwa.git
and go to Chapter 12, 01-credential-management-api folder to find all sample
codes.

It is also a good practice to use the autocomplete attribute on the login form to help
the browser to appropriately identify the fields (Figure 12-1).

```
<input
    matInput
    placeholder="Enter your email"
    autocomplete="username"
    formControlName="email"
    required
/>
```

```
<input
        matInput
        autocomplete="current-password"
        placeholder="Enter your password"
        [type]="hide ? 'password' : 'text'"
        formControlName="password"
    />
```

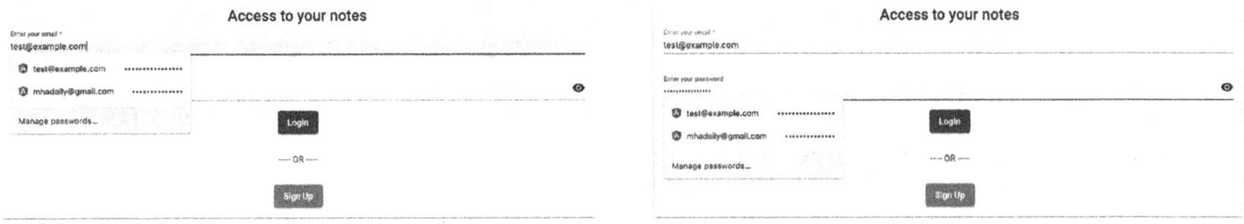

Figure 12-1. *Autocomplete attribute allows browser to show appropriate username and password for the website*

We run the application in a new browser, then we will go to the login page and by entering my credential will log in to the website. You'll see a prompt message that asks the user to save the credential in the browser (see Figure 12-2).

Figure 12-2. *Credential prompt when web app wants to save credential in the browser*

To test my `auto sign-in`, we will open a new clean browser and will go to the login page, then we will notice that we get redirected to the note list, and a `snackbar` message appears that shows we am automatically signed in (see Figure 12-3).

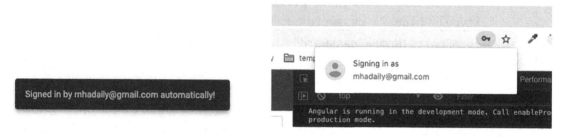

Figure 12-3. *The website snackbar message and a message from browser itself after automatic sign-in occurs*

Finally, the mediation `optional` or `required` will display an account chooser prompt that allows users to select their account of choice, especially if they have more than one account saved (See Figure 12-4).

Figure 12-4. *The account chooser if mediation is optional or required*

Browsers Support

By the time of writing this book, Chrome on Desktop and for Android, Android browser, Opera for desktop and mobile, and Samsung internet browser support this API; and it currently under consideration for Firefox. MS Edge is moving to a Chromium platform and this API should be covered soon.

Payment Request

There is a high probability that all of us reading this book have made a payment on the web – at least once. So we all know that how time consuming, and boring it is to fill out the checkout forms, especially if it has more than one step.

The payment request standard API is developed by W3C to ensure the online payment system for both consumers and merchants remains consistent and smooth with minimal effort. This is not a new way of payment; rather, it's a way that aims to make the checkout process easier.

With this API, consumers always see a native platform UI when they want to select payment details such as shipping address, credit card, contact details, etc. Imagine that once you save all of the information in your browsers, you can simply just reuse them in every single checkout page where this API is supported. How pleasant an experience it will be: ignore the filling out of lots of fields in a checkout form, credit card information, and more. Instead we will be seeing saved information consistently with a familiar native UI. Just a few clicks or tabs to select, and it's done!

Another advantage of this API is to accept different payment methods from a variety of handlers to the web with relatively easy integration: for example, Apple Pay, Samsung Pay, Google Pay.

Long story short, I am going to add a donation button in the PWA note app.

First, we will create a service in Angular called WebPaymentService and import it in CoreModule.

```
export class WebPaymentService {
  public isWebPaymentSupported: boolean;
  private requestPayment = null;
  private canMakePaymentPromise: Promise<boolean> = null;

  private supportedPaymentMethods = [
    {
      // support credit card payment
      supportedMethods: 'basic-card',
      data: {
        supportedNetworks: ['visa', 'mastercard', 'amex'],
        supportedTypes: ['credit', 'debit']
      }
    }
```

```
   // Apple pay, Google Pay, Samasung pay, Stripe and others can be added here too.
  ];

// just an example of a simple product details
  private paymentDetails: any = {
    total: {
      label: 'Total Donation',
      amount: { currency: 'USD', value: 4.99 }
    },
    displayItems: [
      {
        label: 'What I recieve',
        amount: { currency: 'USD', value: 4.49 }
      },
      {
        label: 'Tax',
        amount: { currency: 'USD', value: 0.5 }
      }
    ]
  };

  private requestPaymentOptions = {
    requestPayerName: true,
    requestPayerPhone: false,
    requestPayerEmail: true,
    requestShipping: false
    shippingType: 'shipping'
  };

  constructor() {
    if (window.PaymentRequest) {
      // Use Payment Request API which is supported
      this.isWebPaymentSupported = true;
    } else {
      this.isWebPaymentSupported = false;
    }
  }
```

```
constructPaymentRequest() {
  if (this.isWebPaymentSupported) {
    this.requestPayment = new PaymentRequest(
      this.supportedPaymentMethods,
      this.paymentDetails,
      this.requestPaymentOptions
    );
```

// **ensure that user have a supported payment method if not you can do other things**

```
    if (this.requestPayment.canMakePaymentPromise) {
      this.canMakePaymentPromise = this.requestPayment.canMakePayment();
    } else {
      this.canMakePaymentPromise = Promise.resolve(true);
    }
  } else {
```

// **do something else for instance redirect user to normal checkout**

```
  }
  return this;
}

async show(): Promise<any> {
```

/* **you can make sure client has a supported method already if not do somethig else. For instance, fallback to normal checkout, or let them to add one active card */**

```
  const canMakePayment = await this.canMakePaymentPromise;

  if (canMakePayment) {
    try {
      const response = await this.requestPayment.show();
```

// **here where you can process response payment with your backend**
// **there must be a backend implementation too.**

```
      const status = await this.processResponseWithBackend(response);
```

// **after backend responsed successfully, you can do any other logic here**
// **complete transaction and close the payment UI**

```
      response.complete(status.success);
      return status.response;
    } catch (e) {
      // API Error or user closed the UI
      console.log('API Error or user closed the UI');
      return false;
    }
  } else {
    // Fallback to traditional checkout for example
    // this.router.navigateByUrl('/donate/traditional');
  }
}

async abort(): Promise<boolean> {
  return this.requestPayment.abort();
}

// mock backend response
async processResponseWithBackend(response): Promise<any> {
  // check with backend and respond accordingly
  return new Promise(resolve => {
    setTimeout(() => {
      resolve({ success: 'success', response });
    }, 1500);
  });
}
}
```

Let's break it down.

1. As always, a feature detection for progressive enhancement.

```
if (window.PaymentRequest) {
    this.isWebPaymentSupported = true;
  } else {
    this.isWebPaymentSupported = false;
  }
```

2. For each payment, you need to construct a `PaymentRequest` that accepts three arguments.

```
new PaymentRequest(
        this.supportedPaymentMethods,
        this.paymentDetails,
        this.requestPaymentOptions
    );
```

3. Define `supportedPaymentMethods`, which is an array of all supported payment methods. In the code example, I have just defined a basic card; however, in this chapter's sample codes, you will find more methods such as Apple Pay, Google Pay, and Samsung Pay. You are not also limited to them; you can implement any favorite methods such as PayPal, Stripe, and more that support this API.

```
private supportedPaymentMethods = [
    {
      // support credit card payment
      supportedMethods: 'basic-card',
      data: {
       // you can add more such as discover, JCB and etc.
        supportedNetworks: ['visa', 'mastercard', 'amex'],
        supportedTypes: ['credit', 'debit']
      }
    },
]
```

Each object in this array has `supportedMethods` and `data` property that is specific for the method itself. To have a better understanding, I'll provide an Apple Pay object as an example, too:

```
{
        supportedMethods: 'https://apple.com/apple-pay',
        data: {
          version: 3,
          merchantIdentifier: 'merchant.com.example',
```

```
        merchantCapabilities: ['supports3DS', 'supportsCredit',
        'supportsDebit'],
        supportedNetworks: ['amex', 'discover', 'masterCard', 'visa'],
        countryCode: 'US'
    }
},
```

4. In Define paymentDetails, for instance, in my example, I have a fixed donation number; however, you may have a cart page with different products and other details that need to be added to payment details accordingly.

```
private paymentDetails: any = {
    total: {
        label: 'Total Donation',
        amount: { currency: 'USD', value: 4.99 }
    },
    displayItems: [
        {
            label: 'What I recieve',
            amount: { currency: 'USD', value: 4.49 }
        },
        {
            label: 'Tax',
            amount: { currency: 'USD', value: 0.5 }
        }
    ]
};
```

There are two main properties: total indicates total amount; and displayItems, which is an array that shows cart items.

5. Define requestPaymentOptions is optional; however, you may find it very useful for different purposes – for instance, if a shipping address is required or email must be provided.

```
private requestPaymentOptions = {
  requestPayerName: true,
  requestPayerPhone: false,
  requestPayerEmail: true,
  requestShipping: false,
  shippingType: 'shipping'
};
```

In this example, we ask the payer to provide an email and name only.

6. Last but not least, we show call show method on requestPayment in order to display the payment native prompt page.

```
async show(): Promise<any> {
    const canMakePayment = await this.canMakePaymentPromise;
    if (canMakePayment) {
      try {
        const response = await this.requestPayment.show();
        const status = await this.processResponseWithBackend
        (response);
        response.complete(status.success);
        return status.response;
      } catch (e) {
        return false;
      }
    }
}
```

There is another Promised-based method on requestPayment called canMakePayment(), which is essentially a helper to determine if the user has a supported payment method to make this payment before show() gets called. It may not be in all user agents; therefore, we need to feature detect.

Then we call show(), once the user is done, and Promise will get resolved with the user's selection details including contact information, credit card, shipping, and more. Now it's time to validate and process the payment with the back end.

Open header.component.html() and add the following button (see Figure 12-5):

```
<button mat-menu-item (click)="donateMe()" *ngIf="isWebPaymentSupported">
  <mat-icon>attach_money</mat-icon>
  <span>Donate</span>
</button>
```

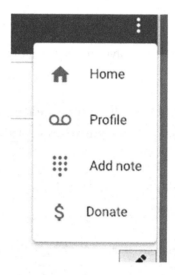

Figure 12-5. *Donate button where it triggers payment native UI*

Lastly, inject WebPaymentService into header.component.ts. donateMe() method should be defined, and it will call requestPayment and display the appropriate message to the user once it's resolved.

```
public isWebPaymentSupported: boolean;

  constructor(
    private webPayment: WebPaymentService,
  ) {
    this.isWebPaymentSupported = this.webPayment.isWebPaymentSupported;
  }
```

```
async donateMe() {
    const paymentResponse = await this.webPayment
      .constructPaymentRequest()
      .show();

    if (paymentResponse) {
      this.snackBar.open(
        `Successfully paid, Thank you for Donation ${paymentResponse.
        payerName}`
      );
    } else {
      // this.snackBar.open('Ops, sorry something went wrong with
        payment');
    }
}
```

We will build application and run and test it in the browser and mobile (See Figures 12-6 and 12-7).

Figure 12-6. *Payment native UI, Chrome, Mac*

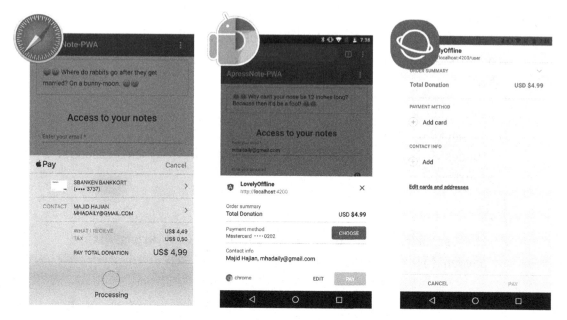

Figure 12-7. *Apple pay in Safari, Chrome, and Samsung internet browser display native payment UI*

Note   Clone `https://github.com/mhadaily/awesome-apress-pwa.git` and go to Chapter 13, 02-request-payment-api folder to find all sample codes.

Browsers Support

By the time of writing this book, almost all major browsers support this API either in production or a nightly build for both desktop and mobile, although they may also support them partially.

Video and Audio Capturing

The Media Streams is an API related to WebRTC, which provides support for streaming audio and video data. This API has been around for a while. New Promised-based `getUserMedia()` is a method that ask for user permission for microphone and camera; and, thus, you will get access to the live stream.

In this section, we will add a new feature to "add note" page, where users can save an interactive video with audio to their notes.

Note, we will not send this video to a server in this example, but the implementation will be ready to communicate to the back end in order to save the video and audio if needed.

In notes-add.component.html, we will add following html snippet:

```html
<div class="media-container" *ngIf="isMediaRecorderSupported">
     <h1>Add video with audio Note</h1>
     <div class="videos">
       <div class="video">
         <h2>LIVE STREAM</h2>
         <video #videoOutput autoplay muted></video>
       </div>
       <div class="video">
         <h2>RECORDED STREAM</h2>
         <video #recorded autoplay loop></video>
       </div>
     </div>
     <div class="buttons">
       <button mat-raised-button color="primary" (click)="record()"
       *ngIf="disabled.record" > Start Recording</button>
       <button mat-raised-button color="primary" (click)="stop()"
       *ngIf="disabled.stop"> Stop Recording </button>
       <button mat-raised-button color="secondary" (click)="play()"
       *ngIf="disabled.play"> Play Recording</button>
       <button mat-raised-button color="primary" (click)="download()"
       *ngIf="disabled.download">  Download Recording </button>
       <a #downloadLink href="">Download Link</a>
     </div>
   </div>
```

This code is pretty self-explanatory. We add the logic to notes-add.component.ts:

```
export class NotesAddComponent {
  @ViewChild('videoOutput') videoOutput: ElementRef;
  @ViewChild('recorded') recordedVideo: ElementRef;
  @ViewChild('downloadLink') downloadLink: ElementRef;
```

```
public disabled = { record: true, stop: false, play: false, download:
false };
public userID;
public errorMessages$ = new Subject();
public loading$ = new Subject();
public isMediaRecorderSupported: boolean;
private recordedBlobs;
private liveStream: any;
private mediaRecorder: any;

constructor(
  private router: Router,
  private data: DataService,
  private snackBar: SnackBarService
) {
  if (window.MediaRecorder) {
    this.isMediaRecorderSupported = true;
    this.getStream();
  } else {
    this.isMediaRecorderSupported = false;
  }
}

async getStream() {
  try {
    const stream = await navigator.mediaDevices.getUserMedia({
      audio: true,
      video: true
    });
    this.handleLiveStream(stream);
  } catch (e) {
    this.isMediaRecorderSupported = false;
    this.onSendError('No permission or something is wrong');
    return 'No permission or something is wrong';
  }
}
```

```
handleLiveStream(stream) {
  this.liveStream = stream;
  this.videoOutput.nativeElement.srcObject = stream;
}

getMediaRecorderOptions() {
  let options = {
    mimeType: 'video/webm;codecs=vp9',
    audioBitsPerSecond: 1000000, // 1 Mbps
    bitsPerSecond: 1000000, // 2 Mbps
    videoBitsPerSecond: 1000000 // 2 Mbps
  };
  if (!MediaRecorder.isTypeSupported(options.mimeType)) {
    console.log(`${options.mimeType} is not Supported`);
    options = { ...options, mimeType: 'video/webm;codecs=vp8' };
    if (!MediaRecorder.isTypeSupported(options.mimeType)) {
      console.log(`${options.mimeType} is not Supported`);
      options = { ...options, mimeType: 'video/webm' };
      if (!MediaRecorder.isTypeSupported(options.mimeType)) {
        console.log(`${options.mimeType} is not Supported`);
        options = { ...options, mimeType: " };
      }
    }
  }
  return options;
}

record() {
  this.recordedBlobs = [];
  this.disabled = { play: false, download: false, record: false, stop: true };
  this.mediaRecorder = new MediaRecorder(
    this.liveStream,
    this.getMediaRecorderOptions
  );
  this.mediaRecorder.ondataavailable = e => {
```

```
      {
        if (e.data) {
          this.recordedBlobs.push(e.data);
        }
      }
    };
    this.mediaRecorder.start();
    console.log('MediaRecorder started', this.mediaRecorder);
  }

  stop() {
    this.disabled = { play: true, download: true, record: true, stop: false };
    this.mediaRecorder.onstop = e => {
      this.recordedVideo.nativeElement.controls = true;
    };
    this.mediaRecorder.stop();
  }

  play() {
    this.disabled = { play: true, download: true, record: true, stop: false };
    const buffer = new Blob(this.recordedBlobs, { type: 'video/webm' });
    this.recordedVideo.nativeElement.src = window.URL.createObjectURL(buffer);
  }

  download() {
    const blob = new Blob(this.recordedBlobs, { type: 'video/webm' });
    const url = window.URL.createObjectURL(blob);
    this.downloadLink.nativeElement.url = url;
    this.downloadLink.nativeElement.download = `recording_${new Date().
    getTime()}.webm`;
    this.downloadLink.nativeElement.click();
    setTimeout(() => {
      window.URL.revokeObjectURL(url);
    }, 100);
  }

  onSaveNote(values) {
```

```
this.data.addNote(values).then(
  doc => {
    this.snackBar.open(`LOCAL: ${doc.id} has been succeffully saved`);
  },
  e => {
    this.errorMessages$.next('something is wrong when adding to DB');
  }
);
this.router.navigate(['/notes']);
}

onSendError(message) {
  this.errorMessages$.next(message);
 }
}
```

This code is straightforward. As always, it is a feature detection for MediaRecorder, and if it is supported by a browser, we will continue and show this feature to our user and will initialize getUserMedia(); therefore, we ask for audio and video permission as shown in Figure 12-8.

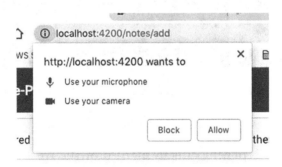

Figure 12-8. *Browser asks for permission for camera and microphone*

Once permission is granted, Promise gets resolved and the stream will be accessible (see Figure 12-9). When user clicks on tab "start recording" button, MediaRecorder constructor gets called with the live stream data and the options that gave already been defined.

We store each blob in an array until `stop()` method gets called. Once recording stops, media is ready to be played. By hitting "play" button, we will simply create a stream buffer of the stream array and by creating a `Blob URL`, we will assign it to an `src` of `<video>` tag.

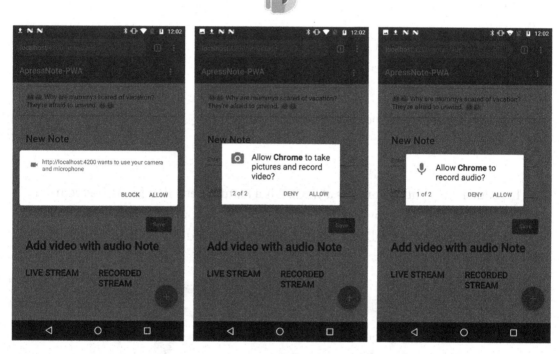

Figure 12-9. *Ask for permission for getting access to video and audio on Android mobile*

Ta-da, now the video is playing directly in the browser. We are also able to work on the downloadable version of this video (see Figure 12-10).

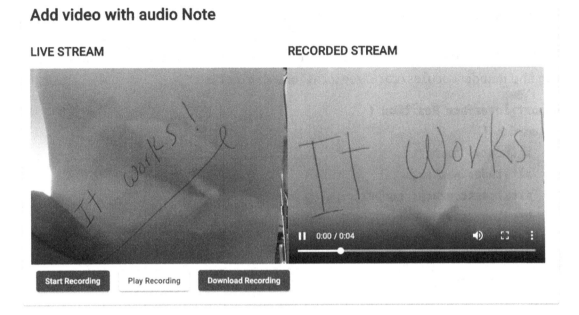

Figure 12-10. *Live stream and recorded playback*

By the tab or click on "Download" button, we will create a Blob from an array of `recordedBlob` and then will create a URL and assign to `<a>` tag thatI have defined in the template with `display: none` and then call `click()` to force browser opening download modal for user in order to ask them where this file must be saved on their system.

Note   Clone `https://github.com/mhadaily/awesome-apress-pwa.git` and go to Chapter 12, 03-camera-and-microphone-api folder to find all sample codes.

Browsers Support

At the time of writing this book, Opera, Chrome, and Firefox on desktop; and Chrome and Samsung internet on Android support most of the standard specs. Microsoft Edge also has this API under consideration. It also works on Safari 12 / iOS 12. I believe the API's future is bright.

Geolocation

The Geolocation API provides the user's location coordination and exposes it to the web application. The browser will ask for permission for privacy reasons. This Promised-based API has been around for a long time. You might even work with it already.

We will explore this API by creating a service called GeolocationService where you can find it under modules/core/geolocation.service.ts.

```
export interface Position {
  coords: {
    accuracy: number;
    altitude: number;
    altitudeAccuracy: number;
    heading: any;
    latitude: number;
    longitude: number;
    speed: number;
  };
  timestamp: number;
}

@Injectable()
export class GeolocationService {
  public isGeoLocationSupported: boolean;

  private geoOptions = {
    enableHighAccuracy: true, maximumAge: 30000, timeout: 27000
  };

  constructor() {
    if (navigator.geolocation) {
      this.isGeoLocationSupported = true;
    } else {
      // geolocation is not supported, fall back to other options
      this.isGeoLocationSupported = false;
    }
  }
}
```

```
getCurrentPosition(): Observable<Position> {
  return Observable.create(obs => {
    if (navigator.geolocation) {
      navigator.geolocation.getCurrentPosition(
        position => {
          obs.next(position);
          obs.complete();
        },
        error => {
          obs.error(error);
        }
      );
    }
  });
}

watchPosition(): Observable<Position> {
  return Observable.create(obs => {
    if (navigator.geolocation) {
      navigator.geolocation.watchPosition(
        position => {
          obs.next(position);
        },
        error => {
          obs.error(error);
        },
        this.geoOptions
      );
    }
  });
}
}
```

Let's break it down.

1. As usual, a feature detection to ensure geolocation is available.

2. Define getCurrentPosition(), I am going to convert geolocation.getCurrentPosition() callbacks into an observable.

3. Define watchPosition(), we do the same with geolocation. watchPosition() and turn its callbacks into an observable.

4. We have already defined my Position interface by which geolocation methods provide.

What I'd like to do is to add user coordination to each note to keep the location as it saves. Thus, we can later show the user's note's coordination or exact address using a third-party map provider like Google Map. Since we are saving all coordination data, we will be able to convert this coordination to a meaningful address using third-party map providers in the back end or even in the front end based on application needs.

At the moment, to keep in simple and short, let's just display the current latitude and longitude to the user.

First, we inject geolocation service into NotesAddComponent, then we will call getCurrentPosition() and assign it to my local location$ variable where we transform a position object into a simple string.

```
public isGeoLocationSupported = this.geoLocation.isGeoLocationSupported;
public location$: Observable<string> = this.geoLocation
    .getCurrentPosition()
    .pipe(map(p =>
        `Latitude:${p.coords.latitude}
        Longitude:${p.coords.longitude}`
        ));

  constructor(
    private router: Router,
    private data: DataService,
    private snackBar: SnackBarService,
    private geoLocation: GeolocationService
  ) {}
```

Finally, add the following html snippet where we use location$ observable with async pipe; however, we first check if geolocation is available by using *ngIf (see permission dialog in Figure 12-11).

```
<h4 *ngIf="isGeoLocationSupported">You location is {{ location$ |
async }}</h4>
```

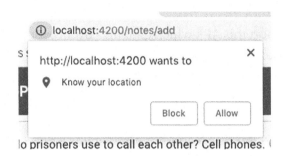

Figure 12-11. *Browser asks for location permission*

Once permission is allowed by the user, the browser will provide coordination data on each method call (see Figure 12-12).

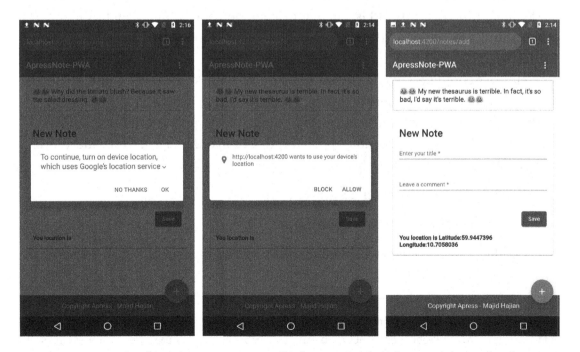

Figure 12-12. *Geolocation permission dialog on Android; once it's resolved, coordination is displayed*

Note   Clone `https://github.com/mhadaily/awesome-apress-pwa.git`
and go to Chapter 12, 04-geolocation-api folder to find all sample codes.

Browsers Support

All major browsers support this API, which globally covers over 93 percent of the market
according to the caniuse.com website.[1]

Web Bluetooth

This Promised-based API is a new technology that opens a new era for Internet of Things
through the web. It allows a web application to get connected to Bluetooth Low Energy
(BLE) devices.

Imagine developing a PWA where we are able to get access to Bluetooth and get
control over devices such as smart home appliances, health accessories, ONLY with web
API consistency across all browsers in different platforms.

Keep in mind that this API is still being developed and API may slightly change
in the future. I recommend the following implementation status documentation on
GitHub.[2]

Before we continue, I would suggest studying the basic knowledge of how Bluetooth
Low Energy (BLE) and the Generic Attribute Profile (GATT)[3] work.

In this section, we simulate a BLE device using BLE Peripheral Simulator[4] app on
Android and will pair my PWA note app to that device in order to receive a battery level
number. What we have done is this:

1. Installed BLE Peripheral Simulator app

2. Select Battery Service to advertise

3. Keep the screen on and put the battery level to 73

---

[1]`https://caniuse.com/#search=geolocation`
[2]`https://github.com/WebBluetoothCG/web-bluetooth/blob/master/implementation-status.md`
[3]`https://www.bluetooth.com/specifications/gatt/generic-attributes-overview`
[4]Search "BLE Peripheral Simulator" on the Google Play store.

Let's get started.

First, we will create my WebBluetoothService and import it in CoreModule.

```
@Injectable()
export class WebBluetoothService {
  public isWebBluetoothSupported: boolean;
  private GATT_SERVICE_NAME = 'battery_service';
  private GATT_SERVICE_CHARACTERISTIC = 'battery_level';

  constructor() {
    if (navigator.bluetooth) {
      this.isWebBluetoothSupported = true;
    }
  }

  async getBatteryLevel(): Promise<any> {
    try {
      // step 1, scan for devices and pair
      const device = await navigator.bluetooth.requestDevice({
        // acceptAllDevices: true
        filters: [{ services: [this.GATT_SERVICE_NAME] }]
      });
      // step 2: connect to device
      const connectedDevice = await this.connectDevice(device);
      // step 3 : Getting Battery Service
      const service = await this.getPrimaryService(connectedDevice, this.
      GATT_SERVICE_NAME);
      // step 4: Read Battery level characterestic
      const characteristic = await this.getCharacteristic(service, this.
      GATT_SERVICE_CHARACTERISTIC);
      // step 5: ready battery level
      const value = await characteristic.readValue();
      // step 6: return value
      return `Battery Level is ${value.getUint8(0)}%`;
    } catch (e) {
      console.error(e);
```

CHAPTER 12   MODERN WEB APIS

```
      return `something is wrong: ${e}`;
    }
  }

  private connectDevice(device): Promise<any> {
    return device.gatt.connect();
  }

  private getPrimaryService(connectedDevice, serviceName): Promise<any> {
    return connectedDevice.getPrimaryService(serviceName);
  }

  private getCharacteristic(service, characterestic): Promise<any> {
    return service.getCharacteristic(characterestic);
  }
}
```

This service is simple. We followed these steps:

1. Detect if bluetooth is available.

2. Call requestDevice() with proper configuration where we ask
    browser to filter and show us what we are interested in. There is
    potentially an option to ask for checking all devices; however, it's
    not recommended regarding battery health.

    To make the service simple, we have statically defined GATT
    service name and characteristic.

3. Try to connect to device once prompt modal appears.

4. Call getPrimaryService() to retrieve battery service.

5. By calling getCharacteristic(), we will ask for battery_level.

6. Once characteristic was resolved, we will read the value.

It seems a bit complex and confusing even though this a very simple device and the
documentation is clear. The more you work with these types of devices and technologies,
the better you will become at figuring it all out.

You can only ask a browser to discover devices by click or tab on a button; thus, we'll add a button under the menu in `header.component.html` and ensure with `ngIf` that the button appears when it's supported.

```
<button mat-menu-item (click)="getBatteryLevel()" *ngIf="isWebBluetooth
Supported">
    <mat-icon>battery_unknown</mat-icon>
    <span>Battery Level</span>
</button>
```

Finally, I will define my `getBatteryLevel` method in `header.component.ts`, which only shows a message with the battery level once all promises are resolved (see Figure 12-13).

```
async getBatteryLevel() {
    const level = await this.bluetooth.getBatteryLevel();
    this.snackBar.open(level);
}
```

Note   Clone `https://github.com/mhadaily/awesome-apress-pwa.git` and go to Chapter 12, 05-web-bluetooth-api folder to find all sample codes.

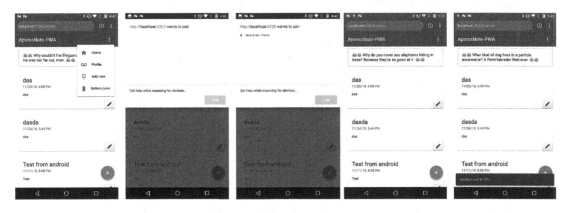

Figure 12-13. *Web Bluetooth API: pair a device and read a characteristic and display a message once all Promises are resolved*

The example above unfolds read possibilities from a BLE device; however, writing[5] to Bluetooth characteristics and subscribing[6] to receive GATT notifications are also another case.

We have reviewed the basics of Web Bluetooth and hope that it excites you enough to get started with this awesome web technology.

There is a great Angular library for Web Bluetooth with Observable API by my community friend Wassim Chegham – and you can install by running the following command:

```
npm i -S @manekinekko/angular-web-bluetooth @types/web-bluetooth
```

Find the documentation on GitHub https://github.com/manekinekko/angular-web-bluetooth.

Browsers Support

Browsers that support this API, at the time of writing this book, are Chrome Desktop for both Windows and Mac as well as Android, Samsung internet, and Opera. I hope in the future, especially when you are reading this section, there will be more browsers supporting Web Bluetooth API.

Web USB

This Promised-based API provides a safe way to expose USB devices to the web via browsers using JavaScript high-level APIs. This is still a relatively new API and may change over time, implementation is limited, and bugs are reported.

Web USB API by default needs HTTPS, and similar to Web Bluetooth it must be called via a user gesture such as a touch or mouse click. Devices similar to a keyboard and mouse are not accessible to this API.

---

[5]https://www.bluetooth.com/specifications/gatt/viewer?attributeXmlFile=org.bluetooth.characteristic.heart_rate_control_point.xml

[6]https://www.bluetooth.com/specifications/gatt/viewer?attributeXmlFile=org.bluetooth.characteristic.heart_rate_measurement.xml&u=org.bluetooth.characteristic.heart_rate_measurement.xml

I believe Web USB opens a new window where it brings a lot of opportunities for academic purposes, students, manufacturers, and developers. Imagine this instead of an online developer tool that can access to a USB board directly or manufacturers who need to write native drivers; instead they will be able to develop a cross-platform JavaScript SDK. Think of a hardware support center who can access directly through their website to my device and diagnose or debug. We can count more and more case studies; however, I should mention that this technology is still growing and, if not right now, will be a mind-blowing feature for the web in the coming future. Truly, the web is amazing; isn't it?

Enough talking, let's get started and explorer the API. To keep it simple and give you an idea how Web USB works, we going to connect my "Transcend Pen drive," and once it's connected, I will just show a message where it displays hardware information including "serial number."

First, I write a service called WebUSBService and import to CoreModule.

```
@Injectable()
export class WebUSBService {
  public isWebUSBSupported: boolean;

  constructor(private snackBar: SnackBarService) {
    if (navigator.usb) {
      this.isWebUSBSupported = true;
    }
  }

  async requestDevice() {
    try {
      const usbDeviceProperties = { name: 'Transcend Information, Inc.',
      vendorId: 0x8564 };
      const device = await navigator.usb.requestDevice({ filters:
      [usbDeviceProperties] });
      // await device.open();
      console.log(device);
      return `
      USB device name: ${device.productName}, Manifacture is ${device.
      manufacturerName}
```

```
        USB Version is: ${device.usbVersionMajor}.${device.
        usbVersionMinor}.${device.usbVersionSubminor}
        Product Serial Number is ${device.serialNumber}
        `;
    } catch (error) {
      return 'Error: ' + error.message;
    }
  }

  async getDevices() {
    const devices = await navigator.usb.getDevices();
    devices.map(device => {
      console.log(device.productName); // "Mass Storage Device"
      console.log(device.manufacturerName); // "JetFlash"
      this.snackBar.open(
        `this. USB device name: ${device.productName}, Manifacture is
        ${device.manufacturerName} is connected.`
      );
    });
  }
}
```

Let's break it down:

1. Feature detection to ensure "usb" is available.

2. Define requestDevice method, it calls navigator.usb.
   requestDevice(). I needed to explicitly filter my USB device by
   vendorID. I didn't magically come up with vendor hexadecimal
   number; what I did was to search and find my device name
   'Transcend' in this list http://www.linux-usb.org/usb.ids.

3. Define getDevices method, and it calls navigator.usb.
   getDevices(); once resolved, it will return a list of devices that are
   connected to the origin.

We add two buttons in header.component.html, which on click call getDevices()
and requestDevice() methods respectively.

```
<button mat-menu-item (click)="getUSBDevices()"
*ngIf="isWebUSBSupported">
  <mat-icon>usb</mat-icon>
  <span>USB Devices List</span>
</button>
<button mat-menu-item (click)="pairUSBDevice()"
*ngIf="isWebUSBSupported">
  <mat-icon>usb</mat-icon>
  <span>USB Devices Pair</span>
</button>
```

Inject `WebUSBService` to `header.component.ts`. Make sure buttons are visible if `isWebUSBSupported` is true.

```
constructor(private webUsb: WebUSBService) {
        this.isWebUSBSupported = this.webUsb.isWebUSBSupported;
}

  getUSBDevices() {
    this.webUsb.getDevices();
  }

  async pairUSBDevice() {
    const message = await this.webUsb.requestDevice();
    this.snackBar.open(message);
  }
```

By clicking on "USB Devices Pair," a list appears where it shows my device and I can pair it (see Figure 12-14).

Figure 12-14. *A device in the list based on the filter options when* `requestDevice()` *gets called. Once paired, based on logic, a message appears that shows device information such as serial number, device name, manufacturer, USB version, etc. Once device is connected, it's ready to transfer data in and out.*

Once the pair is completed successfully, the device is ready to be opened and data can be transferred in and out.

For example, here is an example for a device to communicate with:

```
await device.open();
await device.selectConfiguration(1) // Select configuration #1
await device.claimInterface(0) // Request exclusive control
                                   over interface #0
await device.controlTransferOut({
        "recipient": "interface",
        "requestType": "class",
        "request": 9,
        "value": 0x0300,
      "index": 0 })
const result = await device.transferIn(8, 64); // Ready to
                                               receive data⁷

// and you need to read the result...
```

---

[7]https://beyondlogic.org/usbnutshell/usb4.shtml

This information is specific to each device. However, the methods are an API in the browser.

In general, the Web USB API provides all endpoint types of USB devices:

- **Interrupt transfers:**

  Used for typically nonperiodic, small device "initiated" communication by calling `transferIn(endpointNumber, length)` and `transferOut(endpointNumber, data)`

- **Control transfers:**

  Used for command and status operations by calling `controlTransferIn(setup, length)` and `controlTransferOut(setup, data)`

- **Bulk transfers:**

  Used for large data such as print-job sent to a printer by calling `transferIn(endpointNumber, length)` and `transferOut(endpointNumber, data)`

- **Isochronous transfers:**

  Used for continuous and periodic data, such as an audio or video stream by calling `isochronousTransferIn(endpointNumber, packetLengths)` and `isochronousTransferOut(endpointNumber, data, packetLengths)`

Last but not least, it may happen that users connect or disconnect the device from their system. There are two events that can be listened to and acted on accordingly.

```
navigator.usb.onconnect = event => {
  // event.device will bring the connected device
  // do something here
  console.log('this device connected again: ' + event.device);
};

navigator.usb.ondisconnect = event => {
  // event.device will bring the disconnected device
```

```
    // do something here
    console.log('this device disconnected: ', event.device);
};
```

Debugging USB in Chrome is easier with the internal page `chrome://device-log` where you can see all USB device-related events in one single place.

Note   Clone `https://github.com/mhadaily/awesome-apress-pwa.git` and go to Chapter 12, 06-web-usb-api folder to find all sample codes.

Browsers Support

Browsers that support this API, at the time of writing this book, are Chrome For desktop and Android as well as Opera. While the API is evolving and being developed rapidly, I hope we soon see better support in the browsers.

Summary

In this chapter, we have just explored six web APIs. Although they are not an essential part of a PWA, they help to build an app that is even closer to native apps.

As I wrote in the chapter's introduction, these are not the only new APIs that are coming to web. There are many others that are either under development or consideration to be developed soon.

I am very excited about the future of web development as I can see how it will open endless opportunities in front of us to build and ship a much better web application.

CHAPTER 13

PWA with Angular and Workbox

Up until this point in the book, I bet on the Angular Service Worker module and built on top of that. It has many advantages, including less code; tested in high scale, reliability, and stability; Angular way of communicating with Service Worker; automatic build with CLI; and great support from the Angular team. It truly gives us peace of mind.

However, like every other tool, there are also disadvantages too. One of the downsides is that Angular Service Worker is not extendable in a proper way (at least at the time of writing this book), which means that you are not able to add your own logic to Service Worker if you want; or you may need some of the new Service Worker APIs or features that Angular Service Worker doesn't support yet, and it may take some time until the team provides a public API to Angular developers.

Luckily there are a few tools out there which support generating Service Workers with ease, although they might be more complex than an Angular Service Worker. One of the best is Workbox, a library from Google Chrome team. Workbox is a modular library that provides an extremely easy way to write our Service Worker. Workbox CLI (command-line interface) consists of a Node.js program and can be run from a Mac, Window, and Unix-compatible command-line environment. It wraps the Workbox build module under the hook, which generates an entire Service Worker or just generates a list of assets to precache that could be used within an existing Service Worker.

In this chapter, we strive to explore Workbox capabilities and will build the Note PWA once more with Workbox. You will see what the differences are between Workbox setup and Angular Service Worker. Thus, you will be able to decide, based on your project, which one you have to choose in order to build your next, fantastic PWA.

© Majid Hajian 2019
M. Hajian, *Progressive Web Apps with Angular*, https://doi.org/10.1007/978-1-4842-4448-7_13

Angular and Workbox Setup

Before we go further, we will explorer Workbox and explain how it works.

Workbox is a modular library that helps to generate an entire Service Worker with minimal effort. It can generate an SW automatically or will allow us to write a custom Service Worker, and it will inject scripts based on the configuration (aka manifest) and generate an entire Service Worker.

Workbox-cli provides an easy way of integrating Workbox into a command-line build process with a flexible configuration. To install the CLI:

```
npm install workbox-cli --global
```

Or if you would like to install locally (which I prefer to):

```
npm install workbox-cli --save-dev // to run `npx workbox [mode]`
```

Workbox CLI has four different modes, which are the following:

- **wizard**: a step-by-step guide to set up Workbox for your project.

- **generateSW**: generates a complete Service Worker for you.

- **injectManifest**: injects the assets to precache into your project.

- **copyLibraries**: copy the Workbox libraries into a directory.

Workbox consists of different modules that a developer can decide to use. These modules are the following:

- **Core**: common code that each module relies on, for instance, log level.

- **Precaching**: simplifies precaching app-shell on install event.

- **Routing**: perhaps the most important module, where you can intercept a network request and respond accordingly.

- **Strategies**: provides the most common caching strategies so it's easy to apply them in your Service Worker.

- **Expiration**: allows you to limit the number of entries in a cache and / or remove entries that have been cached for a long period of time.

- **BackgroundSync**: detects a network request's failing due to connectivity issue and queue them in IndexedDB and will retry on a 'sync' event, which the browser fires when a user reconnects. This module also provides a fallback for those browsers that still don't support Background sync APIs. This feature is not available in Angular Service Worker as of the time of writing this book.

- **GoogleAnalytics**: helps to detect failed requests to Measurement Protocol, store in IndexedDB, and retry once connectivity is back.

- **CacheableResponse**: provides a standard way of determining whether a response should be cached based on its numeric status code, the presence of a header with a specific value, or a combination of the two.

- **BroadcastUpdate**: provides a standard way of notifying Window Clients that a cached response has been updated. This module uses `Broadcast Channel AI` to announce the update. In Workbox 4, it will automatically fall back to `postMessage() API` for those browsers that don't support Broadcast Channel API.

- Navigation**Preload**:[1] will handle checking at runtime to see if the current browser supports navigation preload; and if it does, it will automatically create an activate event handler to enable it.

- **RangeRequests**: when making a request, a range header can be set that tells the server to return only a portion of the full request. This is useful for certain files like a video file, where a user might change where to play the video.

We know the basics now. Let's continue and add Workbox to our Angular project.

Note   Clone `https://github.com/mhadaily/awesome-apress-pwa.git` and go to Chapter 13, folder 01-starter does not have Service Worker implementation and is ready to start adding Workbox.

---

[1]https://developers.google.com/web/updates/2017/02/navigation-preload

Workbox Wizard Mode

The first and easiest way to work with Workbox is to use the Wizard mode. Workbox CLI asks you a few questions. Then `workbox-config.js` is created, and you can add or generate a Service Worker to your build process. It is possible, indeed, to do all these steps manually by creating `workbox-config` file.

Run wizard mode with Workbox CLI:[2]

```
npx workbox wizard
```

And then questions appear, which are listed below:

1. What is the root of your web app (i.e., which directory do you deploy)? (**dist** or could be dist/project-name)

2. Which file types would you like to precache? (Press \<space> to select, \<a> to toggle all, \<i> to inverse selection) (**css,js,txt,png,ico.html.json**)

3. Where would you like your Service Worker file to be saved? (**dist/sw.js**)

4. Where would you like to save these configuration options? (**workbox-config.js**)

Config file will be generated with minimal setup in a file called `workbox-config.js` as you have chosen in the wizard:

```
module.exports = {
  globDirectory: 'dist/', // this could be dist/project-name in an Angular
  project
  globPatterns: ['**/*.{js,txt,png,ico,html,css}'  ],
  globIgnores: ['stats.json'],
  swDest: 'dist/sw.js', // this could be dist/project-name in an Angular
  project
  importWorkboxFrom: 'local',
 maximumFileSizeToCacheInBytes: 4 * 1024 * 1024 // not more than 4MB
};
```

---

[2]https://developers.google.com/web/tools/workbox/modules/workbox-cli

1. globDirectory: the folder that Workbox needs to scan for the patterns or ignore files provided in the next property.

2. globPatterns: an array of globs in order to add them to precache, essentially to generate our app-shell.

3. globIgnores: an array of glob type that will be ignored for app-shell.

4. swDest: folder where sw.js will be placed after generating.

5. imporWorkboxFrom: defines how Workbox library should be imported into Service Worker file.

   a. cdn: script will be imported from Google Cloud storage. For example: https://storage.googleapis.com/workbox-cdn/releases/3.6.3/workbox-sw.js

   b. local: Workbox libraries must be copied to dist folder and be imported into Service Worker. In order to copy Workbox libraries, run npx workbox copyLibraries dist

   c. none: will import nothing.

6. maximumFileSizeToCacheInBytes: a guard if discovered file is oversized.

This configuration is enough for generating a Service Worker to precache the static assets and app-shell. Once the Angular build is done, by running the command below, Workbox will be generating a Service Worker automatically:

```
npx workbox generateSW workbox-config.js
```

Tada! The auto-generated sw.js is in dist folder, so let's glance at it:

```
importScripts(`workbox-v3.6.3/workbox-sw.js`);
workbox.precaching.precacheAndRoute([
  {
    "url": "favicon.ico",
    "revision": "b9aa7c338693424aae99599bec875b5f"
  },
```

```json
{
  "url": "index.html",
  "revision": "ba3375f16e2a5c7fdf36600745e88e98"
},
{
  "url": "styles.356e924fea446d033420.css",
  "revision": "b7a968bbc1b49cd4f6478cae97fed4f6"
},
{
  "url": "1.ee064b5075b0e24f691c.js",
  "revision": "1a0cf93d36be20c46550e5a85a91aeae"
},
{
  "url": "5.902dda00d476d615f591.js",
  "revision": "28265e0a43435a8acebad181a6f02056"
},
{
  "url": "6.58566fec934a1864fc29.js",
  "revision": "33af875f4f0454106aa0e23f66ee13d0"
},
{
  "url": "lazy-fonts.js",
  "revision": "62693c91e34c656d59025a6fb3e22f99"
},
{
  "url": "main.e1f6fe9ffe4709effd6b.js",
  "revision": "6debac0612cf6f10ab6140e18f310899"
},
{
  "url": "polyfills.c1da48c5c45ccdef1eb4.js",
  "revision": "7c508c4c2a0d8521e03909fb9e015ebe"
},
```

```
    {
      "url": "runtime.0c53ce34d2b71056f3b2.js",
      "revision": "ad44f617b496d7cf73f3e6338864abe1"
    }
]);
```

First the Workbox library is imported, then an array of app-shell assets in the precaching module is used in order to put them into a cache on the 'install' event in Service Worker.

Note   Workbox uses a revision hash similar to Angular Service Worker to detect file changes.

Now it is time to register sw.js. We will add my Service Worker registration in the main.ts file where Angular bootstraps AppModule.

```
document.addEventListener('DOMContentLoaded', async () => {
  try {
    const module = await platformBrowserDynamic().bootstrapModule(AppModule);

  const app = module.injector.get(ApplicationRef);

    const whenStable = await app.isStable
      .pipe(filter((stable: boolean) => !!stable), take(1)).toPromise();

    window.onload = async () => {
      if (whenStable && navigator.serviceWorker && environment.production) {

        const registration = await navigator
                        .serviceWorker.register('/sw.js', { scope:
                  '/' });
        console.log(`sw.js has been registered, scope is: ${registration.
        scope}`);

      }
    };
  } catch (err) {
    console.error(err);
  }
});
```

To break down:

1. Once Angular `AppModule` is bootstrapped and promised to be resolved, we'll get access to `ApplicationRef` through a dependency injection to find out if the application is stable.

2. To ensure registration is as performant as possible, we keep the logic in `window load` event.

3. Once the Angular bootstrap is resolved and `AppModule` is stable, which means there is not any kind of recurrent asynchronous task when the application starts: for example, a polling process started with setInterval or Rxjs Interval.

   We will do feature detection for Service Worker as part of progressive enhancement as well as production environment in order to prevent conflicts in development.

Finally, we will add a Workbox command to my build pipeline for generating a Service Worker right after the Angular build for production is done:

```
"build:prod": "ng build --prod && workbox copyLibraries dist && workbox generateSW workbox-config.js",
```

Workbox injectManifest

Workbox `generateSW` is simple, fully configuration based, and makes it easy to generate an entire Service Worker. It works perfectly for many web apps. However, what if we want to add our custom code for any reason to Service Worker? Every time Workbox generates SW file, our custom code will be overwritten. There must be a solution.

Luckily, Workbox provides `injectManifest` mode in which you can stay in control of your Service Worker file and let Workbox generate part of it. All your configuration is written as code in a custom Service Worker instead of a configuration file.

To use `injectManifest`, you need to specify where the source of the custom Service Worker is by `swSrc` property. I have created a `sw-srouce.js` in the `src` folder and add it to the config file.

```
module.exports = {
  globDirectory: 'dist/',
  globPatterns: ['**/*.{js,txt,png,ico,html,css}'],
```

```
  globIgnores: ['stats.json'],
  swDest: 'dist/sw.js',
  swSrc: 'src/sw-source.js',
  maximumFileSizeToCacheInBytes: 4 * 1024 * 1024 // not more than 4MB
};
```

Now we need to create "Source Service Worker." Let's get started. First things first, though; we need to import Workbox.

```
// current workbox version
const MODULE_PATH_PREFIX = 'workbox-v3.6.3';
// to copy workbox files run npm run copyWorkboxModules or 'npx workbox
copyLibraries dist'
// this synchronously load workbox locally, if you prefer CDN use the linke
// mentioned earlier
importScripts(`${MODULE_PATH_PREFIX}/workbox-sw.js`);

if (!workbox) {
  // if workbox for any resson didn't happen simply ignore the rest of file
  console.error(`Something went wrong while loading ${modulePathPrefix}/
  workbox-sw.js`);
} else {
        // OUR CODE
}
```

We can modify the Workbox config and SW update cycle based on requirements.

```
// set module path prefix
workbox.setConfig({ modulePathPrefix: MODULE_PATH_PREFIX });

// overwrite cache name details if you like, if you don't write this line,
// Workbox uses default settings.
    workbox.core.setCacheNameDetails({
    prefix: 'angular-aprees-note-pwa',
    suffix: 'v1',
     precache: 'install-time',
     runtime: 'run-time',
    googleAnalytics: 'ga'
    });
```

```
// Modify SW update cycle
// forces the waiting service worker to become the active service worker.
  workbox.skipWaiting();
// ensure that updates to the underlying service worker take effect
immediately // for both the current client and all other active clients.
  workbox.clientsClaim();
```

Workbox still will generate precaches assets; however, we need to tell Workbox explicitly where assets (manifestEntrys) should be concatenated in the source file. We can configure this in two ways:

- By adding a different RegExp containing two capture groups. The manifest array will be injected in between the capture groups.

  For example: injectionPointRegexp: new RegExp('(const myManifest =)(;)'),

  default is: /(\.precacheAndRoute\(\)\s*\[\s*\]\s*(\))/

- Or, we can add a placeholder in the source Service Worker file by using a precaching module that calls precacheAndRoute([]) by passing an empty array.

  ```
  /* PRE-CACHE STERATEGY */

  // this is a placeholder. All assets that must be precached
  will be injected here
  // automatically
  workbox.precaching.precacheAndRoute([]);
  ```

In Chapter 4, we defined assetGroups in ngsw-config.json. If you forgot, please quickly review Chapter 4 where ngsw-config.json assetGroups was explained.

For prefetch installMode, I had a list of globs that can be written in the Workbox config file, too.

```
globPatterns: [
  '**/favicon.ico', '**/index.html', '**/*.css', '**/*.js'
],
```

We have done precaching so far by instructing Workbox to add app-shell resources to cache where it actually happens during the 'install event' in Service Worker. Now we need to write our logic for a runtime cache with different cache strategies. The Workbox routing module allows us to register routes by defining a regular expression that matches a specific request and then assigns a cache strategy to it.

Before we continue, let me remind you that we had explored advanced cache strategies in Chapter 4, and basically the Workbox strategy module provides them to you effortlessly.

- Stale-While-Revalidate:`workbox.strategies.staleWhileRevalidate()`

- Cache First (Cache Falling Back to Network): `workbox.strategies.cacheFirst()`

- Network First (Network Falling Back to Cache): `workbox.strategies.networkFirst()`

- Network Only: `workbox.strategies.networkOnly()`

- Cache Only: `workbox.strategies.cacheOnly()`

All of these methods are configurable by passing an object argument containing the following:

- `cacheName`: the name of the cache to use in the strategy.

- `plugins`: an array of plugins that will have their life-cycle methods called when fetching and caching a request. We can use all Workbox plugins such as `expiration`, `cacheableResponse`, `broadcastUpdate`, and `backgroundSync` as well as a custom plugin by passing in instances.

Let's register two routes for caching images and Google fonts requested dynamically in `sw-source.js`.

```
workbox.routing.registerRoute(
  new RegExp('/(.*)assets(.*).(?:png|gif|jpg)/'),
  // cacheFirst for images
  workbox.strategies.cacheFirst({
    cacheName: 'images-cache',
```

```
  plugins: [
              // set cache expiration restrictions to use in the
              strategy
      new workbox.expiration.Plugin({
        // only cache 50 requests
        maxEntries: 50,
        // only cache requests for 30 days
        maxAgeSeconds: 30 * 24 * 60 * 60
      })
    ]
  })
);
// we need to handle Google fonts
workbox.routing.registerRoute(
  new RegExp('https://fonts.(?:googleapis|gstatic).com/(.*)'),
  // stale-while-revalidate for fonts
  workbox.strategies.staleWhileRevalidate({
    cacheName: 'google-apis-cache',
    plugins: [
              // set cache expiration restrictions to use in the
              strategy
      new workbox.expiration.Plugin({
        // only cache 50 requests
        maxEntries: 10,
        // only cache requests for 10 days
        maxAgeSeconds: 10 * 24 * 60 * 60
      })
    ]
  })
);
```

Having looked at ngsw-config from Chapter 4, in dataGroups, we defined
api-network-first and api-cache-first. Let's register those routes with Workbox.

```
// API with network-first strategy
 workbox.routing.registerRoute(
   new RegExp('https://firestore.googleapis.com/v1beta1/(.*)'),
   workbox.strategies.networkFirst({
     cacheName: 'api-network-first',
     plugins: [
       new workbox.expiration.Plugin({
         maxEntries: 100
       })
     ]
   })
 );
 // API with cache-first strategy
 workbox.routing.registerRoute(
   new RegExp('https://icanhazdadjoke.com/(.*)'),
   workbox.strategies.cacheFirst({
     cacheName: 'api-cache-first',
     plugins: [
       new workbox.expiration.Plugin({
         maxEntries: 20,
         maxAgeSeconds: 15 * 60 * 60 // 15 min
       })
     ]
   })
 );
```

A routing module allows us to add a whitelist or blacklist for a particular navigation route. We will use the same Regex from the Angular manifest file.

```
// Register whitelist and black list
 workbox.routing.registerNavigationRoute('/index.html', {
   whitelist: [new RegExp('^\\/.*$')],
   blacklist: [
     new RegExp('/restricted/(.*)'),
     new RegExp('^\\/(?:.+\\/)?[^/]*\\.[^/]*$'),
```

```
    new RegExp('^\\/(?:.+\\/)?[^/]*__[^/]*$'),
    new RegExp('^\\/(?:.+\\/)?[^/]*__[^/]*\\/.*$')
  ]
});
```

Time to build the application. To simplify the build process, we will add two npm scripts to packge.json and add injectManifest to the production build script.

```
"injectManifest": "workbox copyLibraries dist && workbox injectManifest",
"copyWorkboxModules": "workbox copyLibraries dist"
"build:prod:shell": "ng run lovely-offline:app-shell:production && npm run
injectManifest",
```

Let's build and run the app. After the first visit, test the application in offline mode (see Figure 13-1).

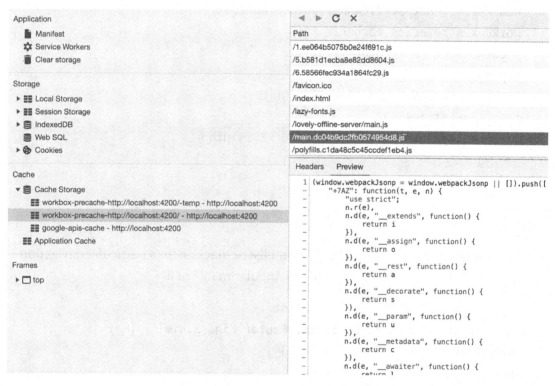

Figure 13-1. *Cache storage after writing our logic for Workbox*

Note   Clone `https://github.com/mhadaily/awesome-apress-pwa.git` and go to Chapter 12, 02-workbox-setup folder to find all sample codes. You can build the application and test in your browser by running `npm run prod`.

Summary

In this chapter, we managed to set up an Angular project with Workbox and generate our custom Service Worker where it caches app-shell resources and intercepts network requests based on the pattern that we have defined, along with an appropriate strategy.

You may read this chapter while Workbox 4 is being released. There are a few breaking changes in Workbox 4, and many of the techniques that have been revealed in this chapter can be used for version 4, too, although there might be additional features.

In the next chapter, we will explore advanced features such as background sync, which helps to retry failed requests due to no connectivity; push notifications for engaging; update flow notifications that inform users to refresh an application in order to receive the latest update; and offline analytics.

CHAPTER 14

Advanced Workbox

In the previous chapter, I taught you how to use Workbox in an Angular project whether you have used Angular Service Worker and you want to replace it with Workbox, or you simply want to start a new project from scratch.

In this chapter, I will show you how to implement Background sync, push notification, offline analytics, and how to notify a user if there is a new update available.

Dealing with Updates

When responding to a request with cached entries, while being fast, it comes with a trade-off that uses my end up seeing stable data. Workbox provides broadcast update module, which helps to notify Window clients in a standard way when there is an available update for a cached responded. While Workbox, by default, compares `Conent-Length`, `ETag`, and `Last-Modified` headers for detecting updates, we can still define our custom headers to be checked.

We start implementing a channel for broadcasting a message if there will be an update available for precached assets. In `sw-source.js`, we will add the `broadcastUpdate` plugin to the precaching module in order to open a new channel to receive an update notification message:

```
workbox.precaching.addPlugins([new
workbox.broadcastUpdate.Plugin('app-shell-update')]);
```

Or we can use this plugin along with `staleWhileRevalidate` caching strategy since that strategy involves returning a cached response immediately, but also provides a mechanism for updating the cache asynchronously. While the first argument of the plugin is channel name, the second one is an object that provides options to the function.

© Majid Hajian 2019
M. Hajian, *Progressive Web Apps with Angular*, https://doi.org/10.1007/978-1-4842-4448-7_14

For instance, we can pass headersToCheck, which is an array to define all the custom headers that must be checked for detecting changes and notifying throughout the channel.

```
workbox.routing.registerRoute(
  new RegExp('https://fonts.(?:googleapis|gstatic).com/(.*)'),
  workbox.strategies.staleWhileRevalidate({
    cacheName: 'google-apis-cache',
    plugins: [
      new workbox.expiration.Plugin({
        maxEntries: 10,
        maxAgeSeconds: 10 * 24 * 60 * 60 // 10 Days
      })
      // new workbox.broadcastUpdate.Plugin('apis-updates', {
      //    headersToCheck: ['X-Custom-Header']
      // })
    ]
  })
);
```

In the Angular app-component, we need to listen to the channels that we have opened in Service Worker in order to receive the message and perform an action accordingly. For instance, a snack bar that has update action button will be shown when a message is received. Once clicked or tabbed on the "update me" action button, we will force the window to be reloaded, which helps that a new update gets in place automatically.

```
ngOnInit() {
  this.joke$ = this.db.getRandomDadJoke();
  this.checkForUpdates();
}

checkForUpdates() {
  const updateChannel = new this.window.native.BroadcastChannel
  ('app-shell-update');
  updateChannel.addEventListener('message', event => {
    console.log(event);
```

```
  this.snackBar
    .open('Newer version of the app is available', 'Update me!')
    .onAction()
    .subscribe(() => {
      this.window.native.location.reload();
    });
  });
}
```

The `window` object may not be available everywhere that Angular is running such as mobile or web workers; therefore, you notice that we are using `WindowRef` service injected in app-component instead of getting a reference to `window` object directly to change the concrete runtime instance of a given object based on the environment. It may look overworked for this project, but let's do it in the Angular way.

```
// app-component.ts
constructor(private window: WindowRef){}
```

And wrap `window` by creating `WindowRefService` as below:

```
// window.service.ts
function _window(): any {
  // return the native window obj
  return window;
}

@Injectable()
export class WindowRef {
  get native(): any {
    return _window();
  }
}
```

It is good to mention that there is an alternative way to listen to an update during the install event in Service Worker. The onupdatefound property of the ServiceWorkerRegistration interface is an EventListener property called whenever an event of type statechange is fired; it is fired any time the ServiceWorkerRegistration. installing property acquires a new Service Worker.

```
if ("serviceWorker" in navigator) {
  // register service worker file
  navigator.serviceWorker
    .register("service-worker.js")
    .then(reg => {
      reg.onupdatefound = () => {
        const installingWorker = reg.installing;
        installingWorker.onstatechange = () => {
          switch (installingWorker.state) {
            case "installed":
              if (navigator.serviceWorker.controller) {
                // new update available
              } else {
                // no update available
              }
              break;
          }
        };
      };
    })
    .catch(err => console.error("[SW ERROR]", err));
}
```

The code above is an example that we can listen to for purposes of an update.

Let's build and run the application. To see the notification, first make sure you are running the app in supported browsers such as Firefox, Chrome, and Opera on both Android and Desktop.[1] When an update is available, snackBar will show a message with an action button (Figure 14-1).

---

[1]As of writing this book, Broadcast Channel API is only supported in these browsers, but it may change later. However, in Workbox 4, there will be a fallback to another method if this API is not supported. At the moment, we are using Workbox 3.6.3.

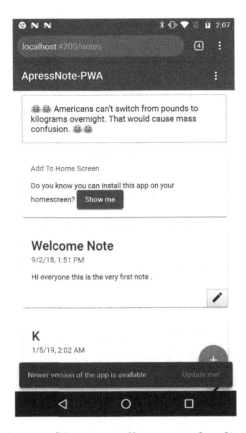

Figure 14-1. *The "Update me" button will trigger reloading page*

Background Sync

The BackgroundSync API is an ideal solution to those requests that fail due to no connectivity or when server is down. When a Service Worker detects that a network request has failed, it can register a sync event that gets delivered when the browser thinks connectivity has returned. Thus, we can save the requests and when the sync event happens, retry to send the requests. This is more effective than a traditional strategy to resolve this issue because even if the user has left the application, we still can deliver the requests to the server from Service Worker.

Workbox provides a background sync module that helps to intercept network requests that fail and save it in IndexedDB to retry them when a sync event happens. It also implements a fallback strategy for browsers that don't yet implement BackgroundSync.

The best candidate for implementing a background sync is the POST and DELETE method in Note PWA. To demonstrate back-end APIs, we will create a simple express app that provides POST and DELETE APIs:

```
const express = require('express');
const bodyParser = require('body-parser');
const axios = require('axios').default;
const app = express();

app.use(express.static(__dirname + '/dist'));
app.use(bodyParser.urlencoded({ extended: false }));
app.use(bodyParser.json());

app.post('/api/saveNote', async (req, res) => {
  try {
    const result = await axios.post('https://us-central1-awesome-apress-
    pwa.cloudfunctions.net/saveNote', req.body);
    return res.status(201).json(result.data);
  } catch (error) {
    return res.status(500).json({ success: false, error: { message:
    'something went wrong with the endpoint' } });
  }
});

app.delete(`/api/deleteNote/users/:user_id/notes/:note_id`, async (req,
res) => {
  try {
    const { user_id, note_id } = req.params;
    const { authorization } = req.headers;
    const result = await axios.delete(
      `https://firestore.googleapis.com/v1beta1/projects/awesome-apress-
      pwa/databases/(default)/documents/users/${user_id}/notes/${note_id}`,
      {
        headers: {
          Authorization: authorization
        }
      }
    );
```

```
    return res.json(result.data);
  } catch (error) {
    console.log(error);
    return res.status(500).json({ success: false, error: { message:
    'something went wrong with the endpoint' } });
  }
});
```

```
// redirect all routes to index.html since we are running single page
application
app.get('*', (req, res) => {
  res.sendfile('./dist/index.html');
});
```

```
app.listen(4200);
console.log('SEVER IS R'EADY -> PORT 4200');
```

You can run this server as simple as "node simple-express-server.js" in the terminal. As you remember, DataService was in charge of making http requests; therefore, we are going to slightly modify the two methods and endpoint in this service to point them to new back-end APIs.

We will data SaveNote endpoint to be pointed to our back end.

```
protected readonly SAVE_NOTE_ENDPOINT = '/api/saveNote';
saveNoteFromCloudFunction(note: Note): Observable<{ success: boolean;
data: Note }> {
  return this.http.post<{ success: boolean; data: Note }>(this.SAVE_NOTE_
  ENDPOINT, {
    user: this.auth.id,
    data: {
      ...note,
      created_at: this.timestamp,
      updated_at: this.timestamp
    }
  });
}
```

I will also define a new method for deleting a note pointing to my back-end API.

```
deleteNoteDirectly(id): Promise<any> {
  return this.auth
    .getToken()
    .pipe(
      switchMap(idToken => {
        return this.http.delete(`/api/deleteNote/users/${this.auth.id}/
        notes/${id}`, {
          headers: {
            Authorization: `Bearer ${idToken}`
          }
        });
      })
    )
    .toPromise();
}
```

Finally, we will use these methods while saving and deleting a single note. Once you cloned https://github.com/mhadaily/awesome-apress-pwa, go to Chapter 14, then 02-background-sync. You will find all the sample codes including all the new changes in NoteModule, DataService and sw-source.js.

We will register two routes in order to intercept network requests that fail and use the backgroundSync plugin to retry those requests.

```
workbox.routing.registerRoute(
    new RegExp('/api/saveNote'),
    workbox.strategies.networkOnly({
      plugins: [
        new workbox.backgroundSync.Plugin('firebaseSaveNoteQueue',
{
          callbacks: {
            queueDidReplay: StorableRequest => {
// Invoked after all requests in the queue have successfully replayed.
              console.log('queueDidReplay', StorableRequest);
```

```
// show notification
            self.registration.showNotification('Background Sync
            Successful', {
              body: 'You notes has been saved in cloud! '});
          },
          requestWillEnqueue: StorableRequest => {
  // Invoked immediately before the request is stored to IndexedDB.
// Use this callback to modify request data at store time.
            console.log('requestWillEnqueue', StorableRequest);
          },
          requestWillReplay: StorableRequest => {
  // Invoked immediately before the request is re-fetched.
// Use this callback to modify request data at fetch time.
            console.log('requestWillEnqueue', StorableRequest);
          }
        },
        maxRetentionTime: 60 * 24 * 7 // 7 days in minutes
      })
    ]
  }),
  'POST'
);
```

Let's break it down now that the argument has been passed into the registerRoute() function:

1. First argument is regular expression to match network request, which is /api/saveNote in this example.

2. Background sync has been added to plugins. The first argument is the queue name, and the second one is options, which is optional. In the options, there are a few properties such as maxRetentionTime that indicate how long this request should be retried and callbacks where you have access to life-cycle methods.

    a. queueDidReplay: Invoked after all requests in the queue have successfully replayed.

355

b. requestWillEnqueue: Invoked immediately before the request is stored to IndexedDB.

c. requestWillReplay: Invoked immediately before the request is re-fetched.

3. Third argument is the HTTP methods.

We will register a new route for intercepting failed DeleteNote network requests.

```
workbox.routing.registerRoute(
  new RegExp('/api/deleteNote/(.*)'),
  workbox.strategies.networkOnly({
    plugins: [
      new workbox.backgroundSync.Plugin('firebaseDeleteNoteQueue', {
        callbacks: {
          queueDidReplay: _ => {
            self.registration.showNotification('Background Sync
            Successful', {
              body: 'DELETE is done!'
            });
          }
        },
        maxRetentionTime: 24 * 60 // Retry for max of 24 Hours
      })
    ]
  }),
  'DELETE'
);
```

Sadly, testing BackgroundSync is somewhat unintuitive and difficult for a number of reasons. One of the best ways to test is by using the following steps:

1. Build and run application in production as Service Worker is registered.

2. Turn off your computer's network or turn off back-end server, which is simple-express-server.js. Please note that you cannot use offline in Chrome DevTools as it will only affect requests from the page. Service Worker requests will continue to go through.

3. Make network requests that should be queued with Workbox Background Sync. For example, add a note or delete a note.

4. You can check the requests have been queued by looking in Chrome DevTools > Application > IndexedDB > workbox-background-sync > requests.

5. Now turn on your network or run the web server (node simple-express-server.js).

6. Force an early sync event by going to Chrome DevTools > Application > Service Workers, enter the tag name of workbox-background-sync:<your queue name> for example workbox-background-sync:firebaseSaveNoteQueue, where "" should be the name of the queue you set and then clicking the 'Sync' button.

7. You should see network requests go through for the failed requests, and the IndexedDB data should now be empty since the requests have been successfully replayed (Figures 14-2, 14-3, 14-4, and 14-5).

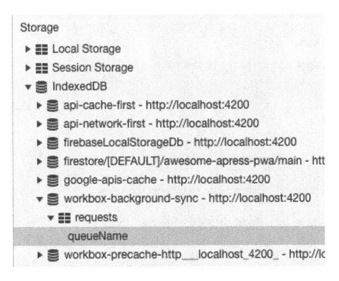

Figure 14-2. *Queue databse in indexedDB*

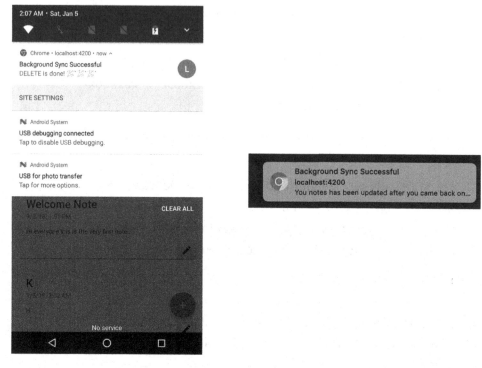

Figure 14-3. *Successful notification when network requests succesfully synced*

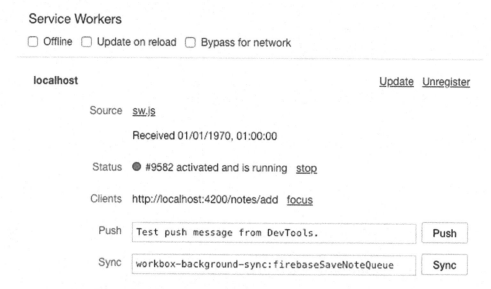

Figure 14-4. *Simluate background sycn in Chrome dev tools*

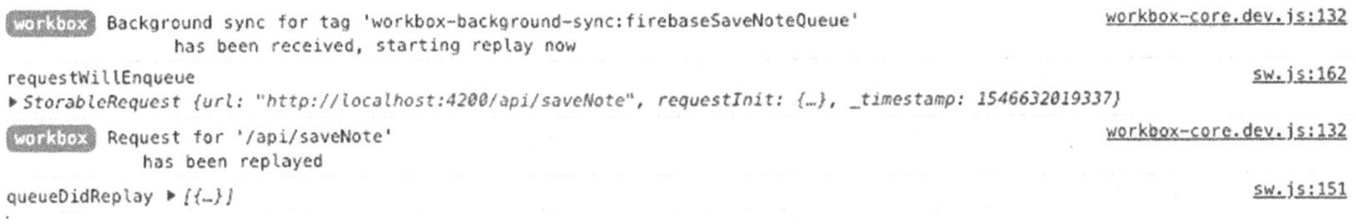

```
workbox  Background sync for tag 'workbox-background-sync:firebaseSaveNoteQueue'      workbox-core.dev.js:132
         has been received, starting replay now
requestWillEnqueue                                                                           sw.js:162
▶ StorableRequest {url: "http://localhost:4200/api/saveNote", requestInit: {…}, _timestamp: 1546632019337}
workbox  Request for '/api/saveNote'                                                  workbox-core.dev.js:132
         has been replayed
queueDidReplay  ▶ [{…}]                                                                       sw.js:151
```

Figure 14-5. *Workbox logs in callback functions for background sync*

If you check console when you are in localhost, you will be able to see logs, too.

You should see a notification when sync is done since we have used
showNotification() in queueDidReplay callback.

Push Notification

In Chapter 8, I explained the basics of a web push notification and taught you how to use Angular Service Worker SwPush service. Since we have taken out this module, we will first create a service called SwPushService that provides the same methods that Angular provides and use it in our components.

```
@Injectable()
export class SwPushService {
  constructor() {}

  public async checkSW(): Promise<{ isEnabled: boolean; subscription: any
  }> {
      if (navigator.serviceWorker) {
        const registration = await navigator.serviceWorker.getRegistration();
        let subscription;
        if ('PushManager' in window && registration) {
          subscription = await registration.pushManager.getSubscription();
        }
        return { isEnabled: true, subscription };
      } else {
        return { isEnabled: false, subscription: null };
      }
    } else {
      return { isEnabled: false, subscription: null };
    }
}
```

```
  urlBase64ToUint8Array(base64String) {
    const padding = '='.repeat((4 - (base64String.length % 4)) % 4);
    const base64 = (base64String + padding).replace(/\-/g, '+').
    replace(/_/g, '/');
    const rawData = window.atob(base64);
    const outputArray = new Uint8Array(rawData.length);
    for (let i = 0; i < rawData.length; ++i) {
      outputArray[i] = rawData.charCodeAt(i);
    }
    return outputArray;
  }

  async requestSubscription({ serverPublicKey }) {
      const registration = await navigator.serviceWorker.getRegistration();
      return registration.pushManager.subscribe({
        userVisibleOnly: true,
        applicationServerKey: this.urlBase64ToUint8Array(serverPublicKey)
      });
  }

  async unsubscribe(): Promise<boolean> {
      const registration = await navigator.serviceWorker.getRegistration();
      const subscription = await registration.pushManager.getSubscription();
      return subscription.unsubscribe();
  }
}
}
```

Let's break it down:

1. We need to first check if Service Worker is ready and PushManager is available. We use this to ensure that the "subscribe" button in UI is shown when the browser supports web push notification.

2. requestSubscription() method accepts serverPublicKey. We use it when subscripting to pushManager. Server public key must be converted to Uint8Array by calling urlBase64ToUint8Array().

3. Unsubscribe() to unsubscribe from push manager.

Now we just replace this service with Angular Service Worker. Since we have provided the same methods, we don't need to change too many things, only run checkSW() on component initialization.

```
constructor(
    private auth: AuthService,
    private swPush: SwPushService,
    private snackBar: SnackBarService,
    private router: Router,
    private dataService: DataService
  ) {}

ngOnInit() {
    this.checkSW();
  }

  async checkSW() {
    const { isEnabled, subscription } = await this.swPush.checkSW();
    this.isEnabled = isEnabled;
    this.subscription$.next(subscription);
  }
```

The rest of the header will be as same as what we have created in Chapter 8. Let's continue to add our push notification event in sw-source.js. As we discussed earlier in this book, push event fires when a push notification is received. Thus, we need to listen to this event in Service Worker.

```
self.onpush = event => {
    const { notification } = event.data.json();
    const promiseChain  = self.registration.showNotification(notification.
    title, notification);
    event.waitUntil(promiseChain);
  };
```

We also need to handle click event on notification actions. In Chapter 8, we implemented a logic in Firebase function method that a notification will be sent while saving a note is successful. The sent notification will have two custom actions: open and cancel.

```
// Custom notification actions
  self.onnotificationclick = event => {
    event.notification.close();
    switch (event.action) {
      case 'cancel': {
// do something if you want, e.g sending analytics to track these actions
        break;
      }
      case 'open': {
// we can track these actions in Analytics
        const URL = `${self.registration.scope}notes/${event.notification.
        data.noteID}`;
        event.waitUntil(clients.openWindow(URL));
        break;
      }
      default: {
        event.waitUntil(
          clients
            .matchAll({
              includeUncontrolled: true,
              type: 'window'
            })
            .then(clientList => {
              clientList.forEach(client => {
                if (client.url == '/' && 'focus' in client) {
                  return client.focus();
                }
              });
              if (clients.openWindow) {
                return clients.openWindow('/');
              }
            })
        );
      }
    }
  };
```

```
// Closing notification action
self.onnotificationclose = event => {
  console.log('Notification Close Event', event);
  // do something if you want!
};
```

Once you build and run the application again, add a note. A notification will be sent to the browser and shown to the user if you have a valid subscription (see Figure 14-6).

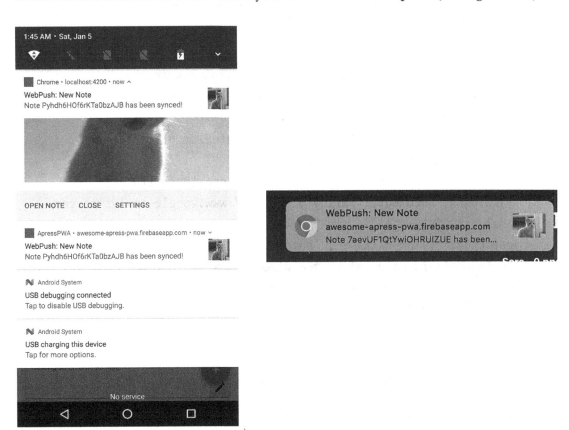

Figure 14-6. *Web push notification after saving note in both mobile and desktop*

Please note that you can clone `https://github.com/mhadaily/awesome-apress-pwa`, and all the sample codes can be found in Chapter 14 ➤ 03-push-notification folder.

Offline Analytics

Offline analytics is a module that will use background sync to ensure that requests to Google Analytics are made regardless of the current network condition; this is especially useful while a user is offline.

Whether you use Google tracking tag directly in index.html or using a module such as angulartics2, you should set a custom dimension to determine when the app was offline or when it was online. Let's add the script in index.html.

```
<script>
    /*
    (function(i, s, o, g, r, a, m) { i['GoogleAnalyticsObject'] = r;
      (i[r] = i[r] || function() {  (i[r].q = i[r].q || []).
      push(arguments);}),
      (i[r].l = 1 * new Date()); (a = s.createElement(o)), (m =
      s.getElementsByTagName(o)[0]);
      a.async = 1; a.src = g; m.parentNode.insertBefore(a, m);
    })(window, document, 'script', 'https://www.google-analytics.com/
    analytics.js', 'ga');
    ga('create', 'UA-XXXXX-Y', 'auto');
    // Set default value of custom dimension 1 to 'online'
    ga('set', 'networkstatus', 'online');
    ga('send', 'pageview');
    */
</script>
```

Enabling offline analytics can be as simple as in sw-source.js:

```
workbox.googleAnalytics.initialize({
  parameterOverrides: {
    networkstatus: 'offline'
  }
});
```

On googleAnalytics initialization, we will pass in parameterOverrides that we define to overwrite the dimension that we have defined already to determine the tracking has received when the app was offline.

Summary

In this chapter, advanced topics have been implemented in both Angular and Service Worker with Workbox. We walked through how to send a message to a `window` client in order to inform the client that there is an update in the cache. Background sync helped us to retry sending a failed request to the server once the connection or endpoint is back online. Engaging is one of the main characteristics of the PWA that we have achieved by implementing push notifications. Finally, Workbox Google Analytics module provides a mechanism that we can track our application while it is being used offline. With that said, let's move on to the next chapter and see what the next steps for building PWA will be.

CHAPTER 15

Next Steps

Congratulations! You have completed Angular PWA education, which enables you to build a Progressive Web App with Angular and have a good understanding of how PWA works. But, wait! This is just the beginning! From now on, you have to keep learning and trying to do things better and better. You don't have to stop at this point but should continue your path, which you have come with me until this point in the book. There are a lot more things to learn. Some of the concepts that we have explored together in this book were just the surface for an ocean of knowledge and information. You should continue diving deeper and deeper.

As a developer, we all know that what we write today might be obsolete in the next five years. You have probably also noticed that I mentioned a few times in different chapters that many of these APIs are still evolving and changing over time, which means we need to embrace these changes and keep ourselves updated.

In this chapter, I will write a few pages about learning resources, case studies, and PWA examples in the real world as well as introducing a few new technologies and tools that you should keep an eye on.

Learning Resources

There are tons of articles, videos, tutorials, blogs, and podcast about PWA. In the list below, I introduce you to a few resources that you can help you learn more about PWA and Angular and dive deeper if you want:

1. `https://developers.google.com/web/progressive-web-apps/`

   I believe you have seen this website before. Google Developer has a dedicated section for PWA under Web. Just check it out!

© Majid Hajian 2019
M. Hajian, *Progressive Web Apps with Angular*, https://doi.org/10.1007/978-1-4842-4448-7_15

2. `https://web.dev`

   In Chrome Dev Summit 2018, Googlers announced a new website dedicated to web and, in particular, PWA. This website not only helps you to learn more but also provides tools to measure and audit your web application.

3. `https://serviceworke.rs`

   This website is powered by Mozilla and provides a collection of working, practical examples of using Service Worker in modern websites.

4. `https://blog.angular.io/`

   Ensure you are getting the latest update from the Angular blog. Also, it's good have an eye on Angular documents, especially the PWA guide.

5. `https://developer.mozilla.org/en-US/docs/Web/Apps/Progressive`

   Mozilla MDN website is familiar to all developers. Keep your eye on PWA sections.

Case Studies

In my opinion, it's always great to read about other developers' and teams' experiences and follow their journey. I always find many tips and tricks that help sometimes to avoid bugs and errors, or many times speed up my development process. I will write no case studies here, but I will encourage you to read up from the following resources:

1. `https://developers.google.com/web/showcase/2018/nikkei`

   Nikkei achieves a new level of quality and performance with their multipage PWA.

2. `https://developers.google.com/web/showcase/2018/asda-george`

   George.com enhances the mobile customer experience with a new PWA.

3. `https://developers.google.com/web/showcase/2017/eleme`

   Ele.me improves performance load times with a multipage PWA.

4. `https://developers.google.com/web/showcase/2017/bookmyshow`

   BookMyShow's new PWA drives an 80 percent increase in conversions.

5. `https://developers.google.com/web/showcase/2016/aliexpress`

   AliExpress increases the conversion rate for new users by 104 percent with a new PWA.

You can find a lot more on the Google website if you just simply search PWA case studies or check out `www.pwastats.com` to see more use cases in the context of business advantages.

Example Applications

If you are interested to see who is using PWA in production now, you can find a list of PWA websites on this website: `https://outweb.io/` or `https://pwa.rocks/`.

I encourage you to check out Hacker news as PWAs: `https://hnpwa.com/` website where you will find a lot of different implementations of PWAs with different technologies and tools. It's a good resource to learn and study more, especially about techniques that are being used to boost initial load and application performance.

Tools and Technologies

Although throughout this book I have mentioned a lot of tools and technologies and reviewed them, there are still tools and technologies that I'd like to write a few lines about here.

1. **Desktop Progressive Web App**

   As we already talked about, one of the main advantages of PWA
   is that we create only for browsers and we can ship it to different
   platforms. Mobile users are the most important target for our
   Angular PWA; that's why we have focused on mobile refinement
   and mentioned that many times. However, we don't have to forget
   that our desktop users will benefit from our optimization, too.
   In fact, Desktop PWAs are supported on many platforms already
   such as Chrome 67+ on Chrome OS, Linux, Windows, and Mac.
   Even better, we are able to submit our PWA app to the Microsoft
   Store; and once published, our customers can install to Windows
   10 as an app. That's huge. Imagine your PWA will be discovered by
   millions of active Windows users.

   So, when you build your PWA with Angular, you should think of
   a wide variety of customers from mobile to desktop. I think we
   may see Google Play or Apple Store! Also we might be able to
   submit our PWA to their store in the future – who knows! Just even
   thinking of that makes me so excited.

   In order to learn more about the Windows store and PWA, follow
   this link: `https://developer.microsoft.com/en-us/windows/pwa`.
   Also, Google has a dedicated page regarding this topic, which
   is accessible here: `https://developers.google.com/web/`
   `progressive-web-apps/desktop`.

2. **Trusted Web Activities**

   Trusted Web Activities are a new way to integrate your web-app
   content such as your PWA with your Android app using a protocol
   based on Custom Tabs. Read more about it on https://developers.
   google.com/web/updates/2019/02/using-twa.

3. **Web Share APIs**

   This is one of my favorite API that I hope will see better support
   soon, especially on iOS. This method provides a simple high-level
   JavaScript API that invokes the native sharing capabilities of the
   host platform. The API is Promised-based and has only a single

method. It accepts configuration objects that at least need to have text or url properties.

Here is an example:

```
// a method which gets invoke by user mouse click or tab (touch)
async openShare(){
    if (navigator.share) {
    try {
      const result = await navigator.share({
          title: 'Apress NG-PWANote',
          text: 'Check out Apress Angular PWA Note!',
          url: 'https://awesome-apress-pwa.firebaseapp.com',
      })
        console.log('Successful share')
    } catch(error) {
      console.log('Error sharing', error)
    }
    }
}
```

Chrome for Android supports this API. There is no more support as of writing this book, but I hope that by the time you read this book, this API is supported widely across different platforms and browsers.

4. **Offline Webpack Plugin**

   You may, for some reasons, use webpack or are using webpack for your Angular application. If so, there is plugin in the webpack ecosystem that brings offline capabilities.

   Find it here https://github.com/NekR/offline-plugin

5. www.pwabuilder.com

   This website is founded by Microsoft and helps you to take data from your website and use that to generate a cross-platform PWA.

   If you like automation and have no configuration for your website, you may find this website useful!

6. www.webhint.io

   Another great website from Microsoft developers.

   Webhint is a linting tool that will help you with your site's accessibility, speed, security, and more by checking your code for best practices and common errors. Use the online scanner or the CLI to start checking your site for errors.

7. **Background Fetch**

   This is a web standard API that handles large uploads/downloads in the background with user visibility. The problem is when you fetch something, Service Worker must be alive and the process should be short; otherwise, the browser will kill Service Worker due to a risk for a user's privacy and battery.

   This is extremely useful for tasks that may take a long time to be finished, like downloading a movie or podcasts. At the time of writing this chapter, this API was introduced as an experimental web platform feature flag to Chrome 71.

   Keep your eye on this API and find more information on it here:

   https://developers.google.com/web/updates/2018/12/background-fetch

8. **Web Performance**

   We build PWA because we want users to have native-like experiences that are fast, reliable, and engaging. Thus, web performance is always a topic that we never have to stop learning about it. The more you learn, the faster the app you build. A lot of resources, including those that I have mentioned earlier in this chapter, provide performance-related topics, too; however, in addition, you can find the following link helpful:

   https://developers.google.com/web/fundamentals/performance/why-performance-matters/

9. **Web Components**

Web Components is a suite of different technologies allowing you to create reusable custom elements while their functionality is encapsulated away from the rest of your code and lets you utilize them in your web apps.

This is a great technology that Angular supports by Angular Element. You can find more about it here: `https://angular.io/guide/elements`. After Angular Ivy[1] (pretty soon), Angular Element will be even better. Don't forget to keep your eye on it.

10. **Web Assembly**

Web assembly (abbreviated WASM) is designed to help with the compilation of high-level languages like C/C++/ Rust along with JavaScript, which means with Web Assembly JavaScript APIs, you can load WASM modules into a JavaScript app and share the functionality between the two. This is amazing technology that has, of now, been shipped to all major browsers.

The developer documentation is available here o nth Mozilla MDN web docs website:

`https://developer.mozilla.org/en-US/docs/WebAssembly`

Last Words

Web is evolving rapidly. PWA, in particular, is growing quickly. We hear about new technologies literally every day. Even during the time that I was writing this book, there was a lot of new news regarding PWA and Angular, and I probably should have revised what I have written. I personally love it. I love to see new APIs that make me excited and thrilled as a web developer. What I want to point out is that, even though the it takes great speed to catch up sometimes, the concepts and principles of Progressive Web Apps with or without Angular that have been taught to you throughout the book will remain the same. An Angular PWA must be fast to load, reliable to work with, and engaging as

---

[1]`https://github.com/angular/angular/blob/master/packages/core/src/render3/STATUS.md`

native apps were in the past and now. It must run on all browsers and platforms and must be developed and deployed progressively.

Thank you for reading! We had a long journey together. I hope you enjoy building amazing Progressive Web Apps with Angular (or maybe without!) as much as I enjoyed writing this book.

All the best.

Index

A

addPushSUbscription() method, 209

AddToHomeScreenService, 154

Android and Chrome, 161–164

Android Studio, 8

Angular App Shell
    Angular Universal, 174
    bootstrapped, 171
    built-in functionality, 172
    JS and CSS files, 172
    performance
        audit tab, Chrome
          DevTools, 184–187
        bundle sizes analyze, 187–189
        optimizations, 187
        webpagetest.org, 182–184
    in production, 179–182
    project repository, 173–174

Angular CLI, 143, 169
    app generation, 4
    installation, 4
    material design, 5–7

AngularFire, 22–27

Angular firebase, 248–250

Angular Router module, 197

Angular schematics
    @angular/cli, 90
    @angular/pwa schematic, 97
    app structure, 90
    modifications, 90–95

Angular service worker, 285–288
    appData configuration, 134
    build project, 101–104
    chrome DevTools, 258–259
    clear storage, 89
    data groups, 122
    external resources, 116–120
    firebase URL, 88
    firefox DevTools, 259–260
    forward cache/CDN edge, 88
    Network-First strategy, 125–129
    network request, 131
    resource revalidation, no hash, 121–122
    runtime cache, 116, 130
    SwUpdate class, 134–137
    Web App Manifest, 89–90

Angular universal
    angular CLI, 175
    angular.json file configuration, 178–179
    app-server-module, 176
    CLI configuration file, 175
    route shell, 176
    server-side application, 177
    SSR, 174

app-server-module, 176

app-shell.component, 177

App Shell model, 169–171

Audit panel
    lighthouse, Chrome launcher, 275–276
    lighthouse, Puppeteer, 277

© Majid Hajian 2019
M. Hajian, *Progressive Web Apps with Angular*, https://doi.org/10.1007/978-1-4842-4448-7

B

C

D

Printed in the United States
By Bookmasters